DRIVE

WOMEN'S TRUE STORIES

FROM THE OPEN ROAD

EDITED BY JENNIE GOODE

SEAL PRESS

Published by Seal Press
An Imprint of Avalon Publishing Group Incorporated
161 William St., 16th Floor
New York, NY 10038

Library of Congress Cataloging-In-Publication Data has been applied for.

ISBN 1-58005-066-2

Cover design by Joseph Kaftan
Text design by Anne Mathews
Cover photograph by Tony Hopewell, courtesy Tony Stone

9   8   7   6   5   4   3   2

Printed in the United States of America
Distributed to the trade by Publishers Group West

For Beverly Anne
May reading and the road take you where you want to go

acknowledgments

Many thanks to the women of Seal Press who contributed their considerable talents to this project: to Leslie Miller, for her decisive insights and steady encouragement; to Anne Mathews, for her obsessive attention to detail (and willingness to humor mine), fabulous design and all-around good humor; to Faith Conlon, for the opportunity to do this book; and to Christina Henry, for her behind-the-scenes coordinating efforts. Thanks, too, to cover designer Joe Kaftan and copyeditor Jessica Hoffman, for their good work. I also extend my deepest appreciation to the entity that is Seal Press, including its founders Barbara Wilson and Rachel da Silva, for a quarter century of feminist books and, for me personally, five years of indispensable editorial experience. I wish Seal the best as it enters a new era.

I couldn't have taken on this project without the backing of friends and family. Thanks especially to Wendy, for her thoughtful comments on the introduction; to my parents, for their interest in and encouragement of my various and sundry endeavors; and to Kristin, for her unwavering support, remarkably bendable ear, astute perceptions and steady love.

Finally, an anthology, both in process and final product, is wholly dependent upon the contributors. I am fortunate to have worked with an amazing group of strong, responsive and talented women, including quite a few whose work I was unable to include. Thanks to all of you for making this book what it is and rendering the process so rewarding and enjoyable.

contents

IX   Introduction   JENNIE GOODE

3   In the Land of the Saltbush   SHELLY WHITMAN COLONY

18   Tooling Along   KATHRYN MORTON

30   Small Gifts   ANDROMEDA ROMANO-LAX

42   Substitution Trunk   MARTHA GIES

65   Tequila Sunrise   JANET MASON

79   Sunshine Girl   CAROLYN MACKLER

90   My Mom Across America   TINA YUN LEE

112   Changelings   MARIAN BLUE

121   Mourning Ropes   MONIFA A. LOVE

131   Messieurs Monsters Hit the Road   ALEXANDRIA MADERO

149   The Grapevine Passport   MOE BOWSTERN

165   Bridging the Waters   KAREN SBROCKEY

178   An Adventure's Tale   LORRAINE CAPUTO

192   Mapping Home   DEBORAH GITLITZ

206   Inheritances   JEFFE KENNEDY

216	Good for the Long Haul	ALICE EVANS
230	Cruising in My Caddy	KARI J. BODNARCHUK
246	Ride to Live	ANNE STONE
257	The Punxsutawney Pilgrimage	BELINDA FARLEY
268	Damsels on the Highway	TARA KOLDEN
288	Driven	SHARON B. YOUNG
298	Contributors	

introduction

jennie goode

i took my first road trip when I was eighteen months old. In late August, my parents packed my four-year-old brother and me into our brand-new 1973 Travco, the original Dodge motor home. It took only five minutes to get from the driveway of our house in St. Louis to the on-ramp for Interstate 70. Dad drove, and Mom navigated. We headed west, aiming for Rocky Mountain National Park, fourteen hours away. We stayed on the road for six weeks, traveling the spine of the Rockies up into Canada, then aiming for the nearest ocean and following its coast down to Oregon, and finally pointing toward home, back over the hump of mountains and across the plains' flat expanse.

A few times a year for the next fifteen years, the motor home served as our rolling abode and my introduction to America's highways. What I remember from those trips is falling asleep in the pitch black, lulled by my father's late-night driving to our next destination; waking to the smell of gas heat seeping from the floor vent below my bunk; pushing back a corner of the curtain next to my bed and rubbing away the early-morning condensation to see the view of our new home: the occasional parking lot, but more often a quiet campground umbrellaed by trees; watching the road's yellow hatch marks disappear behind us as I stared out the rear window. And I remember leaving behind the skirts I detested wearing to first grade in favor of hand-me-downs from my brother; scrambling, bare-chested, over boulders and sloshing across shallow glacial streams; lagging behind on hikes so I could learn from my mom the names of countless wildflowers, which I can still recite today; singing aloud, hopelessly off-key, to the John Denver cassette repeating in the tape deck.

These trips were my window on a wider world; our particular view was of mountain meadows rather than city streets. The America I saw was wild. Maybe because of that, my parents allowed a little more wildness in me. From within the safety of my family, I was able to explore new territory and catch a glimpse of myself as something other than the quiet and somewhat awkward good girl I was at home. But the trips always ended; we always returned to the stifling landscape of suburban St. Louis. And somehow, I couldn't translate the freedom I'd felt on the road into the rest of my life.

The motor home trips ceased when I was in high school, about the time I happened upon Kerouac. He offered a vision of the road so different from my own. My road had been marked by slow meandering, careful itineraries and, always, the reality of returning home. I was infected by his story of zipping back and forth across the country at will, in search of newness, experience, life itself. He'd managed to turn the road into life, or life into the road; I wasn't sure which, but I knew there was no separation between the two. It was all just one long high. His story appealed to my angst-ridden adolescent self, ready for a life of adventure after adventure to begin. Instead I was busy being a good student/daughter/friend with an overdeveloped sense of responsibility. As I read, I underlined passages like this one: "The only people for me are the mad ones, the ones who are mad to live, mad to talk, mad to be saved, desirous of everything at the same time, the ones who never yawn or say a commonplace thing, but burn, burn, burn . . . " I wanted to *be* one of those people; I wanted to jump in a car and drive, find that place of freedom and transcendence.

But when I finally took that mythical road trip, I wasn't burning— I was burned out. Two decades after my introduction to the road, I retraced most of that first western trip with a friend from college. Running from a months-long bout of depression, I'd left school and ended up in the twin bed of my childhood. But my parents couldn't fix my numbed mind, so I sought to escape it. We drove my friend's eighties-model Subaru station wagon long into the night and spent early morning hours sleeping in roadside fields as often as campgrounds. I hiked up mountains and got altitude sickness; hitchhiked in the pouring rain around small island communities; slept fitfully in deserted parking lots; watched over my shoulder for bears. Though I discovered the freedom of controlling my own route, transcendence still eluded me. I was always just myself, on the road. All of me—my fears, my weaknesses, my doubts—accompanied me, wedged between the cooler and sleeping bags in the back seat. It was a valuable lesson. No matter how far I traveled, I could never escape myself, or the responsibilities of life.

The trip was the opposite of what I'd gone looking for. Instead of outrunning myself, I crashed head-on into my depression. I'd been busy trying to please others for most of my life, going along with somebody else's already mapped-out itinerary. Given the chance to decide what to do with each day—where to go, how to get there, when to stop, what to eat, whether to sleep—I realized that I wasn't used to doing what I wanted or needed. Like many women brought up in a culture that emphasizes taking care of others, I didn't even *know* what I wanted. I'd lost my connection with my gut, and with it the instinct for self-preservation. On the road, aware of both the possibilities and dangers that awaited two young women each day, I gradually learned to listen to my intuition and trust myself. I took risks and found my limits. And along the way I quenched my old lust for adventure. Watching lightning storms from above the tree line; pitching our tent a foot from the high-tide mark on an Oregon beach; burning dinner on the side of a Wyoming road, too mesmerized by the sinking sun to notice—I discovered adventure at my own speed, quiet and beautiful. For once, returning home wasn't so difficult.

That was the last time the road was my main destination; these days my trips are more directed. Now, nearly a decade later, I find it more difficult to get away. I haven't entirely shed my good-girl skin, so instead of waking to the question, "What do I want from this day?" or "What new thing do I want to see today?" I rise to yesterday's list of unfinished tasks, ordering my days according to the responsibilities—and rewards—of work and relationships. Check-marking my way through the day, it's all too easy to forget to lift my eyes, look around and see the range of options for my day or my life.

But instead of dreaming of a complete escape, when the page seems too full, the list too long, I load up my car and take to the road, for a weekend, a week at most. From my home in Seattle I drive to Portland, Vancouver, the Oregon coast, the Olympic Peninsula or eastern Washington, and even on these short jaunts the power of the road returns for a brief time. As the miles tick by on the odometer, the world's colors begin to seem more vibrant, and I smile more easily. Away from expectations of who I am or who I should be, my vision of my life clears, sharpens. As I put more distance between myself and the pull of other people's needs, I remember to focus on my own. The physical movement of the road dislodges me from my mental or emotional inertia. And the unpredictability of the road reminds me that though I may have choices, I don't have control. My grip on the wheel loosens.

I'm lucky to have discovered myself out on the road. Women haven't always had the opportunity to take such journeys, to explore the world or themselves. For most of American history the road has been a man's world and women have been tied to the home, kept in place by the responsibilities of caretaking. But decades have passed since women began taking to the road in greater numbers. I began to wonder, Where are the women? Where are their stories? Looking back at Kerouac as an adult, I could no longer find myself in his version of the road-trip tale. In his book, women were girls, and girls were characters to leave behind or sleep with along the way. And indeed, women are largely absent from the American literature of the road, which has been primarily written by men, from Jack Kerouac to Hunter S. Thompson to William Least Heat-Moon. I wanted to know what the road looked like to other women, and what it taught them about themselves. I imagined that putting women at the center of the road-trip narrative would expand and change it. I wanted a road story with a baby in the back seat; a walk on the wild side that openly acknowledged vulnerability and risk; a good old-fashioned female-bonding road-trip tale.

Of course, mainstream American pop culture does offer one example of the latter. The first time I saw *Thelma and Louise* I was completely riveted. It portrayed an experience of the road that I could recognize (though taken to extremes I hadn't experienced). I was captivated by the characters' elation and empowerment at shedding propriety, their excitement at trying on new personas, their anger and vulnerability at being a target of harassment and abuse, and the quiet transformation that occurred in the wide open spaces of the West. But then, Thelma and Louise do die in the end. As an acknowledgment of the odds facing women who challenge a misogynistic culture, it's a realistic close to the story. But I didn't want it to be the only end; I wanted to be able to see and read and imagine other conclusions, other futures for women. I wanted more stories, true stories, that followed many different women on widely diverging roads. I wanted to know what other women were looking for when they climbed behind the wheel—and what they found.

This book is the result of that curiosity. The women here are driven to the road by many events and exigencies in their lives: the desire to shed routine or push limits, the longing to reconnect with an old friend or revisit family history, the need for space to think or time to mourn, the simple wish for some fun or a nice long drive. Sometimes they find what they're looking for; other times they happen upon the unexpected. For these women, the road offers perspective—a sense of independence, a new view of one's place in the world—and it serves up breakdowns and snowstorms as well. It presents fear as well as freedom. It is a rich and complicated place, and it is a different place for each woman.

Each of us imbues the road with meaning, layering our own experiences and expectations like blacktop. Each traveler, each writer, experiences and records a different cultural and geographical landscape. The road looks different depending on whether we're female or male, black, brown or white, queer or straight; whether we have a car and money for a motel room, or just a thumb and a backpack; whether we blend in with the people we're passing, or are visible as "outsiders" just passing through. Our personal stories interact with the histories of the regions through which we travel, and it's this intersection that tells us who we are as individuals and as a community.

As with the road, there are as many views of America as there are people to view it. Among the Americas presented here are depressed mining towns of the West; heart-opening mountain sunsets in Wyoming; rural Mississippi, where Jim Crow once reigned; cold, isolated towns in Alaska; rural Canada as viewed from the window of a tour bus; wide-open stretches of Texas highway; the side of the road in the Middle of Nowhere, Mexico; an end-of-the-line garage in the California desert. These are the places, away from the comfort and predictability of home, where the women in this book find something new, something worth noting, a reason for a trip or a tale.

Like all forms of travel, road trips are ultimately about exploration and discovery. They are about opening one's eyes to the surrounding world. I hope that after accompanying the writers in this collection on their journeys, readers will return transformed, inspired and ready to go somewhere new, somewhere unexpected.

Jennie Goode
November 2001
Seattle, Washington

DRIVE

in the land of the saltbush

shelly whitman colony

> I will leave you alone to look out on the desert. What makes you want to leave now is what is trying to kill you. . . . Moving on is not important. You must wait. You must take things down to the core.
> —Barry Lopez, *Desert Notes: Reflections in the Eye of a Raven*

a marked transition occurs in the landscape of southeastern California. Here, crustal forces at work deep beneath the surface truncate the roots of the Sierras as the Pacific plate grinds north along the margin of North America. The effect is as sharp as a knife blade drawn across the earth, leaving the forested mountain slopes of the Inyo Range juxtaposed against tawny valleys of the Mojave Desert. This suture defines a boundary between tectonic plates, between ecological domains, between worlds.

I had been on the road for a couple of months, carving a giant arc westward from my home in Montana, and now following the great continental backbone of the Sierras southward. I eased the van into a pullout that overlooked the Panamint Valley and stepped out into the dry November wind. A few miles to the south, the Panamint Range loomed like a jagged pink scar against the pale blue sky. Rock outcroppings lay exposed like bone jutting from the lean flesh of the mountains, and great skirts of detritus at the mouths of the canyons spilled together to form a gravel plain, or *bajada*. Below the bajada, salt pans lay like sheets of dirty white paper spread across the valley floor. I sat on a big rock and looked out upon this lonely hard-bitten landscape, hunch-shouldered and forlorn.

The idea for this trip began with the desire to run away from home the winter before, when it became clear that the man I loved drank too much, smoked too much pot and loved his best friend too much to be able to be a husband. My next man sent roses and left poems on my answering machine. He seemed perfect until he decided he really didn't want to leave his wife. I had loved both of them and had grown weary trying to be loved in return. So with the vague idea that what I needed was a complete resetting of my life, I sold my house, quit my job, closed my consulting business and packed everything I'd need for twelve months alone on the road into six Rubbermaid totes and left my home in Bozeman. My hope was that by the end of a year to myself, I'd know how to break the spell of bad luck and poor judgment I had had with men. I hoped to discover how to love, how to attract love, how to find and live with happiness. Tears spilled out of my eyes as I sat on the rock, and the cold November wind blew them dry.

Easing the van down a series of switchbacks, I intended to cross the salt pans and Panamint Range beyond to spend the night at Furnace Creek in Death Valley National Park before crossing into Arizona, where I would winter. Dropping into the Panamint Valley was like falling off the known world. Roads came and went, intersecting the highway like silent, nameless actors crossing a stage. I chose a road that headed east. On the map it warranted no name or number; it was simply designated "Other Road," one step in substance above the generic "Unpaved Road."

So far the trip had been unexpectedly miserable. For one thing, I hadn't counted on vehicle repairs in my otherwise carefully constructed budget. The van had broken down in Spokane, then Portland, then Tillamook, on the rain-drenched Oregon coast. With each repair the cash supply in the ashtray dwindled by a couple hundred dollars. At this rate my trip would be over before it started, before I had found the wisdom I was looking for. It's not supposed to work that way, I fumed to myself as I drove across the deserted valley. When you set out to gain insight and commit yourself so fully and plan so well, it should work. You should get some benefit. My dream shouldn't be derailed by mechanical problems—how stupid.

Suddenly a loud alarm screeched from under the dash. The needle on the battery voltage gauge went limp.

"Shit!" I yelled.

Frantically looking for a road sign, an intersection, a dry wash, anything, I tried to pinpoint my location. The last sign I remembered was an authoritative green highway sign marking the dirt road to Darwin. Stopping the van, but leaving it running, I groped for the map on the passenger seat. Studying it, I realized many of the "towns" marked on the map were actually ghost towns. Throwing the worthless map across the van, I cursed every Rand McNally mapmaker, every mechanic, every person who lived now or ever had lived in California. The alarm continued to screech. It was driving me mad.

I looked under the dash and ripped the alarm's voice box out. Stepping out, I stood by the side of the road in the sudden and deafening desert silence, shaking, knowing I probably didn't have much time until the main battery went dead and I would be camping wherever that happened to be, for as long as it took to ride my bike to a real town. I stood in the middle of the highway. There was no other vehicle, no town in sight, and I felt the panic of loneliness and fear rise up in my chest. Oh God.

They say strange things happen in the desert. Visions and prophecies, revelations of truth. The soul, stripped of the distractions of daily life, can finally know what has been driving it, the name of the beast it has been running from. I felt that I had come up to the very edge of something, as if, like the crust beneath my feet, I was strained to the breaking point. The trembling in my arms seemed to come up from the depths of the earth, a great breaking and shaking, the beginnings of a shift in understanding. A saltbush stood alone within a white circle of sandy dirt, a gray plastic bag stuck in its branches. It seemed to whisper.

Back in the van I retrieved the map. With shaking hands, I held the torn pieces together. Darwin lay behind; Trona lay an equal distance to the south. Both dots were the same size; both might be ghost towns. I jerked the van into gear. An eternity later I coasted to a dead stop in the dirt driveway of an unmarked shop in Trona, California.

Trona looked like hell.

The town lay at the southern end of the Panamint Valley, hunkered in a small corridor between two halves of the China Lake Naval Air Weapons Station, a military complex devoted to developing and testing bombs and missiles. Military aircraft used the surrounding desert for training, and as I drove into town, a swarm of fighter jets appeared suddenly above the ridge behind the grade school. White salt from the three trona processing mills blew across the bare dirt playground and coated the corrugated tin-roofed buildings that cropped up along Main Street like eroded tombstones. The town had an ugly, no-nonsense demeanor.

A stout woman with long red hair and pink eye shadow came out of a cinderblock shack. She smelled of cigarettes and held her arms wrapped around her body to shrug off the afternoon's chill. I was glad to see her.

"I've been having electrical problems," I said thickly.

"There's no one here right now." She looked at me. "But you can wait. Mike'll be back." The telephone rang and she turned to go back in the office. "You're welcome to come inside for a cup of coffee."

The place reminded me of the yards of hardscrabble ranches back in Montana. Unpainted cinderblock buildings. Junk strewn about. No landscaping, not even a ragged juniper shrub. A three-sided building with two bays served as the shop, where a young Latino kid was working on a muscle car. Three strands of barbed wire topping a high wall circled the whole outfit. It was nothing like the coolly competent, efficiently managed dealerships I had been visiting.

I followed the woman into the tired shack. She sat heavily at an oily, paper-strewn metal desk and talked loudly on the telephone in a dark room that used to be a living room. In the kitchen, dirty dishes flowed out of the sink and over the counters like black lava, piled and solidified, a welded ceramic and aluminum breccia. The place reeked of spoiled food, automotive and fried grease, stale cigarettes and body odor. I picked my way through cases of air filters, bags of trash and piles of greasy parts to the tiny restroom.

"I haven't had time to clean it for a while. The guys are so messy," she shouted apologetically.

The bathroom smelled like an alkaline lake, a rotting combination of algae and hard-boiled eggs. Bright red rust and grimy black grease stains coated the toilet and basin. Old hoses, boxes and trash filled a bathtub. I didn't bother to line the seat with paper. I didn't care anymore.

The woman was still on the phone, trying to soothe an irritated customer or get money out of someone, I couldn't tell.

"You hungry?" she called out. "There's burritos in the fridge."

I looked at the mummified bean mush and crusty tortilla on the paper plate on top of the microwave.

"No thanks."

She got off the phone and came around from behind the desk. I wondered if she lived as well as worked in this dump. I felt sorrier for her than I did for myself at that moment, because it was obvious that whoever took care of this place didn't give a damn about much.

"Can I just have a cup of hot water? I have some tea out in the van."

"Oh sure. Don't use the tap water, though. We drink bottled water." She picked up an open gallon jug from the counter; a fly buzzed lazily off the rim.

"Thanks," I said. "I'll go get my cup."

I drank tea with Gloria. She was excited to be going to Los Angeles at Thanksgiving to visit one of her kids, a daughter she hadn't seen for a while. She picked up a framed photograph from the edge of the desk. "I'm a grandma now. Doesn't that baby have the reddest hair?"

"Yeah," I agreed flatly. "Pretty cute."

"You goin' anywhere for Thanksgiving?"

"No. I don't know. I'm on the road. I'll probably be in Arizona for Thanksgiving."

I was surprised to see her looking at me with genuine sadness. How could she feel sorry for me? She worked here. The most colorful thing in town—the nearest thing to a mural, or sculpture, or tree—was the green tower of the American Chemical Company mill. The water was unfit to drink, summer temperatures soared to 120-plus degrees. The whole damn place was a salty version of hell. I'd be leaving soon, but she was stuck here for the rest of her life.

"You're welcome to join us . . ." her voice trailed off, embarrassed, I suppose, to be so eager to invite a stranger to Thanksgiving.

"Oh," I said, trying to muster some enthusiasm, "I like being alone. I'll be just fine. Anyway, I'll be home for Christmas." I lied to make her feel better and make myself seem less pathetic.

"I appreciate the tea. May I have another cup?"

"Sure," she said brightly. "I work for Mike. He should be here anytime now. He went out to tow some people in. They've been stranded five days."

"I would have been stuck a while, too, if I hadn't made it right to your door." I smiled weakly at her and went out to the van to wait.

Eventually Gloria came out. We talked about what might be wrong with the van. Her family. She flitted back and forth to the office, catching the phone, doing her business. I had hours to kill. I ate Fig Newtons. Drank some tea. Talked with Gloria.

A man and woman pulled into the far end of the driveway. The woman, dressed in a startling pink and orange dress and fuchsia shoes, got out of the passenger side and started rummaging through the open trunk of the 1970s Town Car, its paint blasted to an indeterminate blue or black.

"I love her shoes," I said to Gloria. My leather hiking boots, wool-felted Sorels and running shoes seemed poor and unimaginative in comparison.

"That's crazy Mavis. She comes 'round thinking somebody stole her clothes."

The woman was rifling through the trunkload of clothes and cursing loudly.

"How ya doin', Mavis?" Gloria called.

"I know you took it, you bitch! I know you have it!" Mavis screamed, her face red, eyes dazed. One shoe was missing a heel, which gave her a canted, off-center stance. "Son of a bitch!" Mavis glared at us.

A bent old man in a white T-shirt came around to escort Mavis back into the car. He nodded matter-of-factly at Gloria. She waved.

I felt as cracked as Mavis. When I sold that cursed Chevy van, I'd be as homeless as she, with my Rubbermaid box of clothes in my lap, riding the Greyhound to somewhere else.

Thinking of the Greyhound, I confided to Gloria, "I hope nothing much is wrong with the van. I've already spent several hundred dollars on this problem and I don't have a lot to spare. I'm thinking maybe I should just sell it, get on a bus and get the hell out of here."

"Don't you have a job?"

"No, actually I don't."

"Well, what are you good at?"

"I'm a geologist."

Her eyes widened. "Oh, a geologist," she said. "We got lots of geologists here. Why, I'm sure you could get a job over at the mill." She jerked her head to indicate the American Chemical Company offices down the street. "Those are good jobs, too."

I knew about those kinds of jobs. I had worked for a Canadian mineral exploration company one summer. Living in motel rooms in Idaho, I worked fifteen-hour days on a drill rig and drank beer with the drillers in bars at night. I never took my hair out of its braid that summer and finally had to cut it off to get a comb through it. But on my days off I thumbed through a mail-order catalog and thought about ordering fancy bath products—bath salts, moisturizer, facial scrubs, toner. I had never used anything like them; they seemed so beautiful, so gentle, so feminine. I'd thumb through the catalog, dog-earing the pages and filling out the order form in pencil over and over. I never ordered a single item.

The only other female geologist was a sweet Christian from the Midwest who drafted maps in our makeshift basement office and made corn chowder for her husband. They rented a small house, and she had a garden. She didn't associate with the drillers and roughnecks, and I'm pretty sure she never spent an evening in the Atomic Bar. She also made twenty dollars a day less than her husband, who worked a drill rig like I did. Women made women's wages unless they could work and behave like men, and men didn't order bath salts.

I imagined working at the mill, the harsh ugliness of that life, and almost started crying just thinking about it.

"Thanks for the tip," I said to Gloria. "It's always good to have a plan for when things don't work out."

A mechanic wheeled into the yard and shouted at Gloria, "I'll be right back. I have to go pay my cable bill."

"Is he going to look at my van?"

"Oh, he could," Gloria said, not looking at me, "but Mike's really the one you need."

Eventually, the mechanic, whose name was Tom, came back and looked under the hood. "It's a loose wire, see?" He jerked on the cable to the isolator. I watched closely. The cable didn't move in its fitting.

"I don't think so," I said quietly.

He ducked his head under the hood again. "It's probably the alternator."

"Can't be. I just had it replaced."

"Sometimes the rebuilt ones are bad."

"Yeah," I allowed. I looked under the hood so as not to threaten him. "Maybe you could put a voltmeter on it."

"Yeah," he said brightly. "That'd be the thing to do." He trundled off into the dark shop.

Tom's ineptitude didn't bother or surprise me. The day before I would have been indignant, thinking he was trying to pull one over on me, take advantage of me because I'm a woman and presumably don't know much about the mechanics of automobiles. But indignation is a luxury of the ego, a way of exhibiting one's superiority. Without realizing, I had been stripped of this self-righteousness. Like every surface exposed to the salt-laden desert wind, the veneer of who I thought I was had been eaten away. I had nothing left to prove, and no one to prove it to.

Gloria was fussing around the van, ignoring the ringing telephone. "Don't do anything until Mike gets here," she said, bossing Tom, who didn't seem to mind.

"Yeah," I said, "I guess I'll just wait for Mike." Tom seemed relieved.

"We're a Ford place, we don't really work on Chevys," he mumbled as he faded into the blackness of the shop.

Watching the late-afternoon light turn the underbellies of the clouds shades of golden pink, I waited.

I had come to the desert to be alone, to hear myself think in the spare stillness. To eliminate the distractions that seemed to wrap themselves around my life, like pythons around a rabbit, until I couldn't tell up from down. The desert's sparse vegetation and exposed rock evoke subtle thoughts and feelings that civilization and greenery stifle. A young Navajo woman once told me she loved living on her place in a remote part of northeastern Arizona, a land so bleak as to be almost uninhabitable. "One thing about living on the reservation," she had said, "you can scream out your troubles and no one will hear you." The desert is a private place because the light and heat draw out all preconceptions, leaving the soul lean and clear. Distractions here can mean mistakes, and a mistake can mean death. Having death so palpable makes it easier to organize one's priorities.

Wallace Stegner said the West isn't a garden, that you have to change your longing for greenery to appreciate the western landscape. But to me, having grown up and lived in small western towns all my life, the natural landscape is the only garden I've ever really known. Deserts have been meticulously designed by millennia of evolution, the space shaped and rendered in a way no gardener could ever achieve.

Creosote bushes stand alone like diaphanous specimen shrubs regularly spaced by the chemical warriors in their roots. Wildflowers and shrubs bloom after a freshening thundershower, a red, orange, yellow, white and purple carpet of tiny color spots. Frozen plugs of terra cotta granite form ragged, scaled features, drawing the eye out, away. The desert is mulched with ventifacts, wind-burnished and faceted cobbles thousands of years in the making. Too big to blow away, they cover the fine soil underneath, forming a desert pavement of precisely interlocking stones, more finely wrought than a cobblestone path. Unpopulated western landscapes soothe and center me for what I don't understand in the complexities of life with other people.

My experience of deserts didn't fit with what I saw of Trona. The land here had been hard-used. The beautiful desert pavement had been tilled under by off-road driving, military exercises and mining. Salty dirt blew constantly, eating at every man-made surface. I was told vehicle batteries have a life span of only two years: the blowing salt corrodes the terminals like sprayed acid.

Trona and the surrounding land were ugly, and I realized I was horrified and frightened by ugliness. Ugliness was unlovable and I had been running from the belief that *I* was unlovable. I was forever running, trying to escape to a more beautiful place, to a more beautiful man, where the external conditions of ordinary life would not remind me of my secret belief. The fear of being unlovable cornered me at every turn. It panted behind as I ran blindly through every relationship. In Trona, the beast had caught me. I could no longer run. There was no one left to fight, nothing beautiful in which to take sanctuary. I gave up and began to find what I was looking for.

The clouds started to turn slate blue on the undersides as reddish-purple stains played out in the tops. Gusts of wind brushed against the van, and I thought I could hear the sound of tiny particles raining against the sides and roof. I walked to the edge of the yard and looked out at the salt pan.

Salt pans develop from evaporation of shallow freshwater lakes. Water from underground springs bubbles to the surface under the lakes, causing salts to precipitate and form a crusty deposit like hard-water scale. Algae living in the lakes help the process along. Bubbling and precipitation continue until a vertical tube is formed, a soda straw that channels fresh water to the lake surface. The chemical-rich salts are called tufa, and salt with abundant sodium in it is called trona, a type of tufa. Here, the fossil tufa towers are one hundred feet high and form irregular pinnacles on the desert floor, ghosts of deceased Pleistocene lakes.

As I looked longer, I could see the mounded outlines of desert salt-bush, a weedy plant with sage-green leaves that grows in soil too toxic for most plants. Water in desert soil is three times saltier than seawater, and draws moisture out of most plants until they die. Desert saltbush reverses this process by storing salt in its leaves, making the plant even saltier than desert water, and thereby drawing moisture into the plant. The plant collects so much salt that minuscule hairs on the leaves burst, releasing tiny salt crystals on the surface, making room inside for yet more salt, making room inside for yet more poison.

This plant has adapted to the harshest, ugliest environment. It thrives here and in fact could not live in a more hospitable place. The benevolence most plants enjoy would kill saltbush. I had always thought I was unsuccessful at relationships because there was something wrong with me, but now I saw that I had just been trying to live in the wrong climate. Perhaps I was a saltbush and not the tropical flower I had imagined. And what is wrong with that? I thought. It's far better to know what you are and live accordingly than to wear yourself out with the unhappiness of trying to fit into a life that never satisfies.

Mike arrived in the tow truck just before dark. He went into the office, grabbed a burrito and a can of Coke. I watched him wolf his dinner as he walked across the yard. He was a boyish-looking middle-aged man in dark blue jeans, a flannel shirt and a black foam baseball cap. He smiled.

"Havin' some trouble?"

I recounted the entire history of my electrical problem, which had begun some eight hundred miles and three Chevrolet dealerships earlier. Tom came over to offer his opinion about loose wires and bad alternators. Mike patiently explained what the different readouts on the voltmeter might indicate. While he and Tom puzzled over the van, I stood with Gloria.

"You have a place to stay? You could have my couch," she offered.

"If they get the van working, I'll camp out in the desert."

Misinterpreting the look on her face in the waning light, I added, "Course, if it's late, I'll just get a room." It was the wrong thing to say.

"Oh, where will you stay?" she asked, her voice unnaturally nonchalant.

I named a motel I had passed as I came into town.

"Don't go there. They overcharge and the rooms aren't that good. Go into Ridgecrest, it's only a few miles further on."

Mike was beckoning from the front of the van. "Give 'er some gas."

I got in and revved the engine. The voltage needle jumped.

"Okay," he said.

"What do you think it is?"

"I think you have a bad cell in your battery, but all these test okay. Is there another battery in this rig?"

I took him around back to the auxiliary battery cabinet. He was working by flashlight now.

Despite his long day, Mike was quick to smile and full of stories. He'd grown up here. He told me about his boyhood explorations of lost caves and abandoned mining camps in the hills around Trona. He told me how to get to some of them, although the information seemed to evaporate before I could picture the route. He described the kinds of rock in certain canyons and I speculated on the names, offered facts about their origins or history. He told stories about the predicaments he had pulled people out of in the backcountry. Like this latest couple who had high-centered their sedan and had to walk for two days. They had waited for help for three. A thin laugh scratched out of me; I had so narrowly missed a similar fate.

A 1960s Oldsmobile pulled into the yard. Mike walked over to the driver's side and leaned down. After a while the owner got out of his car and came over to me. His black hair was slicked back. He sported Elvis-like sideburns and wore a thin white short-sleeved shirt over a white T-shirt. He was either way ahead of or way behind the fashion curve. I imagined he had just come from the bowling alley and the 1965 men's league.

I chatted with him. He wanted to talk politics.

"I hope they pass that anti–affirmative action law. It just ain't fair. A man can't get a job around here unless he's a spic or a nigger." I winced and glanced over at the shop, where the Latino kid lay on a creeper.

Speeches began to form in my mind. A few choice words, a narrowed look and closed gesture would tell him I disapproved of him, he was wrong, he was unworthy of my time, he was disgusting. But then I understood I couldn't change this man's opinions any more than I could make someone love me. I stood there and suddenly felt free of the compulsion to make the man be as I wanted, as he "should" be. The shadow over my shoulder slipped away; I no longer heard the panting, nor did I feel like running anymore. I felt light.

"It must be difficult," I said quietly.

That simple phrase uncorked him.

"You remind me of my daughter," he blurted. "She's out in Reno. I haven't seen her in years."

He told me all about her. I stood in the dark and listened to this man talk so tenderly about a daughter who probably didn't think much of him. I wished she could hear how he spoke of her. I guessed that she would probably like to know that her father really did love her.

How do we learn how to love? I still don't really know, but I learned more about love from that odd collection of people in that ugly little town than I ever learned in the arms of a beautiful man. I left that night relaxed, as if released from a great tension. I felt as if I had made love. And it was more satisfying than anything any lover had ever done for me.

Driving onto the salt flats south of town, I made my way through the soft patches and hard ruts toward a group of tufa towers. After setting up camp I stood out in the moonlight. The wind was blowing hard, but the desert was still, the crust firm. I licked the salt off my lips, satisfied.

tooling along

kathryn morton

S haped like an egg in the era of acute angles and razor-edge tail fins, colored dull blue when metallic shine was the fashion, gas-efficient when nobody cared, foreign when even VWs were still considered exotic, my first car was perfect. And topping it was the first sunroof I had ever seen, a plasticized folding canvas lid that could be shoved back so far that sky shone straight down into the back seat. I drove that car all over the eastern seaboard the summer of '67, mostly alone. I named it Henryjames because, like its name-sake novelist, the car had strength of character and a tendency to take longer to get where it was going than one could reasonably imagine.

It was a 1962 Saab with only fifty thousand miles on it. A guy from college (who drove a thirty-five-dollar Chevy) had spoken of the Saab as the ideal car: front-wheel drive, solid body, dual-diagonal brakes, built-in roll bars and a front-end engine. And what an engine! Only three cylinders, six moving parts, no separate lubrication system. Too simple to go wrong. Mechanically, it was the equivalent of three lawn mowers under one hood or three motor scooters linked together. Anomalous and marvelous, it even had a hand starter in addition to a hand choke. It had a freewheel lever for those long, downhill glides when the car might as well coast without wear and tear on the clutch. Its engine box had other idiosyncrasies, like the window shade behind the grill, with a handle inside the car to make it possible to protect the engine from road spray on stormy days—a necessity because the distributor was located right behind the grill. Anything more than a mist would spritz the wiring where the electricity runs its course to spark each piston in turn to fire and move the car. In short, it shorted in the rain.

Fair weather was best. But I was at that time of life that sought the storm. I had been through college. Assigned to analyze the narrative structure and devices of irony in the novels of Tolstoy and Faulkner, I had instead gotten sozzled on the angst of Anna throwing herself under a train and drugged on the ineluctable and myriad outrage of Addie living in such a way as to get ready to stay dead a long time. I looked like a choirgirl and ached like a torch song. So far, life had not left me any interesting memories or scars.

After college I had moved back home to Norfolk, Virginia, to the bed of my childhood. I got a job evenings and helped care for my invalid grandmother by day. I lived under the watchful care of my parents, who knew every danger and pitfall within twenty miles and worried on my behalf about each one. Sometimes at night, I would climb out the dormer window and sit on the roof for a little air. I worried my parents. But theirs was a kind of emotional myopia: Up close every ominous splinter or pinprick loomed large, but when I could get some distance between us, my surroundings became to them a luminous blur. Their worry quotient was inversely proportional to the square of the distance between us. If I was in the same room, didn't my face look flushed or maybe pallid? Did I feel okay? If I was just in the same town, they wanted to know where I was after dark. If I could get one hundred miles away, they had daily concern. A thousand miles, and all the wrinkles were airbrushed away by the weather zones that came between us. I could relax and we could smile at each other long distance. So, after my grandmother's death, and between jobs, I found reasons to be other places: there was a course to take in North Carolina, a friend to visit in Georgia, a reunion in Indiana, a former roommate in New Hampshire, the World's Fair in Montreal. The car got forty miles per gallon on the open road. I could go 120 miles on a dollar's worth of gas.

While living under guard at home, I would wonder what had become of me, where was the *me* that I had started to become. Alone on the road, I was present. Whatever road I took, I was never lost. Whatever hill I was on, that was where I was. Whatever valley, whatever bridge I was crossing, all of me was in that very place. The car was my carapace as I happily turtled along. I could even retract inside for sleep. The front bucket seats could be shoved all the way forward. The back of the back seat lifted out. I would wrestle the cushions into a kind of pallet and stretch out lengthwise in the car with my feet in the trunk: the ultimate trundle bed. To achieve privacy, I clothes-pinned blue gingham to a ridge that extended above the side windows. Another piece of the cloth hung over the visors to curtain the windshield. The rear window was obscured by clutter. By wadding jeans and sweatshirts for padding and marshaling considerable inattention, I could lie in an attitude of comfort, and even sleep. I was young.

But I liked to drive at night. It is a secret time beyond the hedges of the day. The orange crowd in the West would finish its party. The hard-to-see lilac time passed into solid dark. The small highways emptied of cars. A dashed line down the center of the road gave a rhythm to my speed. Occasionally a neon tavern blared in the darkness. And once in a while, set back from the road, a house would have a light on inside: somebody sick, or dying, or being born, or just waiting. I would smile in their direction without slowing down. Stoplights in small towns blinked yellow after midnight. Some towns left the main road's stoplight set on green. In those days the hue of the green varied from state to state as though made by local recipe, anywhere from sour apple to a sweet mint.

In the small hours there is a coziness: the stars lie low. The air opens its night smell of earth and green. In a bog or from a culvert, frog croaks would ring as loud as a bowling alley's smack and twang with the bombast of the big bulls and the *scree* of peepers. Henryjames had no radio. I sang. I replayed out loud recent or long-ago conversations with men, and even if I changed my dialogue, the outcome would be the same. The past has an inevitability. Resigned and notably alone, I would ride silent for miles in the cushioned darkness, pulled by the pool of light that lured Henryjames and me along the macadam.

Eventually, a bird would begin to sing in the darkness. Trees would drip. Wraiths of mist gauzed the road. I would take the challenge of the blackness and try to catch it giving up to the encroaching light. I would try to name the moment when now—now!—night is over. But, as though I had slept or had glanced at some other horizon for an instant, I would miss it. And looking up, I'd see that light was already there, silhouettes in the woods were forming. And above, the whole black sky had begun to fade. Alone, at such times, you can feel the world's motion, as the shoulder of the earth heaves toward morning, you and the planets and nebulae and galaxies all moving toward something and away from something. Like a child who comes to the head of the stairs to hear the talk of grownups below, you can eavesdrop on the universe.

Then night was over. With hunger beginning to grab at my innards, and shivering with a chill that comes with sleeplessness, in the washed-out light of early morning, I'd watch among the fading stars for that great afterthought: sunrise.

To arrive somewhere at breakfast time felt like appearing out of the mist.

The problem in those days was that I would not always arrive. I might. Or dawn and a patronizing policeman might find me asleep in my car on the shoulder of a country road, or squeezed up against a highway guardrail that blocked my retreat from the battering wind-blast of every truck that soared past, or in an otherwise vacant parking lot, or mired in the median mud between rivers of rolling traffic six lanes wide. I would be wherever I had had enough momentum to get to when I felt the engine quit. I would coast off the road and stay there. Or, if nearing the top of a rise, I would rev the starter, pop the clutch and oomph my way to the top, coasting down the other side. In that way, sometimes, I could reach a turnoff or at least a wide place and get clear of the road. That maneuver got me off a New York thruway one night. It was plain blind luck that got me off the interstate below Cincinnati in the pounding rain the night the wipers went out and the windshield ran like a dappled river of red taillights. When the tires hit the median, I braced for the crash, but instead there was sudden stillness with just the sound of tire-shine on the highway behind me and the battering of rain on the canvas roof. A state trooper, valiant as a knight on a flashing steed, tried to push Henryjames out of the mud. All wet, pride hurt, he finally called a tow truck.

Dry in the bright and quiet garage, I watched a pair of mechanics lift the hood and pretend not to be surprised. The younger one poked and prodded in a general sort of way, then swaggered over to let me know that I needed new spark plugs. I looked at their wall chart of what a good plug looked like (burned clean like the rack of an efficient barbecue grill) and what bad ones looked like (gunked up or bent or busted). I asked to see my old plugs. Cute little things. They looked good, like the chart. The young mechanic said the gap must be wrong and leaned in close so that I might benefit from his cologne. I turned on my choirgirl, eighty-IQ, gee-gosh smile and aimed it at his elder partner. Could he show me how to check a spark plug's gap? He showed me a gauge, a bundle of little bent wires of different thicknesses. "You read your owner's manual to git the distance. And then you slip that right-numbered wahr between here and here, where the spark's gotta leap. If the gap's too wide, you take whatever you got handy—a wrench or screwdriver handle or sump'n—and you whap the little sucker like that, to bend it tighter." Thus began my education.

By the time I was out of the shop, the sky had cleared. Temporarily. Fifty miles further on, a cloud broke open and my car coughed and drowned in the flood. I was wisely away from the six-lane traffic. Now on a quiet country road, I managed to coast and coax the car up under the carport of a weedy, defunct filling station. It made no sense to think the new spark plugs had suddenly gone awry. Something else was wrong. I opened the hood and just looked. A gray metal thing with wires running into it was wet. Surely it wasn't supposed to be wet. The wires were wet. Wires are not supposed to get wet. I dried them off with a sweatshirt and sat down to have a sandwich and think. As I thought, I smoothed the aluminum foil sandwich wrapping against my thigh. It probably wouldn't help much, but what could it hurt? It wouldn't catch fire. Back under the hood, I molded the foil over the distributor, got back in and drove on.

A day later, at my alma mater, a couple of acquaintances saw the car and sought me out. How was it doing? What were its problems? They told me about the window shade. They showed me how to use a rubber glove to cover the distributor: thumb for the incoming wire, three of the fingers for the wires to the spark plugs and the pinky finger extended like that of a lady sipping tea.

After I learned how to protect the engine against the elements, it found other ways to die. A three-cylinder motor does not have any lagniappe. One gunked plug, one shorted wire, one clogged fuel inlet and the car crawled and stalled. Nothing daunted, I kept taking trips and adding to my tool kit.

A person with more leeway in her life would have acknowledged her transportation problems and either stayed home or learned to drive only short distances by daylight, glad to trade the intergalactic mysteries for plain mortal safety. She would not have longed for different time zones as though Oz awaited in each one. She would not have added unsanctioned side trips to her authorized itinerary. Or if she were determined occasionally to visit men or horizons her parents did not approve of, she would have learned to stand up and argue her own turf, claiming a right to possess her own intentions.

None of those options seemed open to me. My parents *expected* me to live the life they imagined for me. "We *expect* to hear from you by five; we *expect* you to have a good time at your girlfriend's and call us." Long-distance phone calls left a record. The point of origin for each call would be known. If I clonked a handful of change into a pay phone instead of calling collect, there was a lecture on false economy, so I often took a roundabout way so the record would show I had been in the approved place at such-and-such a time. My parents' expectations had for me an import and irrevocability like that of gravity. Breaking the law would have broken apart the known universe. To be the me they loved, to be their Kathryn, I could not argue. Other people in their lives argued. Other people disappointed them. Other people hurt them. I was the good girl. I did not disappoint. If there was an increasingly active part of me that could not actually *be* good, I would at least *appear* to be good, and I'd make up the difference by driving all night, keeping my dark side turned away from their life-sustaining sun.

They had bought me the car. I took what advantage I could of the rewards of being a good daughter. It was expected that I would. And besides that, the car was part of my father's hopeful expectation that my years of exploration should include new geographical horizons. Guys I might go visit on the way—or out of the way—were not part of his idea of expanding my vistas.

Instead of learning to be good, honest or safe, I fictionalized my life and learned to keep a blanket in the car. And gradually I learned about auto repair. Fixing the car myself was just another way of side-stepping authorities who everywhere seemed ready to position themselves in my path, telling me what I could or could not do. While my parents had their version of my best interests at heart, auto mechanics had other motives. To get a mechanic's permission to go on required not only obeisance, but cash. Ultimately, I resented paying the cash less than playing the role of rescued damsel to a series of yahoos.

Among these would-be rescuers was one lad who struggled to look lordly while asking, "Whuch en's yur enjun at?" and the guy who tried to sell me an oil change—in a car whose only oil went in the gas tank with the gas, lubricating the pistons as it burned. There were the hopeful gas-pump jockeys who told me that I wouldn't need to put oil in the tank if I would just use a higher grade of gas. There was the sharpie in Williamsburg who saw my car stalled out across the street from his garage and said his towing charge was thirty dollars regardless of the distance, and there was his cousin-in-spirit in Georgia who said the air in my tires needed changing.

Still, had my first time under the hood been different, the course of my future might also have been different. Early in our relationship, before I had gone far enough to have engine trouble, Henryjames's hood blew off. It hinged from the front fender in such a way that, sitting behind the wheel, you could see into the bowels of the engine. A prop-stick held it up for work, and a restraining strap was supposed to keep this clamshell from opening all the way. At some point, mechanics had lifted the whole hood off to improve their access to the engine. When they replaced the hood, they failed to bolt down the restraining strap. Indoor or quiet-day checkups did not betray the hood's potential for flight. But one afternoon at Wrightsville Beach, as I went under the hood to investigate a rattle, a gust off the ocean took hold of the hood and took it sailing. It came to rest on its back, half a block away, free, detached and holding up little bouquets of colored wires like flowers in a corpse's hands. The raw copper ends of the wires hinted at an earlier relationship with headlights and hood-mounted car horn. The surety of color-coding had been eliminated by someone's earlier repairs: All the wire covers were now the same color. I feared I might reattach them incorrectly, so that the lights would blink when I hit the horn, and the horn would honk when I tapped the turn signal. But reattaching the wires in the right configuration was just a matter of matching available lengths. The easy success gave me an unwarranted sense of competence: have pliers, will travel. I bought a bolt and reattached the restraining strap. And I traveled.

I did meet one honest mechanic, in South Hill, Virginia. He showed me how to unclamp the air filter, unbolt the top of the carburetor and blow dust out of the needle valve. In Kentucky a Sunday-morning cop showed me how to siphon gas out of my tank without swallowing any, and how to use it to clean motor parts. A pair of motorcyclists in the Carolina mountains delighted in revealing to me my car's ability to be started from under the hood. A one-legged man driving a hand-controlled Volvo on the New Jersey Turnpike diagnosed a laboring fuel pump and showed me how to clean the filter and reinsert it by feel (much like inserting a tampon, though he did not offer that comparison).

After that encounter, believing the fuel-pump diagnosis, I sought out a Saab dealership outside of Washington, D.C. Yes, they had a reconditioned fuel pump that would fit my old car, but no, nobody could help me put it in. The mechanic was booked till a week from Thursday. My folks expected me home that night, and they expected me to be coming from the west, not the north. I bought the pump and pushed my car to a quiet piece of parking lot.

If a component does not work, you just remove it, noticing the sequence of events. Then by reversing the sequence, you put the new item in place. Pretty simple—when you can reach the thing you are working on and you have the tools. I had an adjustable wrench. Unfortunately, the fuel pump was attached inside the engine housing, with its bolts sticking into the wheel well. If the front right tire had been off, I could have seen where to put the wrench to take the nuts off. The front right tire was on, however, right smack in my way, and I did not want to take the time to jack up the car and remove it. Nor did I fancy getting down and dirty with the automobile while it was balanced on my little jack.

I reached in behind the tire and got the four mud-crusted nuts off. There is some satisfaction in blood on blackened knuckles. Perhaps I was beginning to live. Sweat was changing the color and texture of my T-shirt as I lay under and hunkered over the car. I noticed that the mechanic who was booked till a week from Thursday had come out to watch me kneeling on the July blacktop, embracing my car's front bumper. The hard part was holding the new pump with its bolts in place on the inside of the engine housing with my left hand while I embraced the fender and stretched my right hand double-jointedly in behind the tire to feel where to put the nuts on the out-of-sight bolts. Kneeling, squatting, twisting, sprawling, I dropped sweat onto the blacktop where it rose as steam. If I had been alone, I would have cried. The mechanic watched. I did not cry. Maybe if I turned the wheels all the way left? The bumper shone with sweat smears. My arm came out streaked tire-black from the close negotiations. Maybe if I cocked the wheels all the way right. The service-department supervisor joined the watching mechanic. The sweat-wet fuel pump slipped out of my fingers again and again. I quit to dig in the trunk. All I had were paperbacks. It took several tries to find the right combination of thicknesses to form a prop to wedge the pump in place so it wouldn't move while I got the nuts on. Walt Whitman and Langston Hughes did the job, books that still show the smudges of blood. Of course, either of the live men standing there could have taken one step forward, reached out and held the pump for me, but they were tied up till a week from Thursday. I could have asked for help. If I were somebody else. When the pump was on, attached and running, I drove away without looking back.

My only higher triumph happened one mile from home. I had used the car's last momentum to coast into a filling station. Coming out from under a hydraulic lift, wiping his dirty hands on a dirtier rag, the man whose name was on the filling-station sign diagnosed the problem as being in the "reeds" way down in the engine. In lugubrious tones, he conjured the labyrinthine murk of a bayou or Grendel's cave. I said I didn't need help, I was just going to clean the carburetor and be on my way. A crowd began to form from the people waiting at the bus stop. The mechanic said he would have to tow me to Richmond, ninety miles west, that that was the nearest dealership. I've never known if he spoke from ignorance of the dealer a mile from where we stood, or if his knowledge of Saab dealers was as homegrown as his knowledge of the simple engine. I repeated that I was just going to clean the carburetor's needle valve and be on my way. He leaned in to get a better view of the carburetor (or of my V-neckline), till a liberal gesture with my screwdriver inspired him to reposition himself. I had the air filter clamps up, the lid off, the filter out, the carburetor top loose and then off. He reached his dirty hand toward the clean interior of the carburetor, where only air and gas should blend. At my "Hey! Don't touch that!" he stopped and the crowd giggled.

In counterattack the mechanic repeated his forecast of incapacity and the long tow job. I blew out the needle valve, re-lidded the carburetor, and before putting on the air filter, I put my hand over the air-intake to choke the motor and pulled the starter lever's nether end the way the bikers in the mountains had shown me, and—oh sound that echoes in my best dreams, oh sound that brought the assembled crowd to outright laughter, oh sound of life at last getting underway— *RRrrRRR-RRRR!* The motor revved, resonating on all of its three cylinders. I replaced the air filter, shut the hood and drove on.

It has been decades now since that summer. Life has happened, and is still happening. My parents lived to see and fret about their first grandchildren before Henryjames finally died for good and became spare parts for needy cars. That filling station near home changed hands, closed and was replaced by a dry cleaner; now a chain drugstore is going up on the spot. My current car is too dependent on computers and sealed units for me to mess under the hood—except when I jump-start somebody or check the fluid levels. But the lessons I learned with Henryjames are part of my way of life: don't crowd your children; do ignore naysayers; if something's broke, fix it; look to the horizon as a dependable source of interesting uncertainties; and never drive a car too heavy to push.

small gifts

andromeda romano-lax

*M*aybe you could wait until after Hanukkah," my mother-in-law suggested as we juggled boxes and baby, hauling load after load of our belongings into the chill air of a midwestern December. My own mother, representing the Catholic contingent of our multifaith family, asked if we couldn't wait until after Christmas.

Really, they wanted to detain us until spring. Who would move north with a three-month-old infant, faithful but fretting dog and distinctly unfaithful secondhand car at this time of year? The binding on our new Alaska atlas was uncracked. Our stiff-tongued, rubber-soled Sorel boots, unsullied by snow or wear, squeaked with every step, broadcasting our inexperience. Brian and I had never visited Alaska—had barely even read about it. Wait a few more months, friends and relatives suggested delicately, wise enough to know we wouldn't listen.

Our stay among family in the Midwest was to be temporary, a stopgap between graduate school on the East Coast and a bolder move somewhere else—anywhere else—after the baby was born. But a carefree interlude wasn't in the cards. Both Brian and I spent my pregnancy working temporary, suburban corporate jobs: he took a pharmaceutical research position, though he really wanted to teach environmental science somewhere beautiful and wild; I typed and filed, though I'd published a book and couldn't wait to write again. We both scratched around for more serious career offers, but nothing materialized. Then tragedy struck, dwarfing our petty professional dilemmas. My husband's father died unexpectedly, struck down in his prime by a cardiac aneurysm.

I attended his funeral five months pregnant, and spent the following months waddling around my in-laws' basement, sifting through decades of family papers and mementos, to help prepare my mother-in-law for her own move north to Toronto. Brian reminded me that it was his father who had first injected the idea of Alaska into our minds, by clipping a classified ad that promised job opportunities on the Last Frontier.

During those months, it was hard to distinguish the painful weight of grief from the normal ponderousness of pregnancy. My husband and I were sad for so long that I worried we had infected our unborn son. When Aryeh was born, we named him after my deceased father-in-law, but added a second name, Itzhak—Hebrew for laughter—as an antidote to sorrow.

But a high-spirited name for our newborn son wasn't enough. Brian and I knew we needed a dose of adventure to kick-start all three of our lives (four, if you included our mutt, Marco, named for another world traveler who didn't balk at long distances).

Why Alaska? Not because of jobs—we'd gotten no nibbles on résumés we'd sent—but because it was clean and far and flush against the Pacific Ocean. Why now? Because we'd already put our lives on hold for a year, and we felt like another month would unhinge us completely. When we read that the highway might actually be safer in winter—fewer tourists, no axle-busting potholes since they'd all be filled with snow—we clung to this questionable assertion with the desperate giddiness of prisoners ready to make their break.

Waiting was out of the question, even with holidays and the year's shortest days around the corner. Hanukkah and Christmas paled next to the allure of this adventure. We were tuning our hearts to the compass, not the calendar. Little did we know that the holidays, too, would shape our days, adding meaning to a nearly disastrous trip north.

"Your first Hanukkah, Aryeh," we said to our son, cradling his sagging neck so that he could ogle the menorah. Three flames flickered—and we weren't even out of my parents' house in suburban Chicagoland yet. We'd intended to celebrate the first night of the Jewish festival of lights on the open road. Maybe even celebrate the last night in Anchorage. Okay, that was dreaming.

But the Maccabees had also been wildly optimistic. How else could a small band of Jews have conceived of defeating their Greek conquerors, liberating Jerusalem and reclaiming their temple almost twenty-two hundred years ago? When the Maccabees entered the temple, they found only one cruse of oil, enough to last one day. They lit the menorah, preparing to resume worship nonetheless. What happened next—the miracle of the lights that kept burning—is all that many Jewish children remember of the Hanukkah story.

We lost two days at my parents' house, packing and repacking our small rental trailer, unable to cram even half of our belongings inside. With each effort to reorganize our possessions, the dog paced in ever-tightening circles and Aryeh cried more frequently. On day three, we'd had enough. We said goodbye to the boxes that would not fit.

Finally, with butterflies in our stomachs, we pulled out of my parents' driveway.

In Wisconsin, a first dusting of snow lined the roadside ditches. Temperatures dipped as our station wagon struggled to tow our trailer north and west. Within hours the engine began to cough. We peeked under the hood, adjusted fluids and kept driving, trying to banish thoughts of more serious car failure.

Near the Minnesota border, we checked into a motel and plugged our car's engine into the outlets that served every parking space. We'd never seen public plug-ins before. It was a taste of northern exotica, like the aurora borealis and Montreal's underground malls.

En route to North Dakota, icy winds blew across rolling farmland. Here we met true winter—not just the season, but the culture. We'd left behind arugula and radicchio, skinny dresses and open-toed pumps. In Fargo, women in bulging stirrup pants drowned their iceberg salads in ranch dressing and ordered seconds of pecan pie. The heaviness of the people—their food, their footwear, their thighs—communicated directly to my own feelings of frailty. This was cold country, and I didn't feel prepared for it. Back on the road, we strained to hold the steering wheel steady against sideswiping winds and listened to the overloaded trailer shift and creak.

At a motel in Grand Forks, Minnesota, we had kindled a fifth Hanukkah candle. At the Saskatchewan border we lit a sixth. Fatigue replaced excitement. All day, as one of us drove, the other sat in the back with Aryeh, shaking rattles in front of his face or playing peek-a-boo. He was a tough audience. The car's magic ability to put a cranky baby to sleep was waning, and its heater was no match for subzero temperatures. Aryeh was infuriated by the restraints of his car seat and increasingly suspicious of this entire trip. His colic flared.

In restaurants, Brian left the table to pace with Aryeh while I gulped my meal. Then we switched. Sometimes it seemed as if we burned more calories than we consumed. Luckily, the meals kept getting bigger. We could judge our latitude by the thickness of a local piece of toast.

We weren't making the speedy progress we'd anticipated, but that was all right. After all, how did the Maccabees proceed? On faith. They lit their oil lamps, and the lamps kept burning. For six days, then seven, then eight. That was the miracle of Hanukkah. Somehow, the oil lasted. Somehow, Aryeh's patience would last. Ours, too.

Then there was the matter of our car, and our money, an ever-dwindling stack of dollar bills. Where the Maccabees had faith, we'd soon be turning to credit cards.

In addition to a small menorah and quick-burning candles, Brian and I had brought a few gifts for each other. They were usually edible, always portable and inevitably cheap.

"Bagel chips? You shouldn't have," I said to Brian, handing him his gift: six packets of instant cocoa and cider mix. "Now can we eat that jar of hot peppers you gave me last night?"

"Still frozen on the back seat," he said.

I went to sleep and dreamed of hunger, and the cold.

In Saskatoon, our worst fears were realized. We pulled into a restaurant parking lot, stepped inside and ordered our dinner. On the Canadian plains, temperatures had plunged to thirty degrees below zero. We were grateful to be inside, rubbing our hands together as a waitress laid out our meal in front of us.

Suddenly the lights went out. Not just in the restaurant, but across town. We sat, stunned, surrounded by inky blackness. The baby started fidgeting. Waitresses shuffled and clattered, swinging flashlights in disoriented arcs.

"The blackout is for miles around. Last time it happened, it lasted for hours. Got pretty cold in here," the manager finally told us. Already we could feel a chill spilling under the doorways and around the window frames. "Your best bet might be to get in your car and keep driving."

We wanted to follow his advice, but our car wouldn't start, even with a jump. We slouched back into the restaurant and prepared to eat our meal, which still sat on the table—barely touched, already gelled with cold.

Sympathetic to Aryeh's loud protests against the dark, the restaurant manager checked on us several times and then exited the building. We heard a car start up, and saw him pull into a space just opposite the picture window next to our table. We watched, curious but uncomprehending. Suddenly, headlamps flared, sending cones of light through the window and over our cold plates. The manager had found a way to illuminate our meal and soothe our child. It wasn't romantic candlelight, but it would do.

We stayed in the adjoining hotel that night, and the next, celebrating the final night of Hanukkah disappointingly far from our promised land of Alaska. Until that night, the Hanukkah metaphor had grown in my mind, lending a narrative resonance to our slow, steady trip. But now the metaphor backfired. We had more than half of our trip to go, almost no money and a broken-down car. The festival of lights was over. Even the Maccabees' miraculous oil lasted only eight days. The hardest parts of the trip—mountain ranges, even deeper cold—lay ahead. What story would guide us now?

A Saskatoon mechanic towed our car, made us wait two days and finally popped the hood. When he did, he couldn't find anything wrong. The car started up again on its own. This problem would repeat itself in every major town that followed. We'd stop, the car would die, and no mechanic in British Columbia or Alaska could diagnose the problem correctly. We'd question car experts, wait for parts ordered from distant states or provinces, sign credit-card slips and hope for the best. Meanwhile, we'd kill time in cheap motel rooms, reading aloud from John McPhee's *Coming into the Country*—his seminal work about backcountry living in the forty-ninth state—or tracking the ominous predictions of the Weather Channel.

The latter pastime, in particular, began to consume me. "Watching the weather again?" Brian would ask, exiting the bathroom to find me perched on the edge of a sagging motel bed, staring at the television. "Has it changed in the last hour?"

Finally, the car would reawaken and face the road again. Goodbye cable TV, hello real winds and ice, real clouds gathering menacingly on the lavender horizon.

Behind the wheel, days were short and the landscape, haunting. The hillsides shimmered under a glaze of hard-packed snow, embroidered by the tracks of big game. The white, frozen highway reflected the sun, a smoky disk hovering only inches above the horizon. On bright days the effect was blinding. On overcast days the air looked hazy and surreal. We slowed to a crawl through herds of caribou near the Prophet River, and saw moose standing near steaming meadows, where natural hot springs thawed the frosted earth. We drove through snowstorms and fishtailed up and down icy roads. Only a few cars passed us each day, and night came on suddenly, alarming Aryeh, who by now hated nothing more than driving into the darkness.

North of Fort Nelson, we slid and strained up a steep mountain pass, stopped at the first gas station we'd seen in hours and groaned when the car wouldn't start again. Our car always managed to conk out in a sheltered place with a public phone. If we'd broken down on the open road, who would have found us? And how long would our baby, who still weighed less than a good-sized Christmas turkey, have lasted in the cold?

A tow truck pulled us one hundred miles back to Fort Nelson, and told us along the way how lucky we'd been. "Valleys get sixty below, seventy below," he said. "Man's car broke down and found him dead in a ditch, just the other day."

We spent four days in Fort Nelson, awaiting repairs. Signs at the local grocery store announced upcoming sled dog races, but not for a week. Meanwhile, nothing else was happening in town. More McPhee. More Weather Channel.

It happened again in Watson Lake, and in Whitehorse, and in Tok, where we arrived on the winter solstice. We hung out at Fast Eddy's diner for days, soaking up the ambiance of the "dog capital of Alaska" and eavesdropping on mushers, whose insulated coveralls, kennel trucks and talk of dog chow impressed us.

We split meals, trying to stretch a single hamburger between two adults and over several hours, just to avoid returning to our small, dark motel room. Our waitress sympathized.

"I got stuck in Tok, too. Stayed at the campground, and learned to catch squirrels for stew and make bannock bread," she said, making our hamburgers seem needlessly extravagant.

"That was years ago," she said. "I never left."

The thought struck fear in my heart. I hadn't planned to become a waitress, or raise my infant son on rodent stew. But then again, how much of the last few weeks had I planned? The shortest, darkest days of the year bred a cruel kind of fatalism.

On Christmas Eve, the car decided to run again and we drove to Glennallen. Anchorage was less than two hundred miles away, but night had fallen, the baby was fussing, the back half of the car was freezing and the dog's shivers had escalated to spasms.

We checked into a hotel—the nicest we'd seen on our trip, and also the loneliest. Except for one young woman tending the front desk, the place was deserted. An adjacent restaurant was already closed, and would remain so for several days. We returned to the car, anxious to find somewhere to eat. Too late. The car was playing dead again, and anyway, nothing in town was open. Even the mini-mart down the street had closed for the holidays. We'd already consumed our small stash of snacks, even the last frostbitten jalapeño pepper.

I briefly phoned home from the hotel room and heard happy sounds at the end of the line in Chicago—the laughter and clatter of family and friends eating, drinking, tearing into presents. Brian sat on the hotel bed while I paced with the baby. Our stomachs growled.

"Will you run out to the lobby's hot water machine this time?" I asked my husband. Those slim packets of cocoa and cider mix that we'd exchanged during Hanukkah, more than three weeks ago, were our only source of sustenance now. It wasn't only the calories we craved, it was the psychological comfort. No, we couldn't really be starving—look, we have cocoa, and cider! How festive! When the baby finally napped, the silence of our hotel room was oppressive.

The next day we faced a whole day without food or diversion. Even homeless people in big cities would fare better. At least they could go to a soup kitchen.

"I hate Christmas," Brian said. At least he wasn't saying that he hated Alaska. Christmas was temporary. At our present rate of travel, Alaska would last forever.

We tried not to talk about the immediate future. We'd spent our last real dollar weeks earlier, and we were only one more car repair away from bankruptcy. No jobs awaited us in Anchorage, and no friends.

That afternoon there was a knock at the door. We jumped to open it. I barely noticed the person standing there—to this day, I can't remember if it was a man or a woman. I remember only large hands, and what they carried. The owners of the lodge had interrupted their own family dinner to send over heavily loaded plates. We stuttered sheepishly, closed the door and fell upon the food like wolves.

It was a classic Christmas feast: ham, creamed peas, yams, green salad and pasta salad. I thought of commenting on the irony of Christians rescuing starving Jews with glazed ham, but I refrained, not wanting to interrupt Brian's enjoyment of the meal.

Perhaps it was the sudden infusion of calories into starving brain cells, or the effect of too many days of squinting at a sun low on the horizon, but my eyes began to mist.

"What can we do to thank them?" I asked Brian.

"I don't know."

"Do you think strangers in Anchorage would have done this?"

He shrugged, and put an arm around me.

I'd been holding on to the hope of Anchorage, fanning a small flame of excitement and optimism that had been nearly extinguished weeks earlier. All the while, I'd been planning to erase all memory of what it took to get there. I wanted to forget Saskatoon, forget Fort Nelson and Watson Lake, forget Tok. But now, I had something I wanted—and needed—to remember: this day, one meal, one kind family. Maybe the Last Frontier really is a different kind of place. Obviously, people don't put up with thirty below without a reason.

Two days and one mechanic later, the car started running again. We drove to Anchorage, and arrived in the middle of what felt like a heat wave: thirty-eight degrees *above* zero. Stepping out of the car to pump gas at a station along the Glenn Highway near the city, I peeled off my coat and scarf, feeling the relatively warm air tickle my wrists, my collarbones, the tops of my ears.

We used the last of our financial reserves to rent an apartment. There was nothing left for food, but we did have some Gulf War–vintage MREs packed in the back of the trailer. We'd received them as a gag wedding gift from my aunt years earlier, and had stashed them in an emergency box with extra candles and a shovel. Some gag gift—they tasted great. If only we'd been able to pry them out of the frozen trailer earlier. We dined on them regally in the warm, bare space of our new apartment, toasting the moose browsing outside our window.

There was one last problem. The trailer we'd rented to haul our boxes and minimal furniture was three weeks overdue. Dreading hundreds of dollars in late fees and knowing I had no cash, I clenched my teeth and stomped into the rental agency, prepared to do battle. Sure, we'd pay—ultimately—but they'd better not hassle or humiliate us, I told my husband.

The store manager dissolved my pretense of toughness. He listened to my story, wiped his hands on his coveralls and fiddled with the computer.

"There you go," he said, handing me a receipt to sign. There was no grand total on the form. I saw only one small zero.

"What do we do now?" I asked him, sure there was more to the deal.

"Nothing," he said, laughing. "Sounds like you've been through enough."

If this had been a Hollywood movie, I would have noticed the name Nicholas on his name badge at the last minute. But this was no movie, just a new Alaskan's true story.

I thanked the rental-agency manager and headed for the door.

"Welcome to Anchorage," he called after me. "You'll like it here."

He didn't say Happy Hanukkah, or Merry Christmas, but he may as well have.

For the first time in my life, the two holidays seemed to have compatible meanings, beyond the simple coincidence of their seasonal timing. Hanukkah was tenacity; Christmas was generosity. The first had pushed us onto the road north; the second had saved us from it. Both had brought us to a new life in a new place, at a fitting time of year.

substitution trunk

martha gies

*t*he want ad appeared on a Sunday in winter, and it was so perfect it made my heart lurch: "Stage assistant for traveling magic show. Three months out of town. The Great Kramien."

I circled the phone number with a felt-tip pen.

The Great Kramien was a portly man somewhere beyond fifty. His thick, dark hair crested in romantic waves above his face, making him look like an old-time matinee idol. I sat in the beige-on-beige living room of his ranch-style home and listened to him reminisce about his most recent stage assistant, who had deserted him, inexplicably, for a job as a bookkeeper.

"This kid was gorgeous," he said. "You know, Chinese." His beefy right hand dipped into a can of peanuts by his chair and he popped a handful in his mouth.

From the next room came the *coo* and *caw* of a large aviary.

A woman came into the room, bringing us coffee, its surface a soapy white swirl.

"Thanks, doll," Kramien said. "This is my wife, Miss Kathleen." Miss Kathleen was half Kramien's age, with showgirl legs and a sculpted bubble hairdo, already an anachronism in 1974.

"Miss Nevada World, 1969," Kramien called after her. "Right, babe?"

Miss Kathleen didn't answer and we proceeded with the interview. Kramien had seven elaborate satin costumes, custom-made for the Chinese girl, awaiting someone who wore size five. They would fit me without alteration, which I took as a sign: I would learn the secrets of sorcerers, passed down through the ages.

Kramien did allude to the salary, but that was not my main concern (though later I was surprised to learn that I had to pay all my own road expenses out of this modest amount). We shook hands. From his itinerary (the expired mining towns of the Continental Divide) and his venues (public school gymnasiums), I understood Kramien was third-rate. It only enhanced the fascination. I was in my twenties, and still believed that authenticity sprang only from the lower depths, an idea I would hold dear right up until I took a job as a sheriff's deputy. But that was to be later on.

I left in early January. My single suitcase held jeans, T-shirts, guidebooks for six states and a paperback biography of Houdini. Mildew freckled its pages, but it had cost me only thirty-five cents.

My mother drove me to a Portland freeway exit off I-84, where I was to meet up with The Great Kramien. At five in the morning the magician pulled up in a white Cadillac, Miss Kathleen in the passenger seat beside him. My mother, whose bravado extends to even the most dubious of her children's pursuits, said simply, "Write if you get work," which was an old gag between us. I climbed into the Cadillac's commodious leather-upholstered back seat and waved goodbye to her through the tinted window.

The entire show followed us in an eighteen-foot truck: prop storage, animal pens, aviary and living quarters for the young driver and his wife, Roy and Iris. With a leer, Kramien advised me they were newlyweds. The truck was painted red, with the magician's name on either side above a top hat and two wands, and represented Kramien's entire fortune. I noticed that whenever he lost sight of it in the rearview mirror, his breathing changed.

Driving east through Oregon and Idaho, Kramien talked me through the show.

"We're talking fifty-six cues in an hour and a half," he said, looking at me sharply in the rearview mirror. I also had seven costume changes, and when I was not on stage, I was supposed to be loading animals into props.

"We do the whole show to taped music, hon," Miss Kathleen said, "so everyone's timing has to be perfect."

Kramien interrupted her. "We absolutely *never* tell anyone how the illusions are done." He shifted his bulk around in the seat and looked me in the eye with this pronouncement. "Remember that, kiddo."

"So as we go through these illusions, just write down the names and your cues," Miss Kathleen said. "The magic will all make sense when you have a chance to see the props and study the gaffs."

A gaff, she explained, was the unseen mechanism that made the magic work, an ingenious device, such as a black velvet pocket or clear plastic inner lining; a false door, ceiling or wall; a secret lock or hidden blade.

When Miss Kathleen finally described the Substitution Trunk, the sensational first act finale, she said, "It's probably the closest thing to magic you'll ever see."

The audience sees a solid, heavy trunk. Also on stage there's a cabinet, which she described as standard magician's equipment: drapes hanging on four sides of lightweight aluminum poles. The audience sees one girl put into a large scarlet satin bag. "That will be you," Miss Kathleen advised me. Men are invited up from the audience to tie the bag shut, put the bag in the trunk, padlock the trunk and wind around it with heavy rope. Kramien and Miss Kathleen pull the cabinet around the trunk, and Miss Kathleen steps inside the cabinet, holding the front drapes closed so that only her face is visible. The magician counts to three. At that moment, my face appears between the drapes and Miss Kathleen has vanished into the cabinet behind me. I fling open the drapes. The trunk is there, but Miss Kathleen is gone. The men examine the knots and testify that they are the very same, and undisturbed. Then they unwind sixty feet of rope, unlock the trunk and lift the heavy cover. The satin bag is intact. They untie it and find inside—Miss Kathleen! All this happens in less than two minutes.

"That trunk is a tiny dark space," Miss Kathleen told me, "and you've got to be fast. I hope you're not claustrophobic."

"Elevators don't bother me," I said, "if that's what you mean."

"It's funny," she said. "The tricks that people think are dangerous, like being sawed in half or run through with swords, usually aren't dangerous at all."

Kramien turned a scowling glance on her, which she chose not to notice, and a heavy silence filled the big car.

Half an hour later, I broke that silence by reminding the magician that I had committed to staying with the show only through Nogales, the southernmost booking.

We sped on toward Montana, no one saying a word.

Having read that the infamous Copper Trust hadn't left enough money in the town to buy uniforms for the police, I was happy to find that

Butte, Montana, did have public schools. Our first appearance was at the elementary-school gym.

Backstage in Butte, I sat at a makeshift dressing table in the school lavatory, brushing on green eye shadow. My first costume was gorgeous, a sort of satin corset, iridescent green, with a long train of green and gold ostrich feathers that swept the ground. I could see the whole effect in the mirror only by standing on a toilet seat and holding open the stall door.

Without knocking, Kramien charged into the girls' lavatory, dressed in his tux and carrying his shoes.

I stepped down off the toilet seat.

"Here's what I'm looking for," he said, and he dipped a dirty rag into my jar of cleansing cream, streaking it with shoe polish and grime. He proceeded to shine his patent leather shoes with my cleansing cream, then slipped them on his feet. He shook a couple of red capsules from a prescription bottle and popped them into his mouth. "Five minutes," he barked, then disappeared.

When my music cue began, I whipped on stage, too disgusted with Kramien to be nervous. The matinee was full of children and parents.

The Guillotine, a sinister machine with vermilion uprights and a heavy, diagonal cutting blade, required a willing child. Kramien invited a boy to come up on stage. No older than six, the boy hitched up his corduroy pants and grinned at his sisters in the second row.

Kramien placed a bunch of carrots on the neck piece of the Guillotine and slammed the blade down, sending carrot slices rolling around the floor. The little boy looked on and, remarkably, did not flee the stage.

"And now, ladies and gentlemen, for the first time since the violent days of the French Revolution . . . " Kramien indicated the boy should kneel, with his head across the neck piece.

Then, interrupting his own patter, Kramien turned away from the mike and muttered to the boy, "Okay, you little bastard, ready to get your head cut off?" The boy's face jump-cut from shy self-congratulation to primal terror. I looked at the audience, but they were still smiling; obviously they hadn't heard the remark.

Kramien slammed the blade down once again, and I held my breath—it felt as though the crowd did, too. After a moment, the boy lifted his head, stood, looking a little dazed, and then scrambled back to his seat amidst loud applause. Afterward, he sat with his face pressed to his mother's breast; I don't think he saw the rest of the show.

Meanwhile, Miss Kathleen and I flanked the magician, moving in unison, handing him props, mugging astonishment and encouraging applause. Every ten or twelve minutes, we'd go off stage and return in dazzling new costumes—violet, indigo, burgundy—all worn with net opera hose and silver high heels.

After my fourth costume change, I came back on stage with a small socket wrench hidden in my bodice. We were approaching the end of the first act, which we closed with the Substitution Trunk.

What made the trunk unique was the requirement that I labor to get out of it. The other illusions required little or nothing on my part; usually it was enough to lie still (as when I was cut in half) or make myself as small as possible (as in the Doll House). Getting out of the trunk was a struggle because I had so little time to work. The first night that I performed the Trunk I was clumsy and hyperventilating, as the frantic seconds ticked by in the dark.

After the show, I walked through the center of Butte. Was the show beautiful enough, the little town interesting enough, the magic promising enough to make up for traveling with this guy?

I climbed the Granite Street hill, which commands a view of the town. I had read that the "richest hill on earth" was now hollow to depths of more than a mile underground. The frail and shattered crust on which the city rests was like an eggshell from which the viper had sucked the egg. After the gold and silver were exhausted, the Copper Trust had moved in. By 1900, the fumes from the big smelters had killed all the grass and trees in town. Valuable ore was the gaff that made a big illusion out of Butte. Now that the ore was gone, the trees were back.

I went back for the eight o'clock show, knowing I'd have to keep some distance between myself and the magician. He was swaggering around backstage wearing only his jockey shorts—not an inspiring sight. When he turned around, I saw he had huge raised white scars across his back.

Afterward, Kramien told me we were going out for a drink with "our sponsors," two local men who belonged to the Lions Club. "No thanks," I said.

In a moment, Miss Kathleen appeared, pleading with me. "They like to meet the people in the show, hon. It's a thrill for them." She had changed into a red sweater and a leather skirt, but still had on her stage makeup.

"How did Kramien get those scars on his back?" I asked.

She stopped fishing in her shoulder bag and looked at me. "He had a chimp act in the circus," she said. "One of the chimpanzees went crazy on him."

"Was that the end of the act?"

"Ask him."

"I'll have one drink, that's it." I slowly peeled off an eyelash the size of a butterfly. "Did you ever see him work with the chimps?"

"Don't take off your makeup," she said. "They like us the way we look on stage."

"I'm not getting paid to wear makeup to a bar," I said. I took off the two-inch rhinestone dangle earrings, tissued off the makeup and slipped my trench coat over my jeans.

"Look," she said. "I grew up in Oklahoma. My folks were so poor that when we came to California, we had our mattress strapped to the hood of our car." She gave me a moment for this to sink in, then told me what I could have guessed. "I'm never going to be poor like that again."

"Kathleen, do you think there might be worse things than no money?"

She gave me a look, but no reply.

On the dark street, Kramien grabbed my arm. "They're going to want to know how the magic works," he said, in his gravelly, side-of-the-mouth voice. "Don't tell them *anything.*"

We were met at a cocktail lounge by the two Lions. Without asking whether the rest of us wanted to eat, Kramien ordered for himself: fried eggs and bacon, fried potatoes and toast, which came slathered with yellow oil. Then he pulled out a deck of cards.

One of the Lions, a ruddy-faced man named Mr. O'Connor, spoke up. "The Doll House. I don't suppose you'd tell us how that was done. Or the Sword Box?"

"Those are just big showy illusions," Kramien said. "This is where the real skill lies. Watch." He asked Mr. O'Connor to select a card from a spread deck, show it to the other Lion, and then hand it back to him, taking care to keep it face-down. Kramien placed it back in the deck, covered the deck with a dinner napkin, then produced the very card by stabbing it with a fork. This was a close-up version of the Card Stab, which he did on stage with a large needle. He was good: even at close range, I could never catch him palming the card.

O'Connor kept looking over at me. When I smiled at him, he told me he had twenty-two years as a produce man for Safeway.

"I guess the union is pretty strong here?" I asked.

"You bet," Mr. O'Connor said.

I rattled the last of my bourbon and water. I was interested in hearing about Butte, which Anaconda Copper had dominated for nearly a century, and how the union had fared with them.

"Say, can I buy you another drink?" Mr. O'Connor asked.

"Put your money away," Kramien said.

Mr. O'Connor hesitated, then put his wallet back in his pocket. I stared at Kramien.

"She'll pay for her own," he said, and he returned my stare with a snort.

I finished my drink, untangled my trench coat from the back of my chair and said good night to Miss Kathleen and the Lions. Kramien was gazing off in another direction.

I walked back to the Travelers Rest Motel and winged my suitcase open on the second double bed. Nothing in the room suggested the city of Butte; the orange shag carpet, triangulated toilet paper and bolted-down TV belonged to the larger kingdom of Motel Land. There was no stopper for the tub, so I took a hot shower, then folded back the tightly made bed and began reading the Houdini biography, hoping to recapture some enthusiasm for my new profession.

I learned that Erik Weisz had been born in 1874, at a time when the world was fascinated with spiritualism, séances and psychics. At twenty, he changed his name to Houdini (after the great French stage illusionist, Robert-Houdin) and took his young wife, Bess, to Coney Island to perform as his partner.

I was startled to read that their very first act was the Substitution Trunk. Perhaps I really was in the great tradition, I thought, as I put the book aside and turned out the light.

At eleven the next morning, I was sitting outdoors on the motel steps, waiting for Kramien and blowing on a Styrofoam cup of coffee. Iris, the truck driver's wife, her long red hair in pigtails, joined me.

Roy and Iris had a tough job: responsible for the truck, they were always in the wake of Kramien's anxiety. At each new town, they set up the show, which took two and a half hours, and they were responsible for the strike, which required another hour after the show. They fed, watered and cleaned up after the ducks, doves, rabbit and rooster. Before the show and at intermission, they sold programs, cotton candy and a cheap book of magic tricks.

Iris was eating a doughnut, which was oozing jelly. "I think you do a real nice job," she said.

"Thanks." I sipped the watery coffee. "That trunk is something else."

"That's the best part of the show!" Iris said. She wiped a glob of jelly off her jeans and licked her finger. "Do you believe in magic?" she asked.

"You mean entertainment-magic, or miracle-magic?" Across the parking lot, I watched Kramien come out of his room, unlock the dusty white Cadillac and start the engine.

"I guess I mean both," she said.

"I'm working on it," I said.

Kramien's car began rolling toward us.

"But do you believe it?" she asked. In bib overalls and a pink T-shirt, she looked about fourteen.

I knew she was going somewhere with this question, but I couldn't tell where. "I guess believing is what makes it work," I said.

Iris stood and turned her back on Kramien's approaching car. "They said Roy and I couldn't have a baby," she said in a whisper, "but we're trying anyway."

"That's great," I said, and I reached up to touch her arm.

The Cadillac stopped; Kramien stayed at the wheel.

Iris reached for my empty coffee cup. "Here, let me take this," she said.

"Hey, I'll see you in the next town," I said.

From Dillon, we dropped down into Idaho, playing school auditoriums and grange halls in Idaho Falls, Pocatello, Burley and Twin Falls. Kramien's red pills came out before every curtain. My guess was he'd been an alcoholic, but pharmaceuticals were his habit now. His face told it all: baby-fat cheeks, eyes alternately glazed and inattentive, then excited and watchful.

He guarded the itinerary as though it were the secret of sword-swallowing itself. Roy somehow discovered that the show had another employee, a promoter, who worked ahead of us on the road. The promoter usually called the magician late at night, Roy insisted, and these phone calls confirmed our engagements.

"So when do we play Nogales?" I asked Kramien.

We were coming into Elko, Nevada, and he signaled to turn in front of the Stampede Motel.

I repeated my question.

"Who wants to know?" he asked.

"Look, I said I'd stay with the show through Nogales. So when is that?"

Miss Kathleen pulled down her visor and got busy refreshing her lipstick in the little mirror.

"When I know anything, I'll tell you," Kramien said. He laughed and winked at Miss Kathleen, who refused to meet his eyes.

After I registered at the motel, I put my bags in my room and told Kramien I'd walk to the high school for the afternoon setup. I couldn't spend another minute with him in the car.

On my way across town, I passed the bus station, where I saw a family of four carrying hand luggage and four fishing poles. The woman was a heavy dishwater blond in baggy blue jeans, the right side of her face reddened and erupted with pimples. The two little boys, maybe five and two, had pimples on the same side, as though they were all facing the same direction when a filthy sandstorm blew through. The little ones carried their belongings, stuffed into pillowcases, which they dragged along the sidewalk.

The father, a thin wispy-haired boy with a pencil mustache, went across the street to purchase a little Styrofoam plate of toast and when he came back, the two boys hurried hungrily to his side. They waited in silence as he spread margarine, and then they each received a toast triangle. Right away, the smallest boy set his toast on the ground while he rearranged his pillowcase. The father elbowed his wife, and together they stared at the piece of toast on the sidewalk. Then the father bent down, picked it up and walked it to a sidewalk trash basket. "It's garbage now, buddy," he said. The child stared in disbelief, and then began to cry.

I realized that family could be right out of Miss Kathleen's childhood. Easy for *me* to think she should leave Kramien.

The next day, riding south on U.S. 95, through Hawthorne, Fallon—alfalfa and cantaloupe country—I sat in the Caddy's wide back seat, mending opera hose. The elasticized fishnet lay shriveled in my lap, the big hole I was looking for now hard to see. It was the size of a silver dollar when I was wearing it, but the size of a dime when I took it off to mend. I separated the longest of the busted strands and carefully knotted them together.

Kramien paid me $125 a week, motels cost at least fifteen a night, and I was eating out of the grocery store—apples, canned fish and saltines. I began to envy Kramien's fat-laced diet.

In Tonopah, Nevada, our next town, I told Kramien I wasn't registering at the Best Western.

"What the hell are you talking about?" He was watching Roy back the truck into a parking space.

"We passed an old hotel as we came through town. That's where I'm staying."

"I'm not driving you anywhere."

"You don't have to. I can walk there."

"We're leaving at nine in the morning, whether you're here or not."

"Whatever," I said.

After the evening show, I got a ride with a Rotarian and his wife, who dropped me at the old Mizpah Hotel, a garish relic of the silver boom, half the price of the Best Western. Built in 1907, it had a small casino and a wide, dramatic staircase.

I pushed through the swinging saloon doors, stood at the bar and ordered a whiskey. Five local cowboys were playing poker at a round table; otherwise the bar was empty. The bartender poured me a shot and I asked him to spin the keno cage, just once. I won eight bucks, slugged back the whiskey and picked up my money. "Night, ma'am," the bartender said, and as I left, two of the card players lifted their Stetsons. I floated up the stairs to my shabby high-ceiled room, climbed up on the old iron bed and resumed reading about Houdini.

According to his biographer, after Houdini broke into the theater circuit, a man named Jim Collins always traveled with him. A jack-of-all-trades, Collins designed the gaffs, then built, loaded and rigged them. Houdini always insisted on twenty-four-hour exclusive access to the theater before a show and absolute privacy backstage. The indispensable Jim Collins would set up his control room somewhere out of sight. Eventually they played the most mammoth theater in the world, the New York Hippodrome, which had an entire lake beneath its stage.

So here was the answer to what I'd been wondering: were there any magicians who didn't rely on elaborately prebuilt effects? And the answer turned out to be no. Even Houdini traveled with his own designer and carpenter. I smiled to think that I'd gone to considerable trouble to learn what most of the world already knew—that magic was a beautiful hoax.

The next day we were back in the Cadillac, flying past sagebrush, old miners' shacks and weathered, collapsing pole barns. Kramien's dreadful gaze was frozen in the rearview mirror whenever I looked up to meet it. Since my rebellion he had had this look on his face, as though he expected me to tell the first filling-station attendant how the whole show worked.

When we stopped for lunch in Goldfield, Kramien and Miss Kathleen went into the café. I took my dinner roll and carton of milk and knocked on the door of the red truck. It was a bright February day; Iris set the rooster's cage out on the ground so he could feel the sun. As we ate lunch, Roy and Iris and I talked about what a good performer the rooster was: he waited quietly in his elegant gold-enameled prop, never crowing until he'd been "materialized" by the magician.

"Keep the goddamn show in the goddamn truck," Kramien yelled. He stood in the doorway of the café, wearing reflective sunglasses. He spit a toothpick out of his mouth and let the screen door slam on Miss Kathleen. "What are you, crazy?"

Iris put the rooster back in the truck, and I climbed into the Cadillac without a word. I noticed Miss Kathleen's mascara was smudgy and her eyes red.

When we pulled onto the highway, Kramien bubbled effusively about Las Vegas, somewhere down the line. "First thing, I'm going to chow down on a hot pastrami sandwich, a real one. How does that sound?"

Miss Kathleen said nothing.

"Caesars Palace," he persisted. "How about that?"

She lowered the visor, pulled out a manila folder and, without a word, handed it over the seat to me. It was the first itinerary I'd seen: a typed list of towns, dates and sponsors.

"Beatty, Nevada," I read. "Jaycees—February 27." I scanned down the page and read, at the very bottom, "Nogales, Arizona, Fraternal Order of the Police—March 21."

"Thank you," I said. I handed it back. Kramien glared at Miss Kathleen in disbelief.

But twenty miles later, he cheerfully began to reminisce about his dancing-poodle act.

"Was that before or after the chimps?" I asked.

"The chimps, hell," he said, and he grinned at me for the first time in two states. "That was just a sideline. The big money was smuggling birds from South America."

I saw signs for Beatty, Nevada, but we sailed right through it.

"Wait a minute," I said. "What happened to our engagement in the 'Gateway to Death Valley'?"

"The dogs bark, but the caravan moves on," was Kramien's only comment. "Ancient Arab proverb."

That gave us a four-day break with no show. I was cloistered in a sprawling concrete-block motel on Interstate 93, not far from the magnesium plant at Henderson, Nevada.

I wrote a hasty note to my mother, admitting that the job was not all I might have hoped for: the magician was a jerk and, on what I was paid, I couldn't save up enough to leave the show. I asked her to write me general delivery, Green Valley, Arizona.

By the second day of our impromptu vacation, I had less than a dollar, was woozy from a diet of coffee and soda crackers, and was running a fever. That night, after a semi rumbled by, I darted across the highway—three lanes of traffic, a ravine and three more lanes—to the Outpost Bar.

Inside the door, a blackboard advertised "Noodle Beef Soup, 45c bowl." A red and yellow linoleum floor rose up to meet lurid green walls. Two midgets shot pool in the back, standing on chairs to sight down their cues. The woman behind the bar, one arm in a sling, sold me an order of soup in an oversized Styrofoam coffee cup.

In bed later that night, I heard a crunching sound. When I sat up and turned on the lamp, a sand-colored rat froze for a moment, then relaxed and nosed deeper into my box of soda crackers. I switched off the light. In my delirium, I saw a second rat walk off the desert and through my motel room wall.

My fever broke two days later, leaving me weak but anxious to get back to work. We climbed back into the Cadillac and rolled on, playing Boulder City, Kingman and Flagstaff, which is set in an exalted land-scape of ponderosa pines, then turned south through a lush valley and played Sedona, Cottonwood and Prescott. I was even glad to hear the theme song for the Substitution Trunk start up and feel that old adrenaline rush return.

At Coolidge, Arizona, I got up early and walked north of town to the ruins of a Hohokam Indian village that had been deserted over five hundred years ago. At this site, which Spanish discoverers named Casa Grande, there are the excavated remains of a tremendous four-story temple/observatory. Interesting to think that magicians had governed entire cultures.

A Zuni girl, employed by the U.S. Forest Service, pointed out a curious thing: when the inhabitants abandoned the village, they removed the observatory's interior floors, so that no enemy tribe could gain access to the upper reaches.

After her talk, I sat in the still landscape of white sand and soft green cactuses, eating an orange and trying to solve this mystery. Why was it important that no one ascend to the top floor of the tower? What was the gaff?

At Green Valley, I had a letter waiting. My mother began with a reference to my old cabdriver job, where my assigned number had been fifteen: alluding to my current employment under the magician's saw blade, she began, "Dear 7-1/2." It was a great letter: she made me laugh and she sent cash. Now I had a way out.

Back on the road, Kramien talked about the show promoter. "Dick will be in Nogales," he told Miss Kathleen.

"Why is he sticking around?" Miss Kathleen asked.

"Nogales is hot. The Mexicans eat this up. He's got three thousand tickets out in Nogales. Now he wants to do El Paso."

I leaned over the back seat of the Cadillac and tapped his shoulder. "Nogales is my last show."

Without answering me, he turned on the radio.

In Nogales, I had just paid for a room when the bell tinkled, the door opened and Kramien burst into the tiny motel office. A Chihuahua dashed out from under the counter and danced, yipping, around his trouser cuffs. Without looking down, Kramien raised one foot, as though to plant it squarely on the animal's back. The little dog retreated to a corner brochure rack, where he furiously scratched his neck with a hind leg.

"You're fired," Kramien said.

"What are you talking about?"

He unwrapped two pieces of gum and folded them into his mouth. "You're fired as of right now."

"You owe me for three days," I said.

"Then you're fired retroactive to Wednesday," he said. He dropped the gum wrappers on the rug and smiled. "I hope you haven't already paid for your room." He went out through the tinkling door, leaving me standing in the office of the Pasatiempo Motel, holding my battered Samsonite, my fingers tightening around the handle where the plastic was splitting away from the metal.

Instead of asking the owner for my seventeen dollars back, I went to my room and stretched out on the bed. From my purse I pulled the Houdini biography, which I'd been trying to read slowly.

Houdini began a war against spiritualism, which put him constantly in the headlines: "Houdini Exposes Table Turning" (spirit rapping, automatic writing, crystal gazing, the Ouija board). From famous séance parlors he confiscated wires, tubes, telescopic rods, hooks, coils, rubber hoses and extension poles—all the gaffs of the trade. But the world wouldn't give up the idea that Houdini's own illusions were supernatural, and that Houdini himself was a reluctant psychic.

I lay back and closed my eyes. Kramien, I knew, had the same disdain for spiritualists. But then, his cynicism made him disdainful of almost everyone.

Someone knocked on the door. I opened it to find Roy and Iris standing in the gravel parking lot.

"She's been throwing up," Roy said.

"Does this mean you're pregnant?" I asked Iris.

She stared at her sandals and shook her head.

"It means Kramien is putting her in the show," Roy said.

"I'm really scared," Iris said. "Maybe if we could go over the Substitution Trunk?"

"I can't be away from the truck," Roy said. "I'll come back and get you in an hour." He kissed her hair.

My room had no chairs, so we sat on the pink chenille bedspread. "Okay," I said. "So you and Miss Kathleen bring the trunk on stage, and Kramien invites two men up to examine it. It's solid."

"I know it's solid," Iris said. "I put that thing away every night."

"Then Kramien unfolds the huge red satin bag, which is in the bottom of the trunk, and you step into it."

"I know all about the bag," she said. It was Iris's job to re-stitch the bottom of the bag each night with a single long thread. It had a breakaway bottom; it was the *top* they tied with those extravagant knots.

"So you sit down in the trunk, and the lid is put on, then all six padlocks, then the ropes.

"Meanwhile, Miss Kathleen and Kramien will be pulling the cabinet around the trunk, so you can't be seen when you climb out.

"The important thing for you to remember is, as soon as the lid is on that trunk, you slit open the bottom of the bag with your fingernail and crawl out. Make sure you roll the bag and leave it in the right position at the foot of the trunk.

"I forgot to say you have a tiny socket wrench down the front of your costume. You can't forget that, or it's all finished. There's a concealed trap door on the top of the trunk."

Iris gave me a look of surprise. "There is?" Even she and Roy, who packed this object every night, had never detected the elegantly concealed trap.

"So you need the wrench to remove four bolts in the trap. You have to work *very fast!*

"Once that trap is loose, you hold it in place until you get the signal. When it's time for you to get out, she'll kick the trunk. You've got to drop the trap and *move.* Make sure you leave the wrench and the bolts in the upper corner of the trunk, where Miss Kathleen can find them in the dark."

"How long do I have?"

"You'll hear Kramien yelling at the men to hurry up and rip those ropes and locks off, but don't worry about it. They've got sixty feet of rope to unwind."

"So how long do I have?"

I put my arm around Iris's shoulder. "About ninety seconds."

"I don't know how I got into this," she said, and she stood to go.

"I'll come down to the gym later and see how you're doing," I said. I still had two chapters left.

On his deathbed, I read, Houdini had warned Bess that the psychics would swarm all over her after he died. He gave her a secret password that only the two of them knew. Never believe it's me, he told her, unless you hear this word.

In 1926, Houdini died. Sure enough, Bess was set upon by mediums, and every one of them claimed to be in touch with the great magician.

But none of them knew Houdini's secret word. And Bess held out, waiting for the signal.

At three o'clock, I walked down to the gymnasium. Roy was setting up the show amphitheater-style, on a tarp covering the gym floor, facing one wall of bleachers. Kramien was rattling a prescription bottle and shouting instructions. Two black velvet wings, hung from break-apart aluminum poles, were used to frame a stage on the occasions we worked without a proscenium. Miss Kathleen and Iris were walking through the umbrella routine, which opened the second act. I scanned bleacher capacity: if even half the tickets turned up, Kramien would have to put on two shows.

"Hey! Get her out of here. The public's not allowed backstage," Kramien yelled when he saw me. "Kathleen, look alive."

Miss Kathleen walked me toward the big double doors. I gave her a piece of paper on which I'd written my mother's address. "Kramien owes me for three days," I said. "Here's an address just in case."

"I'm sorry," Miss Kathleen said.

"Kathleen, there really *are* worse things than no money."

Miss Kathleen gave me that look of hers, but this time I saw affection along with it.

I turned and nearly walked over a little guy who looked like a square-dance caller, in a brown double-knit suit with yellow piping around the lapel, and wearing a toupee.

"Have you met Dick?" Miss Kathleen asked.

"Hey, doll," the man said. "How's it going?"

Kramien yelled at Miss Kathleen to get back to work. The promoter followed me outside.

"So you're the man responsible for moving us around the West," I said. "What happened to Beatty, Nevada?"

He opened a monogrammed cigarette case and took out an oval Delicado. "The Jaycees figured out only 15 percent of the ticket sales were going to their Underprivileged Children's Fund. For a minute there, they wanted to have me arrested." He lit his cigarette with a matching Ronson lighter. "I don't know what the big deal was. Hell, some charities *lose* money on fundraisers."

"I hear you've done very well here."

"Got a great sponsor here," he said. "The Fraternal Order of the Police." He grinned. "Stick around, doll, and I'll buy you a drink." He strolled off toward the stage.

"Right," I muttered to myself.

I checked out of the Pasatiempo and carried my Samsonite to the bus station, where I stashed it in a locker. At a cigar stand, I bought a copy of the Santa Fe newspaper, for old time's sake. Four years before, I had worked a season at the Santa Fe Opera, constructing fountains, gold-leafing chandeliers and covering Louis XV divans with brocade, while the orchestra in the pit rehearsed Verdi, Menotti, Donizetti, Stravinsky and Mozart.

I bought a ticket north. The night bus didn't leave until ten. I still had time.

This was my chance to see The Great Kramien. I stood in line with an excited, talkative crowd numbering in the hundreds. In this poor border town, every merchant who bought a ticket book saw that the tickets got used. Children of all sizes, clinging and bold, scrubbed and scruffy, spoke Spanish and English. "Would the *mágico* have a real *elefante?*" one child asked.

When the line began to move inside, I could see the velvet drapes and the shining brass dove perches. From the crowd there were cries of "*¡Ay, que hermosa!*"

I had figured the gym would take eight hundred, but a thousand people must have crammed in for the first show. Girls sat on the laps of their sisters, and children rode their fathers' shoulders.

At seven o'clock sharp, the music blared and Miss Kathleen and Iris strutted rapidly in from either wing, decked in glittering headdresses and trailing green ostrich plumes. They raised their arms welcoming The Great Kramien, portly and commanding in tuxedo, cummerbund and top hat. He skinned off his white gloves, slammed them into a drawer, yanked it open, and a live dove rose into the spotlights.

He stuffed a rainbow of silks into a tube, and another dove fluttered up to join the first, and together they circled the gymnasium's high rafters.

He chopped the air with a butterfly net and produced a third dove, then a fourth; from a flaming platter bloomed two quacking ducks; from an oriental screen, the rabbit. Kramien was exquisite with the huge Chinese linking rings: his big hands handled seven at a time.

The stage blazed with color and music and light and motion, and the bleachers trembled under the applause.

When the Guillotine fell, and a red-shirted boy still had his head, Iris whisked him into her arms and carried him back to his family in the front row. I wished I'd thought of that.

It was the Substitution Trunk, of course, that I waited for—Iris blew it. She never made it out of the trunk. When Kramien took the lid off, she was still half in the bag. She sat there frightened and exposed, like someone caught in the bath. Kramien shot her a killing look, then signaled for Roy to hustle the trunk off stage.

Yet the audience clapped and shouted their delight, as though Iris's failure only proved the difficulty of doing magic and the nobility of anyone who might even attempt it. Their cheers resounded as the trunk and Iris were dragged across the gymnasium floor.

Kramien let loose a few more doves, got back in sync with the tape and finished the show with a flourish. Applause boomed around him as his final doves fluttered upward, and it echoed around me as I was swept by the crowd into the dark street.

I boarded the Citizen Auto Stage and stashed my suitcase on the rack overhead. The enthusiastic applause of the audience still filled my ears. Kramien would have been the first to tell me the world contained no magic, but the chosen gullibility of those people in the bleachers had shown me where magic truly lay.

The motor, lights and heater came on all at once, and the bus rolled out of the garage. I switched off the overhead reading light and pressed the button to make my seat recline.

Through the window, the Arizona night was clear, the eastern sky filling with the stars of spring. Who knew? Maybe Houdini himself was up there somewhere, lost in the constellations, reconsidering his disbelief and signaling to us like mad.

tequila sunrise

janet mason

*i*t wasn't that we'd planned a road trip. We never planned anything. We just were. And for that weekend we were the road. It was as easy as sticking your thumb out, and that's what we did. I was with my friends Kim and Jennifer. We were either juniors or seniors in high school. Even if I could remember, it wouldn't matter. I skipped so many days of school that both years could have fit into one.

We wanted to be free.

I forget which one of us stuck her thumb out as we stood by the highway. To tell the truth I even forget how we got there. But as soon as one of us stuck out a thumb, we got picked up. It was that easy. The driver was middle-aged. He had a receding hairline and a scar in the middle of his forehead. The scar was puckered and inflamed, so pink it was almost red. The pickup truck he drove was a dark, battered green.

This was before the days of shiny new pickups. It was the late 1970s. Post-recession, pre–gas wars. The steel mill was cutting back. Free trade was gearing up. It was the industrial Northeast. We just thought of it as home.

We got into the truck, the three of us jammed into the cab next to the driver. He passed us an almost-full bottle of tequila. We didn't pass it back. Five miles down the road it was empty. We were headed to the shore. The driver said he would take us there.

He said he'd take us anywhere we wanted to go.

The empty bottle thudded onto the pickup floor. The driver pulled into the parking lot at the Jack in the Box where I worked. It was late on a Friday afternoon. We had skipped school that day and I didn't have much in my stomach, a candy bar or two, and a third of the bottle of tequila. Even before the tequila, I had felt like I was walking underwater. We had spent the day in a haze of hashish, green spongy chunks that drew time to a standstill. I vaguely remember spending the day at the house of someone I had never met before. Wherever Kim and Jennifer went there were always older men around. These guys were about twenty-five and had lots of dope. Most likely they dealt it. Kim and Jennifer were beautiful, so everything was free.

I don't remember if I'd intended to go to school that day. Some days when my friend Denise gave me a lift to school, we'd make it as far as the parking lot. We'd sit there in her dented, metallic blue Cougar, finish the joint we were smoking and contemplate the building in front of us. It was a big brick box. There were glass-and-chrome windows on the first floor that led into the lobby. Up above the windows were narrow little slits, like in a jail. It had been built as part of an office complex and at the last minute the town had decided it needed a new high school. We'd sit there staring at it, a big brick box with smaller boxes inside of it, and a world of bricks would threaten to tumble down on us. We were supposed to fit our minds into the smallest of the boxes, called classrooms. We'd sit there in the parking lot and squint our eyes and stare through the smoke as we sucked on the end of the joint. Then we'd wheel on out of there, headed for freedom.

Sometimes we'd go to homeroom and then wander off to the bathroom. We'd meet there, a bunch of girls crowded into a stall, smoking cigarettes, a joint if we had one. Sometimes we'd pop some pills, snort a line or two of meth. Then we'd check the hallways for the monitor and sneak out the side door of the school, winding our way single file toward the country roads that surrounded us.

I learned to hitchhike on those roads. Most of the time I was with my friends.

We'd stick out our thumbs on roads that led to Kim's house. Her father worked all day and her mother was in a sanatorium. She was a schizophrenic. We'd go up to Kim's bedroom and sit around and smoke weed and listen to Harry Chapin, all the while having these really deep conversations we'd forget within five minutes. Time slowed down, expanded, and—*poof*—it was gone. We'd hitchhike back to school to take the bus home.

Eventually Kim decided she wanted to spend her days somewhere else. Everything was a blur, but I remember Kim's eyes wide with fear when she talked about her mother. She might have been afraid that her mother would escape from the sanatorium and find her way home. Her mother may have been violent. Or Kim may have been worried that her father would come home early from work and find us. Or maybe she was just bored with staying at home and wanted to go somewhere else. Fear and boredom. It was all the same thing.

For years, when I thought of my adolescence at all, I thought of myself as a caricature: hell-on-wheels rebellious, a teenage-girl James

Dean. As a child I had been a bookworm, a thread I picked up again in college. In high school I ran with the wrong crowd, and often I was the instigator. But when I look back I see that I wasn't a bad kid—and it wasn't that I didn't want to learn. I had an imagination as wide as the sky. My mind simply couldn't function in a box.

The only time they let us out was at lunchtime, when we could go out to the patio behind the cafeteria. My friend Denise, the one with the metallic blue Cougar, would do handsprings. In her mind, she was training for the Olympics. They made her stop.

The cement patio was white. From there, the curb dropped down four inches or so to the black asphalt of the school parking lot. That's where the buses sat, big orange cages to take us back and forth. Behind the parking lot was a hill. It was our goal to get over that hill, and reach the back roads that led everywhere and nowhere. First we had to get by whatever teacher or guard was on lunch duty. Anyone who stepped off the patio was threatened with suspension.

I always stepped off.

I don't remember why we stopped at Jack in the Box. I might have been checking to see if I worked that weekend or I may have been swapping hours with someone. What I do remember is that one minute I was standing up in the bathroom looking in the mirror and the next minute I was flat on my back staring up at the ceiling. It was a one-person bathroom, and I'm tall, over six feet. Stretched out on the greasy, red-brown tiled floor, I didn't have an inch to spare on either end of me. It felt like a trap, like the rest of my life. There I was. Vertical. Horizontal. Bam. A domino felled, flat back.

I don't remember getting back up, but I must have. I've always been good at hiding things. High as a kite, my eyes glazed for days, and I could still walk a studious straight line. Somehow I walked through the fast-food joint, a box with windows all around. I worked there for only a few years, but I would dream about it into midlife. It didn't matter that I would go on to work in jobs that were worse and jobs that were better—shift work at a chemical plant, too many factories to name, office after office, cubicles and more cubicles, those damn boxes—I would always dream about those orange polyester uniforms, the yellow name badge, the cash register, the greasy floors, the deep fryer. In my dreams I was always trapped. But that day I walked my studious straight line right out of there, behind Kim and Jennifer, and the strange man with a scar in the middle of his forehead. Back into the battered green pickup.

We were headed for the ocean.

The vastness.

I don't remember most of the trip. There may have been another joint, more tequila. We may have stopped at a liquor store. I may have eaten another candy bar. I was always doing that—having a chocolate bar and a beer. It made me feel filthy: out of control and young. Maybe it was my way of acknowledging that a few years earlier I had been a child, and the same amount of time later I would be an adult.

It was a two-hour drive to the ocean. On the way, it started to get dark. I was sitting between Kim and Jennifer. The driver kept turning to us, saying, "What I'm going to do to you girls." It didn't make any sense but that's what he kept saying. "What he's going to do to us," snorted Kim. The road started feeling like a wave on which we were surfing. Or trying to. My stomach rose up to meet my throat. There was a window behind our seat. Kim turned around and opened it. Somehow I turned around. Then without trying I retched up everything into the back of his truck. The truck was green, but in my mind everything turned red.

"What he's going to do to us," snorted Kim.

Jennifer giggled.

I retched again.

Again my mind colored the night red.

A long stretch of road went by but I don't remember it.

My entire adolescence was one blackout on top of another. A row of dominoes falling. Thinking back is like trying to stand them up again. A feeling, a memory surfaces.

The next thing I remember we were at a marsh, one of those long meandering marshes that are so beautiful at the mouth of a bay. In the daytime wild birds fly in and out. The reeds were taller than I was, sharp. I didn't remember this till the next day, late in the afternoon. I was getting undressed and found long sharp slashes on my buttocks. Jennifer told me I was taking a piss and fell backward into the reeds—down, down toward the quiet, dark water of the bay.

I stood there in our rented room, feeling the slashes on my ass, listening to Jennifer, and then it came back to me: the dark night, the quiet water, the fast headlights of cars whizzing by. There was something else, too. Hands that grabbed me. Kim, Jennifer or both pulling me up from the reeds, back to what for a little while longer was safety, the battered green truck, driven by the strange man with the third eye.

When I think back I feel myself suspended in midair, then tumbling backward toward eternity. I've mythologized my life as a miracle. I may have been jumping out of a plane without a parachute, but somehow a current of air managed to come along and catch me.

The hands that reached out to save me that night belonged to Kim and Jennifer.

I knew I loved girls in first grade. Even then I knew that I shouldn't. I started drinking when I was fourteen and learned to forget. Did I love Kim and Jennifer? I don't think so. But I can't be sure. I always valued my friendships with girls over involvements with boys. In tenth grade I won a poetry contest and was given as the prize a big pink *Seventeen Book of Etiquette.* The worst thing it said was that it was okay for a girl to break her plans with her girlfriends to go out with a boy. I always felt betrayed when my girlfriends were more interested in their boyfriends than in me. But I had staying power. I would be there when the boyfriend left.

I was there when my best friend's boyfriend got some other girl pregnant and then left town. I was there when a few of my girlfriends found out they needed abortions, and when it was too late for one of them. Her father threw her down the stairs and she ended up in foster care. Then her baby was given up for adoption and none of us talked about it again, ever. Unspeakable things happen to teenage girls, and our silences were complicit in the denial that pressed down on us. Beyond that, our silence was a kind of salve. It was our way of pretending that nothing could be as bad as it really was.

I had fooled around with boys. Things would go so far and then they would have to stop. I had a boyfriend in tenth grade and my favorite thing about him was that I got to double date with my best friend. She was in the back seat and I was in the front. When our dates took us roller-skating, we stayed in the bathroom most of the night, smoking and talking.

My girlfriends' lives were perforated with thoughts of boys. To me, the boys seemed like another species. I never got emotionally involved with them. But my girlfriends had gotten under my skin. I felt what they felt. Their shame. Their sadness.

I don't know that I was in love with Kim or Jennifer, with any of them for that matter, but I memorized them. Kim was the wildest, with her frizzy blond hair down to her waist. She was the one who would do anything. She was all eyes. An oasis of blue. To look into them was to forget everything. They sparkled. Her face faded behind those eyes. It was a long oval, covered with pale freckles. She had a long fluted neck and perfect breasts. She was Venus rising on a wave: her flat belly, her hourglass hips, her butt that was an upside-down heart riding low. I marveled at the way she displayed herself, so proud of her full creamy breasts as she walked half-naked around the locker room.

She told us about the time she had ridden topless on a sea of shoulders at a rock concert. She had drunk seventy-two beers that night, ponies, the short bottles. When her boyfriend had lifted her up on his shoulders, she'd torn off her own shirt. She was that free. And when we listened to her before class in the hallway, and later when she told the story again in the bathroom stall packed with girls and thick with smoke, we were right there with her as she bared her breasts and reared, throwing back her long mane of frizzy hair.

Jennifer was fast on her way to becoming a girl who would do anything. Her eyes were yellow-green, narrow, slanted up at the outsides. She watched everything, like a cat. An upturned lip, a knowing smile, more often a sneer. A nose that ended in a precisely rounded little square, skewed off to one side, matching her turned-up lip. Her blond hair was thin and fell just to the top of her collar. It was always swept back. Everything about Jennifer was breezy. Once she told me that she had slept with four guys in one night. This was just before we graduated from high school, about six months before she disappeared. Somehow I was still, in the technical sense, a virgin. I was a little shocked when she told me that. Imagine that—me, the girl rebel, shocked. "Four?!" I exclaimed, sitting on the barstool next to her. Stoned. Disbelieving.

Jennifer shrugged. "Yeah. Four. So what?"

I don't know if I loved Kim and Jennifer then, but I love them now.

I love them for pulling me out of the reeds, away from the dark water that could easily have sucked me under. And I love them for not leaving me passed out in the truck when we stopped at the restaurant.

When I came out of the restaurant bathroom, the man with the scar in the middle of his forehead was gone. He had been getting belligerent. I remember his muttering and Kim's outrage. I remember that the lining of my stomach was again rippling toward my throat. I remember the bathroom. Its cool black and white tiles. The stainless steel sinks. I felt enclosed, safe. I wished I could stay there forever. When I emerged, Kim was standing at the counter talking to the waitress. The waitress had threatened to call the cops and the man with the scar, the third eye, left. She told us to wait, so we did.

After her shift she gave us a lift to a nearby neighborhood. We told her we were going to visit my aunt who lived there. We were always making up stories like this when grownups were around. But this wasn't a story. My aunt actually lived in this neighborhood. Now when I look back, I am amazed that we made it to her house. A sense of direction has never been my strong point. But that night, during that long winding ride when I was mostly blacked out, I had a sense of destination.

Either by intention or chance we landed near my aunt's house. The waitress dropped us off on a dark tree-lined street. We crawled into someone's backyard, flopped down and prepared to spend the night. We must have been making noise. Talking, singing, laughing. Who knows? We must have thought that the darkness, the shadowy outline of the pine trees directly over us, would erase our sounds from the night.

The light from the police officer's flashlight startled us. Somehow we got up and did what he said. All I remember is lying on the damp ground, then suddenly sitting in the back of his car. The light inside the police car was bright. All of a sudden we could see each other. The cop was young. He had a clean-shaven baby face. He started driving fast to impress Kim and Jennifer. They had that kind of effect on men. I started asking where the bars were. Kim and Jennifer were shushing me. Everyone thought I meant the kind of bars where people go to drink. "The *bars*," I said, pointing to the empty space above the seat in front of us. "Oh," the cop said, lowering his voice as he explained that not all patrol cars have bars. I sat back in my seat, silent, disappointed. It was the first time I'd been picked up by the cops. I wanted to see the picture from the outside, and I wanted to look dangerous. I wanted bars framing my face.

I told him we were on our way to see my aunt, that we had gotten lost. I gave him the address, the right one. I had this way of talking to male authority figures and convincing them of my innocence. I reminded them of their daughter, their kid sister. Later, this quality would get me out of countless drunk-driving situations. Other teenagers got Breathalyzer tests, got phone calls home to their parents, got their licenses taken away. I got let go.

I always wanted to look dangerous, like my friend Chrissie who rode a motorcycle and would end up in jail a year later. I at least wanted to *look* hard, like another girl in our crowd, Mary, who had a throaty laugh and was so grown up. Later that year she was killed in a drunk-driving accident.

I was still innocent to the consequences of living dangerously.

The cop dropped us off a few doors down from my aunt's house. He did this so the neighbors wouldn't see—as if people were peering out their windows that late at night. We went up the steps to her house, and pretended to knock on the door. The cop drove away. It was late. My aunt wasn't expecting us. I doubt that we thought about any of this at the time. We just wanted to be free. We headed into her backyard. This time quiet, cautious.

In the morning, our throats were dry. We had to go to the bathroom. We went back to the door and knocked on it. I remember us all standing there, the surprise on my aunt's face. I remember the awkward silence that contained us as we sat around the table. We made up a story about where we had been and where we were going. Later, after breakfast, my aunt dropped us off at the beach, where she thought we were meeting friends.

My aunt was an alcoholic. She and her husband, her fourth, took me on my first major drinking binge when I was fourteen. She had slipped me my first joint when I was twelve. Naturally, I thought of going to her house. I found out later she called my mother after we left. My mother knew where I was. All the while I was thinking I was free, not caring what she thought.

There's a lot I don't remember about that weekend. The fact is I don't remember most of it. There was more booze and drugs. Wherever we went we seemed to find it. Usually it was free. Men offered it to us in the hopes that we would repay them. I would usually start to get sick. That was the cue for Kim and Jennifer to lose interest. "Let's go," they said. And we went.

I remember that we didn't want to sleep outside again. Kim mentioned that it would be easy enough to pick up some guys to find a place to sleep. Jennifer was studying Kim with those cat eyes of hers. She was in training to be a girl who would do anything. She smiled a halfway smile.

The nervousness I felt was a trembling in the pit of my stomach. Sex had always seemed so unnatural to me. I was afraid of its consequences. I dug down deep in my pockets and came up with ten bucks to cover a room.

Kim and Jennifer were amused at my nervousness.

Looking back, I think they were also reassured.

Our lives depended on one another that weekend. They pulled me out of the marsh. I found us a room that had a lock on the door.

Later that night, after I discovered the slashes on my ass, we went out. There were bright neon lights. Bars. We found one on the corner that would serve us.

Everyone there was grown up except for us. The barmaid gave us free drinks. Middle-aged men paid for them. There were middle-aged women there, too. They were happy and singing. Eventually they gathered around us, standing between us and the men, in the way of all that expectation. I don't remember leaving the bar or finding our way back to our rented room. But we did get back there, and one of us was able to turn the key in the lock. I know this because I remember waking up there.

The next day we went to the beach. The sky was so blue, the sand bright and warm. The ocean went on forever. Some guys came by and gave us a big fat joint. They were motorcycle hoodlums and they would have stayed for a while, but some other men in suits were following them. They looked like narcs. We dug a deep hole in the sand and buried the joint.

We sat there looking out at the ocean until the men in suits were tiny stick figures. Then they were gone. What I remember after that is the digging. Digging and digging. Sand flying. We couldn't find that damn joint. We wanted it so bad. That's the sad part when I think back, the fact that we wanted that joint more than we wanted ourselves.

Getting high was always the main thing.

But I remember the sun beating on my back and the surf pounding. And I know we weren't just looking for the joint. If time had been suspended we would have kept on digging, straight through the center of the Earth, straight through to the other side of ourselves. We wouldn't have stopped until the blue sky behind us was the same blue sky in front of us, till we could smell the fresh air through the hole that we had dug with our own hands.

We wanted to be that free.

I remember that we took the Greyhound bus home and that it was my idea. Kim and Jennifer didn't resist. Chances are that we were more terrified of hitchhiking again than any of us would admit. After we got home, life went on pretty much as it had before. I was perpetually stoned and drunk. I took risks with my life I would come to regret. I don't remember having it out with my mother when I got back, but I'm sure that I did. My adolescence had collided with her menopause and it was no picnic. That's what my mother said about everything.

It was no picnic.

I don't recall that Kim and Jennifer and I ever talked about the weekend we spent together. But I did learn a few things that weekend. For one thing, I never hitchhiked again. And I learned that I had a few survival skills. And they came in handy again and again.

Even now I think of myself as not having good brakes. But the fact is that I left skid marks all over the place that weekend, on the adventure in which I was the road.

Our lives were so confining that stepping over the line was the only way we could breathe. Chances are that we never really meant to take things as far as we did. Whoever stuck out her thumb that weekend probably did so on a dare. For years I folded up my memories, put them behind me and thought of myself as a stereotype. Maybe part of the stereotype was true. I was rebellious, but I was not a female James Dean. There was nothing invulnerable about me. Teenage girls who drink are walking targets. I hung out with a circle of girls. Our lives were fragmented. Somehow together we made a whole.

It was when we let go of each other that everything went wrong.

Toward the end of our senior year in high school, Kim moved in with her drug-dealing boyfriend. A few months later she disappeared. Jennifer disappeared, too, a few months after that.

I don't know what happened to them. Kim may have ended up in Florida, where her boyfriend did a lot of business. One or both of them may have ended up dead. Chrissie stayed in jail for a few years. All that was left of Mary after the drunk-driving accident was the memory of her throaty laugh. One girl, a few years younger than we were, was murdered. She was pregnant and her boyfriend dug her a shallow grave. At least three of us were raped, myself included.

Some of the girls in that fragile circle that held me were brilliant. But I was the only one to go to college. I hit rock bottom at the age of eighteen. Then I learned to set my sights ahead, to walk a straight line into a future where I eventually would become sober.

I came this far thinking my life has been a miracle, that I owe a great debt to luck and that I saved myself. This may be true to some extent. But the hands that reached out to grab me that weekend belonged to Kim and Jennifer.

I memorized their faces. Then they disappeared.

sunshine girl

carolyn mackler

$a$pril 1995

People tell me I should carry a gun. People tell me I should carry a cell phone. People tell me I shouldn't drive alone. People tell me I shouldn't camp. People tell me I should take the major interstates rather than the secondary routes. People tell me I should spring for a plane ticket. And, in a last grasping attempt to halt operations, people dredge up anecdotes about women who've been abducted from the middle of nowhere.

Everyone feels entitled to an opinion. Young women, they seem to believe, are wards of the community, needing guidance from the outside, lest they rely on their own decision-making prowess. But my mind is made up. I'm going.

I'm twenty-one. I'm about to graduate from Vassar College. I've done precisely what I was supposed to do for the past four, rather, twenty-one years. Until this spring. While other seniors visit the career-counseling office, interview with Teach For America, print hyperbolized résumés on creamy linen paper, purchase power suits and get adult hairdos, I've been wandering around this farm a few miles from campus, spilling poetry onto coffee-ringed leaves of paper, letting my leg hair grow out.

It has finally dawned on me that I've spent two decades acquiring knowledge, amassing facts, cramming my brain with a U-Haul's worth of ideas. Yet one idea slipped out of a crate, or maybe the movers stole it, or maybe I never had it in the first place: I have no idea who I am.

That's why I'm driving from New York to Washington State, all by myself, camping the whole way across. I don't own a car. I don't own a tent. Hell, I'm not even a member of AAA. But I have a hunch that out there in the middle of nowhere, with the prairie sun toasting my left arm while I munch on caramel popcorn and crank the Indigo Girls, I'm going to figure out who I am. Because there will be no one around to tell me.

June 1976

We're driving cross-country—my mom, my dad, my older brother and I. I'm about to turn three, in July. They call me Peewee Piranha because I'm scrawny but I'll bite the hell out of anyone who reckons with me. My dad is on summer break from law school, and so we've borrowed Moony, his friend's roomy Ford, to follow the setting sun. We make up verses for a special family song, to the tune of "Camptown Races."

Family of four a-driving out west
Do-da, do-da,
Family of four the very best
Oh, a-do-da-day.

It's the days before car seats, so my brother and I roam Moony's back seat, crunching our knees on stray Cheerios, searching for "corners."

Corners are my mom's weapon for getting us through car trips. They are small presents—beads to string or number puzzles or Legos—hidden in a corner of the car, designed to capture our attention for a stretch of highway.

Around the Great Lakes, I receive the grand mama of corners: a set of Sunshine Dolls, the family of height-weight proportional hippies that Mattel produced for a few flower-powery years in the seventies. They are the draft-dodging cousins that Barbie is ashamed to tell the girls at the country club about; she scours the Dreamhouse with Lysol after they swing through town in their VW bus. The dad is *my* dad, wearing leather sandals, an embroidered vest, chestnut sideburns, a peace symbol around his neck. The mom is *my* mom, with a waterfall of hair held back by a headband, a peasant dress and round, foothill breasts. They are young. They are in love. They have a little baby, not quite my big brother, but that's okay, because Sunshine Girl, well, she's me. She's about three. She has my blond, tangled hair. She wears patchwork halters and has a ballooned tummy and skinny legs, just like I do. She is happy and free and chatty, prone to biting people when she can't express what she's feeling. Sunshine Girl keeps me company throughout the long, hot cross-country trek. She licks my Popsicles and whizzes around on the plastic motorcycle my parents have strapped to Moony's roof rack and spends the night in the hood of my Mickey Mouse sleeping bag.

We're somewhere in Nevada. My dad is driving. My mom is singing along with Joan Baez on the radio. I'm kneeling in the back seat, stretching Sunshine Girl out the window for a gulp of desert air. My parents remind me to be careful, hold tight, don't drop Sunshine Girl. I squeeze her in my tiny fist. And then it happens. I loosen my grip, just for a second, but long enough for the sixty-mile-an-hour current to pluck Sunshine Girl out of my fingers and smack her against the dry Nevada earth, again and again, until she's out of sight.

"Sunshine Girl is gone! Sunshine Girl is gone!" I wail. My dad swerves to the shoulder, cars streaking by us. They instruct us to stay put. There they go, my parents, my heroes, retracing our route for a mile at least, surveying the side of the highway for the body of Sunshine Girl.

When my parents return to Moony empty-handed, they are grim. I hug my knees, sucking on my sticky knuckles. We pull into the next town, a western outpost, hardly Sunshine Family country. My parents buy a brand-X doll, a little girl. Her knees don't bend. Her hair is too glossy, like she can sit smugly still through a shampooing. Her orange skin is too synthetic. She's wearing something frilly and pink. The Sunshine Family "adopts" her, but it isn't the same. Sunshine Girl is gone.

May 1995

I keep passing the sign for the used Toyota Tercel. It's taped to a wall in the college center, with most of the tabs already torn off. Not a good omen. Anyway, the price is too high, five grand. With savings from summer jobs and part-time campus work and graduation presents, I can scrape together three, maybe three-five. But I keep passing the sign. It's the drawing of an automobile, very Love Bug, with exhaust bubbling out of the rear pipe, that finally prompts me to rip off the last tab.

Her name is Emily. She lives off campus. She's also a graduating senior. She's willing to negotiate. If I swing by her place this evening, I can keep the car overnight, see if we bond.

The official color is "sea-foam green," but it reminds me of a wad of Extra spearmint gum. It is standard transmission, my favorite, and Emily has replaced the stick shift with a metal pole topped by a glittery orange ball, the kind that truck drivers use. The two-door Toyota is small and oval-shaped, a luminous green egg, straight out of Dr. Seuss. After a twilight spin around Poughkeepsie, I name it Egg. I come from a family of car-namers, so I know full well what this means. We must be bonding.

The next morning, I find a mechanic out on Route 55 who will give Egg a complete physical. His name is Moose. He's young and cute, with a dimple in his chin and half-moons of black grease caking his fingernails. We take an immediate liking to each other, discussing timing belts and oil changes and a new pair of mud flaps. As Moose slides under Egg's belly to scrutinize her innards, it hits me: I am discussing timing belts and oil changes and a new pair of mud flaps! My mom—the family grease monkey—isn't talking shop on my behalf. My dad isn't extracting from his wallet a withered baby picture, reminding people to take good care of his precious little girl. I am going to decide whether to purchase this car by myself. I am going to trust my choices. Granted, I'd never heard of a timing belt until five minutes ago, but I can learn.

Moose gives Egg a clean bill of health, recommending only that I buy her a fresh set of tires for the trip. I use this for leverage with Emily, and by afternoon we have agreed on thirty-five hundred. I write her a check for as much as I have, promising the balance within the week. She signs the title over to me.

So this is really going to happen. I'm going to drive cross-country this summer, like I set out to do. My only plan for the future is to meet up with my friend Jenny in Seattle around the beginning of August. From there, we have visions of minimum-wage coffee-shop jobs that won't tax our brains, an affordable apartment in a hip neighborhood, a revolving door of lovers. But I'm not really thinking about that now. Now I'm thinking about the past.

August 1982

I got the *Annie* soundtrack for my ninth birthday and we listen to it the whole way across the country, from New York to California. We sing "Tomorrow" and "Maybe," but no longer the "Family of Four" song. My dad has taken off a few weeks from his law practice in upstate New

York. His hair is shorter now, no sideburns, and his face is tense, or maybe he's just straining as we drive into the afternoon sun. My mom has begun washing her premature gray strands with Lady Clairol. She's happy to be out on the road, a welcome change from our small town, which she's never really taken to. My brother has clunky plastic-framed glasses and chipmunk teeth. I'm still scrawny, but I was the fastest runner in the third grade, whipping all the boys in a lap around the gym.

I'm wistful as we cross the Midwest and climb the Black Hills in Blaze, our faux-wood-paneled Oldsmobile station wagon. My mom has trimmed a nectarine-colored shag carpet to fit into the folded-down back. I spend hours stretched out, staring through the rear window at the endless sky, tugging stray carpet strands. I am Sally J. Freedman, Judy Blume's heroine, with an imagination as vast as the Plains. I am the spunky, monkey-faced actress who played Annie in the movie. Someday I will live on a ranch in South Dakota. Someday I will own a poodle. Someday I will drive around the country in an RV. I've even picked out the one I want, colossal and white with tan siding, the kind with a sleeping bunk hanging over the cab. I've just turned nine and everything seems possible. Out on the road, it's easy to believe the world is mine for the taking.

My parents always allow for one family fight per trip. It's bound to happen, with all of us cooped in a metal box for days and days and days. It transpires at Devils Tower, a twelve-hundred-foot monolith thrusting up from the deciduous woodlands of eastern Wyoming. We're hiking around the base, a tedious, nearly horizontal stroll that caters to Keds-clad Elderhostel types. No one is around so my brother and I scramble off the trail, onto the loose boulders. My mom follows us. My dad hangs back, insisting we obey the rules of the park. When we don't respond, he steps over the low-hanging chain, slips on a stray rock and tears his knee. Suddenly all that tension pent up in his face surges out.

Tendons bulge from his neck like overly taut guitar strings, and he's shouting. My mom is shouting, too. My brother becomes quiet and withdrawn, tears washing train tracks onto his dusty cheeks. I ricochet back and forth between my parents, tugging at their clenched fists, pleading with them to stop.

There's a picture of the three of us, my dad, my brother and me, on our way back to Blaze. My mom must have taken it. Devils Tower looms ominously in the background, daring us to mount it again. My dad has his long arms around both of us and I'm leaning into him. My legs are so bony I look like I'm propped up on broomsticks. My eyes are puffy. You can tell I've been crying, but I'm forcing myself to smile.

June 1995

That's how it's been all spring, smiling on the outside and crying behind closed doors. It's been two years since my parents split up. We still haven't recovered, none of us. My brother is drifting aimlessly from city to city. My dad has a girlfriend, a younger woman. I've met her. I like her. But I can't reconcile this with the fact that my mom lives alone in a one-bedroom apartment in New York City, where she's trying to start a new life, worrying about being put out to pasture.

This is the spring they finalize their divorce—complete with lawyers and summonses and acrimonious legalese. Most of the time, I'm the only one communicating with every other member of the family. I get migraines, searing, pulsing monsters that land me in the Vassar Brothers emergency room. I go on medication for the headaches, but it makes me so depressed I lie on the wooden floor of my dorm room, staring at the bluish glow of the computer screen, my unfinished thesis. I contemplate the meaning of my existence, coming up with no answers, only a void. So I flush the Inderal down the toilet and the headaches return, but at least I know why I'm here.

Vassar's daisy-filled commencement—where I am more parental referee than proud graduate—is a relief to have behind me. I spend June testing Egg's mettle, ping-ponging back and forth from my mom's in Manhattan to my dad's in upstate New York. I buy a two-person river-runner tent, because you never know. I buy a small gas stove and a portable cooler. I join AAA and highlight my spiral-bound maps with secondary routes, because I want to see the country, not a three-thousand-mile-long strip of McDonald's and Denny's and Jack in the Box.

I have a fling with a guy named George. He is gorgeous, the spitting image of Andrew Ridgely from Wham!, but I won't sleep with him, even though I still love "Wake Me Up Before You Go-Go." I haven't had sex since Stephen, and then it was making love. Or at least that's what he *called* it.

June 1994

I meet Stephen at a gas station in Liberty, New York, off Route 17. It's a few weeks before my twenty-first birthday. I'm driving to New York City, then flying out to California to spend the summer working at a camp in the Sierra Nevadas. He is tall and lean and delicious, with a scruffy beard and chocolate eyes. I notice him, and the bongo drums in the back of his pickup, as I fill my mom's Audi with gas. I catch him eyeing my legs in my cutoff jeans. I wash my windshield. He checks his oil. We pull into a nearby parking lot and talk for an hour. He is twenty-four, has just completed two years of teaching in a low-income school. He's driving cross-country this summer, California-bound. We say how cool it would be to meet up in the Sierras in August and go camping.

August 1994

Stephen picks me up from a lonely stretch of the Feather River Canyon on my last day at the camp. He wrote me over the summer, sending along the number of some friend he'd be staying with in some state on some day in July. I called him and we decided to take a mini–road trip to Tahoe, Yosemite, wherever. Then I'd fly back to New York and begin my senior year.

I've just turned twenty-one. I am going camping for five days with a guy I met on the side of the highway in southern New York two months ago. No one knows I'm here, except for one friend from camp. I feel daring and rebellious, like I'm playing the part of a free spirit in a cinematic tribute to the sixties.

We skinny-dip at a hot spring that first afternoon, along the Feather River. *See how daring and rebellious I am?* I ask the audience. *Stripping down in broad daylight . . . and we haven't even slept together yet.*

Stephen is a bohemian. He listens to Bob Marley and Joni Mitchell and Sweet Honey in the Rock. He pronounces Mexico, "May-he-co." He smells like curry powder and sandalwood oil. His black lab wears a splashy Guatemalan collar. He can't play the bongos yet, but he knows some guy in New Orleans who will teach him. That's where he's heading after he's gotten the road out of his system.

We don't make love until the second night, near the shores of Lake Tahoe. We tumble around in our sleeping bags until we crawl into the brisk air and wrap our sweaty bodies around each other. *See, see, I tell the audience. There's a world beyond term papers and grade mongering. Out here, I'm a free spirit, a woman of the road. Sure, we used a condom, it's the nineties now, but Stephen is showing me a world I wouldn't have discovered on my own.*

On our last evening together, we smoke a joint at the base of Half Dome and talk about past sexual experiences. He tells me that his best lover ever was a luscious hippie chick he met on an organic farm in Hawaii, a one-night stand. I feel woozy from the pot. He has no idea how much this stings. *He* has been my best lover ever. I suddenly hate luscious hippie chicks who have one-night stands on organic farms in Hawaii. I feel like a fraud for casting myself as a free spirit. I feel self-conscious for shaving my armpits.

November 1994

I slide Stephen's letter out of my mailbox. The postmark says New Orleans. He has drawn my name in multicolored markers. In his last note, he wrote of oversized wool sweaters and homemade apple pies and fireplaces and rambles down rural roads, wishing we could "do that" together.

I tear open the envelope. That's when I see the name "Amanda." She is a dancer, moves like a feline. "We're having a groovy time down in the Crescent City," he writes, "smoking grass, doing calisthenics, making love." He thinks she and I would like each other. I think I'm going to puke. I crumple the letter in my fist and sob, right there under the naked, fluorescent lights of the college center.

I have failed at being a hippie chick, a free spirit, a woman of the road. I don't even know what calisthenics are, for God's sake.

July 1995

Two days after my twenty-second birthday, I set off. My mom meets me in upstate New York to be my one-person farewell committee, because anyone leaving for a cross-country trip needs to glance in her rearview mirror and see someone hopping up and down, waving furiously.

I steer Egg through the hilly, fertile Finger Lakes region, back roads, windows down. I don't have a gun. I don't have a cell phone. I am definitely in the middle of nowhere. I open the glove compartment and rummage around for the mix that Jenny made me. I discover a jumbo pack of Cinnaburst, a corner that my mom must have stashed in there. Jenny's tape is entitled "Doing the Independent-Woman

Thing Across the Great U.S. of A." Is that who I am? Is that what I'm doing?

I sing along with Cat Stevens's "On the Road to Find Out" and Liz Phair's "Go West" and Simon and Garfunkel's "America," a must-have for every cross-country mix tape. Within forty-five minutes, I have chain-chewed the entire pack of gum, one right after the next, stashing the crumpled wrappers in Egg's ashtray. Ani DiFranco's "God's Country" is the last song on side one: *I came out here to see some stuff for myself / I mean, why leave the telling up to everybody else?*

Maybe that's what I'm doing, seeing some stuff for myself. I've just turned twenty-two and everything seems possible. Out on the road, it's easy to believe that the world is mine for the taking. I'm driving into the setting sun, no family to spell out my adventure or turn me into the dutiful daughter, no lover to help me be a free spirit. This time I'm doing it alone. I'm going to find Sunshine Girl.

my mom across america

tina yun lee

There once was a mother duck and a daughter duck. The daughter duck never listened to the mother duck. In fact, she always did the opposite of whatever her mother asked. When the mother duck asked her to do her homework, she would go out and play. When the mother duck asked her to come home and eat her dinner, she would throw her food on the ground. When the mother duck was about to die, she thought to herself, "I finally know her game. I am going to ask for the opposite of what I want." Now, the mother duck really wanted to be buried up in the mountainside, but she told her daughter to let her body go down the river. One day, the mother duck died. The daughter duck, looking down on her mother's body, thought to herself, "It's time to get serious. I must do as my mother wishes." And so she took her mother's body, and dragged it to the river, and let it go.

—Traditional Korean folktale

*W*hen I was a kid, my two biggest fears in life were dogs and being Korean. Dogs, because I'm afraid they'll hunt me down and kill me. Every dog is Cujo to me. When I see a dog, I start running and screaming. Being Korean—that's harder to explain. I've never actually screamed in terror from being Korean, so what do I mean? Well, for one thing, I panic that Koreans will come up to me and start speaking in Korean. I don't speak the language, and when they find that out, they start clucking their tongues and say something like, *"Ay-gu, keun-ill nat-neh!"* which means "Alas, what a shame!" I turn beet red and get so stressed out. It doesn't matter that I'm an adult with an adult lifestyle, adult pursuits—when someone starts speaking to me in Korean, I automatically feel like a little kid. It's just one more thing I'm supposed to do that I don't. I am a fake Korean.

When I was thirteen years old, I went to tennis summer camp. I was assigned to room with a girl from Japan. Her name was Hiroko. The camp administrators probably thought she and I would have a great deal in common—we were the only two Asian girls at the camp. Hiroko did not speak a word of English, and I spoke no Japanese. No one spoke to either of us that summer. No one sat at our lunch table at mealtimes. At first, I couldn't figure out why, but then I started to see us the way we must've looked to everyone else: different.

One night, Hiroko came to our room, fell on my bed and cried out some English she had picked up that week:

"I hate America!"

I could've comforted her, but I chose not to.

After that summer, I developed a strategy: if I want to be seen as me, I need to open my big old mouth and talk up my big old New Jersey English. I didn't have any desire to stand out; my goal was to be bland, forgotten, to fit in. So I told everybody I was Jewish.

I grew up in a predominantly Jewish community. Most of my good friends were Jewish; my junior-high teacher was Jewish, and so I just started to tell everyone I was Jewish. I loved going to Passover, asking the four questions, singing from my friends' families' tattered song books. I used to tell people, *"Ga kaffin often yam,"* which means "Go shit in the ocean" in Yiddish. After my first year of college, I came home to visit my junior-high teacher.

"Mrs. Garvin, I'm Asian-American," I said.

She turned to me slowly with a stern look. "You are Jewish. I don't want to talk about it. End of discussion."

And then she fed me.

When my mom asked me to go to Canada with her and my father, I thought, Great! I was in graduate school at the time, getting my MFA in fiction writing. I was trying to be a writer: I had to see things, go to new places. I'd never seen this huge section of North America. The experience would change me, would change what I thought of the world and me in it. Travel seemed like a good thing. I don't do it that often because I don't work for Smith Barney; I'm in the arts. And I love my parents, I love being with them. Most of the time. For limited amounts of time. But all in all, we enjoy each other, and so when Mom asked me to go, I said yes.

We fly to Seattle. The plan is to spend one night with my mother's friends, and then go north to Canada. My father—possibly the most antisocial person on earth—is always irritated with people; so while Mom bonds with her buds, I'll hang out with Dad. He wears sunglasses that make him look like he's from *Top Gun,* and he just stands around, not talking to anybody, chewing his Freedent gum, looking grim. But his jacket pockets are always packed with all this stuff he's not allowed to eat (Mom's rules): Kit Kats, Snickers, all kinds of candy he hands out to every little kid we see. If there's a cute face, he's breaking his back to give out that candy. Before we go to meet her friends, Mom insists on checking what we're wearing.

"You gained weight!"

This is a typical greeting from my mother. It's like, I say, "Good morning," and she replies, "You gained five pounds!"

She's always been critical of what I look like, which she says is in my interests. It is her theory that people treat you with respect when you look nice, pretty. I do have an affection for clothing with holes, but I'm on vacation. I'm here to relax. I could fight back, but I also know that these are my mom's friends, and she likes to make a good impression, so I go change. Dad comes out in a bright orange golf T-shirt and hideous green pants, the belt pulled up to the middle of his chest. Mom gives him a look. He turns around to go change.

By the time we're ready to leave, I'm in a dress and Dad's in a suit. We meet my mother's friends. All three of my mom's friends bring their husbands, so Dad goes over to yuk it up with the men. It's a bunch of old Korean couples and me. Everyone's talking and laughing, in Korean. Then one of them turns to me and asks me something in Korean.

Now, all I know how to say is *"Mi-ahn-hae-yo, han-guk-mal-eun uh-ryu-wo-yo,"* which roughly means "Sorry, Korean is difficult." This is the only thing I remember from a Korean class I once took; that and *"Maek-joo han-byung joo-sae-yo."* ("I would like a bottle of beer, please.") Neither of which I can say to my mother's friends without humiliating myself.

"Um, actually?" I start. "I don't really speak Korean."

"Ay-gu, keun-ill nat-neh!" says Mom's friend. "That is such a shame!"

My mom's friends have planned a "fun" night for us: one of those musical-theater dinner cruises, where the wait staff is also the entertainment. Before the buffet dinner, they sing "Rhythm of the Night" by El DeBarge, and some hits from the sixties like "Leader of the Pack." My mom's friends start to talk about what their kids are doing. One woman's son is a doctor, another woman's daughter is a lawyer and yet another woman's daughter is a Rhodes Scholar who went to England and met another Rhodes Scholar, and now they're getting married and having little Rhodes Scholar babies. They turn to me, and I can guess where this is headed.

"So, Yunny or Tee-na, what is your job?"

"I'm in graduate school," I say hesitantly. "I'm getting an MFA in fiction writing."

They look at each other. No one says anything; no one's really smiling. They're not rude people; they probably just don't know what that means. They probably don't know anyone who's a writer. Mom grabs my arm.

"I want her to go to law school, but she never listens to me."

My mother has asked me to go to law school since, God, I think my first day out of the womb, and though it is clear that I am never going to be a lawyer, she keeps at it. It's like a breakup she never got over. She says it without knowing she's saying it. Once, after a family dinner, we ended up playing Trivial Pursuit.

"Mom? What's the capital of France?" I asked, card in hand.

"Law school!" yells Mom before pausing a moment. "Oh sorry. Did I say again?"

But I also know things would be easier for her if I were a lawyer. People know what that is. It's a real job. It's something her friends can get jealous of. I turn away from the conversation and try to get absorbed in the show, which is a little bit of a mistake, because the band has started playing the Macarena, and the wait staff is really into it. They're grinning, singing and dancing around the tables, trying to get people to join in. Now, I really dislike audience participation. It's too much pressure. Once they pick you, that's it; you've got to go. So I turn my chair and stare at my plate, hoping they'll skip me. No such luck. Two baby-faced boy waiters spot me and quickly surround my chair. I can see them out of my peripheral vision, which has always been excellent. I hear them:

"Oh, come on! It'll be fun!"

I'd really rather, at this point, press the butter knife into my temple than dance the Macarena, but I don't want to be rude. Maybe if I keep staring down at my plate, they'll think I'm deaf. All of a sudden, a powerful spotlight shines on our table, and now the pressure is on—on me and these two boys. The boys start tugging on my arms, and I have to slap my hands onto the table to hold on.

"No, really! I'm fine, thank you!" I smile politely up at them from my death grip, and then Mom butts in.

"Come on, Yunny, you're a good dancer!" I turn to my mother in horror, but she continues. "She has a good voice, too! She was in her high school musical!" She practically screams to her friends. It's either stay here at the table or get up and dance. I end up dancing the Macarena.

Finally, it's time to hit the road. We pull into a parking lot, and I feel enormous relief. Now, I can be myself; I don't have to not know what everyone's saying all the time. We say goodbye to my mother's friends, and it's time for the real vacation to begin. The three of us, driving through the Canadian countryside. No schedule, no homework, no job: I can finally relax.

In the parking lot, there is a big bus with the words "Arirang Bus Tour" written on its side, in Korean and English. A bunch of Koreans are stuffing their suitcases and duffel bags into the bowels of the bus. I stare at them, because . . . well, because they're Korean, and Koreans stare at each other. And then Mom starts heading toward them with her suitcase.

I turn to Dad. "What is she doing?"

Dad doesn't say anything, just puts a peppermint candy in my hand and follows her. I follow them, not really registering what's going on until I get on board and see a sea of Asian faces. I take in a deep breath of air. There aren't many seats left, so I follow my parents as they make their way to the back. Every row is occupied by Asian faces. Senior citizens, parents, kids—and by kids, I mean five years old. I see one girl who's maybe fourteen, but she is the oldest kid on the bus, except for, of course, me. And all of a sudden, I feel like the thirty-year-old seated at the kids' table. That's fine, I tell myself, I can handle this. I just concentrate on Canada, how good it'll be. I keep walking. The seats are all gray, and there are little TVs every five rows, and we get to the back by the bathroom. I grab a window seat, and my mother sits next to me. And then the tour guide gets on the mike and starts speaking in Korean.

"An-nyung ha-sae-yo, an-nyung ha-sae-yo! Yuh-ruh-boon-eui guide Kim Il-Nam im-ni-da. O-neul-eun, teuk-byul-hee a-reum-da-un yuh-sung-boon-ee man-ah-suh, gi-boo-nee joh-seum-ni-da." Something, something in Korean. All in Korean.

People around me all laugh. Apparently, this guy is really funny. And it hits me, just then, that I am stuck for a week on an all-Korean bus trip across Canada.

We stop in Vancouver for a photo opportunity, then drive through the night until we stop for lunch the next day. Our bus is the only vehicle in the lot, and the restaurant is in the middle of nowhere. We shuffle into the dining area like patients released from the psych ward—ten hours on a bus will do that to you. Inside, the place seems completely dead, but as soon as we arrive, a two-man band wakes up and starts to play "Arirang," a traditional Korean folk song, really loudly.

"Welcome, Arirang Bus Tour!"

The two men are in their sixties at least. The lead singer is the accordion player, and the drummer just smiles, both of them seated underneath a sign—this computer printout—that just says "K-O-R-E-A."

We line up for the buffet appetizers and watch. When they finish, we clap. It's nice; someone took the time to learn the song of another country. And then they start to play a series of Billy Joel songs, starting with "New York State of Mind," which is not altogether bad on the accordion.

We sit for the main course, a choice of salmon or steak, served to all forty people on the bus. Dad and I both want to order the steak, but Mom says no.

"No good. Too much fat, cholesterol!"

Dad makes a face and orders the steak anyway.

"You see, Yunny? He doesn't care about his health at all. He eats junk all the time. David Letterman got bypass surgery. He's skinny; he exercises; he still got a heart attack. Same thing could happen to Dad. I want Dad to get bypass surgery."

"Mom, you can't just order surgery. Dad has to get a heart attack first."

"I don't care."

Ahh, I love it when my parents get along. I love when we talk about death before the food arrives. My mother is like Albert Camus trapped in an older Korean woman's body.

"Who?"

"Ca-moo. You know, the French guy who wrote about death. Existentialist. Author of *The Stranger?*"

"Oh, Ca-moose."

She brings up death when it's not even a distant glimmer in the conversation.

"Mom, can you pass the ketchup?"

"We can never catch up. We only live until we die."

We eat. Waitresses come and pick up our plates. The band breaks out into waltzes. "The Skater's Waltz," "The Blue Danube Waltz." There's a loud din of Korean from all the tables. It hangs like a cloud over my head. Two people get up and dance—senior citizens. The man must be the oldest person on the bus. His one shoulder is badly sloped down or missing, and he's doing a one-armed waltz with a woman. They bob up and down with stoic looks on their faces. No sign that they're actually enjoying themselves. Very Korean. I never see Koreans dance. It's an unnatural act.

Everyone is watching. Someone starts clapping, and pretty soon, the whole place starts keeping time as one big unit. Before I know what's happening, my mom gets up and starts dancing, and then my father gets up. Parents, kids, everyone is on the dance floor, bouncing around, laughing, having a great time. It's amazing, but I can't join in. Mom comes over to tug my hand, but I tell her I'm tired. I ask the waitress where the bathroom is and go to the back of the room, and watch everyone from there. Everyone is dancing, everyone is having a good time. Later, when my mom asks me why I didn't dance, I can't explain it. It's a lump in my throat.

In Jasper, Alberta, we stop at a breathtaking lake, the color of turquoise—incredible. We are so nestled in the mountains, you cannot hear a thing. After the lake, the bus drives us to a museum. A wax museum. I happen to like wax museums; there's something so creepy about them. They use real human hair for the figures and glass for the eyes. It's like, Are they alive or aren't they?

The bus drops us off at the museum, and we look around as one big unit. There's a history/politics room, where there are past prime ministers and Laura Secord, Canadian hero and chocolate manufacturer.

Then we go to the Hollywood room. They have John Candy, Michael J. Fox, Harrison Ford, Madonna and Mel Gibson in a Planet Hollywood T-shirt. The figures are all alternately sitting and standing on a platform about a foot off the ground. Behind them, there is mirrored paneling from floor to ceiling, so that you can see your own reflection between the celebrities. When I stand on my tiptoes, I can see my own face above a crowd of Asian faces. Sometimes, when I'm at home alone, I look in the mirror and am surprised by what I see. It's like, Whoa! I'm Asian! Didn't see that coming! So it's extra-startling when I see my own face among these other Asian faces. I mean, these are my people. I stare at our reflection, trying to take it in. After all, this is the only way I'll get to see Asian faces in Hollywood.

Back on the bus, onward to Banff. We have an entire afternoon to wander around on our own. When we get into town, people start to roam the expensive malls, packed with chocolate shops and kitschy, touristy gift stores. Mom and I walk past a pricey-looking beauty salon with a sign that says "free makeover" in the window. Mom drags me in.

"Don't you want to look pretty?"

There is something about the "makeover." I have this secret hope that they'll see something in me that no one else has.

"Excuse me, miss?" A handsome modeling agent stops me on the way out of the beauty salon. "But are you a model?"

"What?" I laugh, flipping my hair from my face playfully. "Who, me?"

So I get sucked in. The salon has these weird, modern computer options. A woman smiles at me and takes a picture of my face with a digital camera. Pretty soon, my image comes up on the computer, and the woman starts playing with it, clicking the mouse over my lines, my freckles, all my imperfections. And then she starts to apply makeup.

"We can start with just a casual look? Or a more dramatic night look."

Mom chooses dramatic. I sit in a special chair; the woman releases a lever so that I tilt back. I see her and my mom, on either side of me. As she applies the makeup, the woman talks over my face, telling my mom what does what.

"Lipstick, blush, eye shadow. Don't be afraid of black," she says, dragging a sharp pencil along my eyes.

"You see how I gently press the brush against the eyebrow? We could pluck these off."

"Yes!" Mom yells. "Let's pluck them off!"

What? The woman whips out a pair of tweezers from her coat.

"Ready for the new you?" says the woman.

"Wait a minute," I try calmly. "Can we talk about this?"

"Hold still, or it'll look *really* bad!" she chirps.

The makeup lady bends over my face and starts plucking. I feel pinch after pinch. It takes me a moment to gather my wits. The makeup lady and my mother seem to hover right above, taking all my air.

"Stop!" I yell from the chair. "Stop right now!"

They back away suddenly as if I've broken a spell.

"Hand me those tweezers. Now."

The makeup lady does. She pushes a lever on the chair so that I sit upright and face my reflection. There are chunks missing from my eyebrows and huge purple circles around my eyes. I look like a deranged raccoon.

We emerge. My father takes one look at me and just shakes his head.

"I know, Dad."

He hands me a Tootsie Roll.

Next, my parents and I take a ski lift up to one of the little mountaintops to take a walk. My mom is trying to tell me my face doesn't look that bad, that my eyebrows will grow back.

"Mom, please, let's just walk."

We walk. It's silent up here, beautiful. No one's around—and that's when I notice that we're not alone. A boy, a teenager, not from our bus, is following us. He keeps darting in and out of view, like he's doing a relay race. Then he skips ahead of us; we stop. He tumbles into a handstand, holds it for a second, gets up, makes eye contact with me and then takes off. It's like some weird squirrel mating dance.

"Mom, I think that kid is hitting on me."

"Who, that fat boy?!" My mother points at the boy as he runs away.

"Mom, can you lower your voice? Some people don't think that's a compliment."

"Yunny, please, when you date, don't have an affair with a married man, and don't go out with a boy with a chip on his shoulder."

"Mom, I don't want to date the kid; I'm just pointing it out."

Dad, sensing tension, hands me a Milky Way. Mom does not let up.

"You don't want to get married?"

I keep silent, hoping she'll drop it. We get to an outlook point. Mom is tired, so they both go into a little café. I stay with the view: the city of Banff nestled in a valley. It's lovely, this moment of quiet. And then, I hear footsteps. It's the boy. He skips up loudly and stands right next to me. I don't look at him; I just don't think it'd be a good idea for him to see my face up close. Doesn't bother him though; he just climbs onto the bench behind me.

"This view is amazing. Doesn't it make you want to fly? Fly like an eagle? I grew up here in Banff. I'm a musician. I play the drums."

We're silent. But how long can I ignore him without seeming rude? I turn around to give him a polite smile.

"What happened to your face?" His smile has dropped. "You know, you don't need to wear all that makeup. You're pretty enough without it."

And I blush. He's so sweet. He's so young. His face is so young, and he's standing so close to me, with that unmistakable look in his eye, that lazy, goofy smile.

"I just wanted to give you this. Something to remember me by."

He hands me something and runs away before I can say anything. I look in my hand. It's a key chain. It says, "Welcome to Canada."

☁

We drive all day to Moose Jaw, Saskatchewan, and spend the night. Today, we get to choose our activity for the entire day. The choices are either an all-day yoga retreat . . . or a tour of the Laura Secord chocolate factory, where we can sample the chocolates for hours and buy them at the end! I am all for sitting on my bum and eating chocolate, but when I wake up, I find that Mom has signed the two of us up for yoga.

Mom reads me the brochure:

"'Yoga works on every individual for his growth and betterment physically, mentally, emotionally and spiritually.' Oh, Yunny, you can lose weight!"

The bus tour has to rent a special van for us because we are the only two people who have chosen the yoga option. We get there. A woman answers the door and says, "Shh. You're late! Meditation has started."

The woman leads us to the yoga studio. At the end of a long hallway, she opens a door to a separate room. Inside, people are sitting on pillows, their backs to us, completely silent. At the front of the room, there's a man beating on an animal-skin drum. We sit. After a few minutes, I start to notice that my heartbeat and the drumbeat are synchronized. The man starts to play slower and slower, until I begin wondering how slowly he can play before my heart just stops. And then I think about peace and nirvana, and all those things I think I should be thinking about during meditation. And then I am filled with a sense of wistfulness and a longing for . . . for . . . for the chocolate factory. My mind is flooded with images of all the bus people, happy, eating chocolate. My father cramming his jacket pockets for later.

They turn on the overhead lights. It's time for the yoga to begin. We start with sun salutations. There is a bunch of stretching, breathing and posturing. And then the yoga teacher tumbles into a headstand. Now, I can barely do a somersault, so I try, but immediately fail. Mom keeps trying; she's kicking up those skinny chicken legs, one after the other. The teacher comes over and picks her legs up. The position is crushing her neck, but before I can say anything, he steps away, and my mother falls. I can see from her face that she's really hurt herself. The teacher, not noticing, prods her to go on. I call the hotel to get picked up.

Mom doesn't say anything. She's never aggressive to strangers, just to me and my dad. On the van ride back, she falls asleep. Later that night, she complains about swelling in her neck, so the tour guide arranges for her to see a doctor.

"Mom," I ask when she gets back. "What did the doctor say?"

"Oh, I'm okay, but doctor said I almost paralyzed myself."

She is officially taking the night off. I go downstairs and get her a sandwich. When I return, she's completely asleep, in her pajamas on top of the covers of the hotel bed.

"Mom?"

Nothing. I put the sandwich on the nightstand and watch her. She's frowning in her sleep. I wonder what she's dreaming about. Her body is skinny, too skinny. She's skeletal. What's going to happen when she's really old or too sick to take care of herself? She's very young-looking, so people don't believe her when she's not feeling well. And her eyebrows look really good. She wakes up.

"Mom, why do you still have eyebrow makeup on?"

"I can't take it off."

"Why?"

"It's a tattoo," she blurts out. "I didn't want to tell you because you're so sensitive about cosmetic surgery!"

"How long have you had it?"

"A couple of years. My friend recommended it. It saves me a lot of time in the morning."

"Okay." I shrug and go to the bathroom to start a bath.

"Oh," Mom calls. "Are you taking a bath?"

"No, this is for you."

"Wow, you rocks, Yunny."

When I wake up the next day, my parents are already downstairs. On my nightstand, there is a plate with a bagel and a note. In neat, petite, pretty handwriting, my mother has written, "Be a good girl Yunny! Don't tell family secrets to friends!"

We drive through Manitoba, a land of lakes and wheat fields. In Ontario, we stop in a little neighborhood outside of Toronto. The bus pulls up at a Korean person's house. We all go to the backyard. I wonder, Is this even legal? This is someone's house, not an official tourist destination. I didn't know there were Koreans in Canada—I mean, other than us. The tour guide tells us that we have one of two options for dinner: *soon-doo-boo-jee-gae,* which is a bizarre primordial broth. It's beige, murky, with clouds of tofu and mysterious claws that poke out, going "Help me," while other unidentified masses float by. And then there's *chja-jang-myun,* this kickass brown-bean-sauce noodle dish. It has meat, potatoes and *lots* of sugar, which I love. Any food that tastes like candy, I'm there. It's not a hardcore Korean meal the way the primordial broth is, so it's more likely to appeal to Americans, non-Koreans and kids. It's the one I pick—surprise, surprise—and my parents pick the primordial broth.

The tour guide then proceeds to *split us up* according to what we ordered. Excuse me? My stomach is suddenly completely knotted. I mean, I didn't have to talk to anyone as long as I was with my parents, and my secret non-Korean language complex could remain a secret. My parents walk away, arm in arm, totally oblivious to the fate that awaits me.

"Mom! Dad!"

Nothing. I watch them as they are led into the house, while my "group" and I wait outside the house in total silence. My dinner companions are all about, oh, half my size. There's a very cute little five-year-old boy, Peter, and three girls: Elizabeth, age six, Annie, ten, and Michelle, fourteen.

We sit at a picnic table, everyone staring out into space. Peter gets restless and takes out a little Matchbox car from his pocket and starts zooming it across the table, across his sister's head. Michelle looks bored. She's slim, pretty, showing none of the adolescent awkwardness I had to go through. And then there's Annie. She's pudgy, wears glasses, looks uncomfortable. After a while, she pushes up her glasses and turns to me.

"So, what grade are you in?"

Suddenly, it's not cool to say I'm in graduate school.

"Uh, they don't have grades where I come from."

I pray she won't ask any more questions. No such luck.

"Do you have a job?"

"No, not exactly."

"Then what do you do?"

The woman of the house comes out for our drink orders. She turns to the kids first; the girls all speak impeccable, beautiful Korean; even the little boy is fluent. And then she turns to me.

"Muo-ma-shil-lae-yo?"

I don't look at her; I pretend the trees are really fascinating. Maybe she'll go away. Maybe she'll assume I don't drink beverages.

"MUO-MA-SHIL-LAE-YO!"

I'm getting redder by the instant. I mean, I understand why she's talking to me in Korean; why would a non-Korean-speaking person take an all-Korean bus tour across Canada? And then there's the pressure of this group thing, the pressure to perform. Can I really stand to get humiliated in front of a bunch of kids?

"Maek-joo han-byung joo-sae-yo." ("I would like a bottle of beer, please.")

She nods and leaves like she's going to get the beer. I'm so excited, I have to give myself a high-five.

"What are you doing?" asks Annie.

"Um, high-fives?"

"So what do you do?"

"Oh. I'm a writer."

"Like Judy Blume?" she gasps.

Eyes widen, and it is the first time that I have ever said these words and received a positive reaction. I mean, this girl is on fire with excitement. "Writer" doesn't automatically equal "poor" or "loser" in her eyes. I've never had this experience before in my life.

"Are you famous?"

"No, not really."

"Do you make a lot of money?"

"No, not really."

"Do you write novels?"

"No, I write short stories," which I feel like no one reads except other people who write short stories.

"What do you write about?"

"Actually, I write a lot about death."

"Death?" she asks, turning away from me.

"Yeah."

Wait a minute, I probably shouldn't be talking about death to a young girl; I could be causing irrevocable damage to her psyche, sending her to years of expensive therapy.

"Well, a lot of my characters die, or they lose someone important to them, and then the story is about how they deal with it, or don't deal with it," I deliver in one breath. I wait, hoping I haven't ruined everything. After a moment, the little girl faces me and grins.

"Wow. It's cool to be a writer."

And she's right. There is something, even when it's the biggest torture, when it's something I'm avoiding at all costs. When I get on a writing roll, something else takes over, and I get surprised by what comes out. It's like those love stories where people find love in the most unexpected places.

"Do you write in Korean?" she asks.

"Actually," I say, "I don't really speak much Korean."

She looks at me. She doesn't look disappointed. She still has that look of admiration in her eyes.

"Can I tell you something? I want to be a writer, just like you."

"You do?" Oh, this girl is warming my heart, making me feel good.

"Or a waitress."

We drive for eight hours. To entertain the kids, they show *Mulan* on those little TVs on the bus. I watch it. Korean subtitles. It's a Disney movie about a war, where the father is about to get recruited. There are all these shots of him hobbling on a cane. He cannot possibly make it through the army. And then Mulan sings about how she's just got to be herself, and she takes her dad's place in the war. She's so pretty.

I look at Mom; she's falling asleep. I look at Annie, and she's enjoying it, so I try to enjoy it too. They show Mulan returning from war. Her father is all huddled over, but as soon as she approaches, she says, "Poppa," and he says, "Mulan." They embrace, and then something happens to me. I don't know, something about watching the frail old man trembling, watching him hug his heroic daughter—it gets to me, and I start to cry. I'm horrified. I try to calm myself down, but it's overwhelming. Then the movie ends, the lights go up and people start getting up to stretch.

"Why are you crying?" asks Mom, now awake.

"I'm not crying," I sniffle.

"Oh yeah, you have tears on your face all the time?"

I don't want to talk about it, so I tell Mom I have allergies. This makes her worry.

We cross the border to Quebec, where three-fourths of Canada's Francophones live. Quebec is the most cosmopolitan territory in Canada; it's like Europe. There are tons of wonderful restaurants in Montreal; there's Chinatown, Little Greece, Little Italy, plenty of neat, interesting places to check out, but where do we go? What do we do? We're tourists; we shop.

Dad knows I'm upset, but feels awkward. He's not good with emotional scenes. He puts a Hershey's Kiss in my hand and stands outside the store to practice his golf swing. Mom and I enter the shop.

"Yunny, do you say 'I'm going for shopping' or 'going shopping'?"

"Going shopping."

"Ugh, why don't you correct me?"

"I don't know. Maybe because you make so many errors, that one didn't seem that bad."

"My English is so bad, I should move back to Korea."

"What are you talking about? Your Korean is lousy, too. Remember how Uncle made fun of your grammar? It's changed over there. You can't go back. You may as well stay here."

"Oh, if you made a lot of money, life would be so easy. I could retire. Why you choose writing? Writing is most difficult job. You have to read everything; you have to experience everything; you have to be sensitive about human nature. You have to be better than human! Why you pick most difficult path? Most kids, they start on the straight path, and then they go to sideways, but you . . . you start sideways. What about law school? You know John Grisham went to law school?"

"Yes, I know, Mom."

"Why don't you write a bestseller? Show me what you write. I want to see if it's any good."

"No."

"Why not?"

"Because you'll think it's weird."

"Oh, it's too sophisticated for me."

"No, that's not what I said."

"Yunny, get something. I'll buy for you. You live only once. Until you die."

I hold up a white cable knit turtleneck that says "Canada" across the front in red yarn.

"What do you think, is it me?"

Mom looks at the price tag.

"Seventy-five dollars? Rip-off! If I get this for you, this is your birthday and Christmas present."

"Christmas? As in nine months from now?"

"Yeah."

I pick up a meat cleaver with the Canadian maple leaf engraved in the handle.

"What about this wacky knife? This will make a good birthday present."

Mom stops in her tracks.

"No, I will never give you a knife," she whispers intensely. "You sever the relationship when you give a knife."

"Okay, don't get me the knife."

"I mean it, Yunny. Don't ever ask me for a knife."

"All right, I won't!"

"Because you sever the relationship when you give a knife! Tell me what's wrong. I saw you crying. It's good to talk. Otherwise, you gonna be like Daddy, and you gonna get a heart attack."

"It's nothing. I just got a little upset at the movie."

"The *cartoon?* You crying about a *cartoon?*"

How do I explain myself? It wasn't Mulan or her adventures; it's just that moment when she returns from winning the war. Her parents are literally shaking, and she runs to hug them. And they love her, and they miss her. She's perfect; she's the best daughter.

"I'm sorry I'm not a lawyer! I'm sorry I don't make truckloads of money! And God, am I sorry I don't speak beautiful, amazing, perfect Korean. I just can't. This is it! This is what you get. I'm me."

Mom listens a moment before answering.

"It is not your fault that you do not speak Korean. You need only English in this country. You did nothing wrong. That is mine and Daddy's fault. We did a bad job."

"Oh, you did a bad job? Good, then can I fire you?"

"You wish! You stuck with me for life! You are my blood!"

Someone once asked me, What is it about mothers and daughters? Why all the commotion? My answer: It's just different. Mothers identify with their daughters. They're trying to rewrite their history with you; that's why it's so important that you end up with the right career, the right partner, the right weight, the right hairstyle. Sometimes, I wish I could trade in my title of daughter. Life would be so much easier if I could be demoted to niece, or aunt, or even distant cousin. There's too much pressure with the daughter part.

Later that day on the bus, Mom gives me a package; it's from the gift store, but she asks me not to open it till I get back home. In New York, I open it: inside is a pair of wooden ducks, a traditional Korean wedding gift. People give ducks because they mate for life. There is a note to explain:

There once was a mother duck and daughter duck. The daughter duck never listened to the mother duck. In fact, she did opposite everything her mother asked. When mother duck asked her to do her homework, she would go out and play. When mother duck asked her to come home and eat dinner, she would throw her food on the ground. When mother duck almost die, she thought to herself, I finally know her game; I am going to ask for opposite of what I want. Mother duck really wanted to be buried up in the mountainside, but she told daughter duck to let her body go down the river. One day, mother duck died. Daughter duck, looking down her mother's body, thought to herself, It's time to get serious. I must do as my mother wishes. So she took her mother's body, dragged it to the river and let it go.

So Yunny, I give you ducks, because I hope you get married one day. Soon. Time is running out; stop fooling around! But you have me for the rest of your life. You have so much to look forward, so relax. Until you're forty. Then it's downhill.

Love,
Mom

P.S. I didn't mention law school once.

changelings

marian blue

i was pitched out of my scrambled dream by a rapid decrease in speed. The first sound I was able to identify came from my seventeen-year-old daughter, Cherie, sitting behind the wheel: "Damn."

I think I gurgled a query. Red and blue flashes strobing the car interior dramatized her succinct answer: "I was speeding and got pulled over."

After the day we had just endured, a speeding ticket—even after I found out we had been zipping along at eighty-four miles an hour—didn't warrant panic. I quieted my instinct to abandon the car and run off into the Nebraska corn fields. If anything, an encounter with the police seemed a comparatively mild event in day three of our nonstop driving tour from Norfolk, Virginia, to Seattle.

A few weeks earlier, my daughter-in-law had called to say she, my son and my new grandson would all be at my brother's home in Seattle in November. Wouldn't it be great if we could come out, too?

We were emotionally en route immediately. For Cherie, the trip would be her first cross-country journey as a driver; for me, it could be a last opportunity to take such a trip with my daughter as a child at home. In a rush, we had the car serviced, cleared Cherie at school and packed. Our day of departure arrived with perfect weather: clear skies, temperatures in the fifties, no storms predicted anywhere in the continental United States, thirteen of which we would pass through on our route.

On schedule, Cherie and I wheeled through the city toward the freeway, where we revved up to cruising speed and drove almost seven miles before hitting a traffic jam at the Hampton Roads tunnel. I took pictures of the lines of cars stretching west as far as we could see. Would we encounter our first sunset sitting in backed-up traffic? We fidgeted with the radio, questioning our resolve. Two hours later cars started and the line began to move. As our speed increased, our energy returned.

I drove the first three-hour shift—a prerogative of parenthood—then turned the wheel over to Cherie. I needed to doze, to relax and to be ready for my next shift. I leaned back, closed my eyes. Cherie went around a corner. My left eye popped open, scanned the speedometer, then the road ahead.

I considered sleep. Then I considered the facts at hand. I was hurtling down the freeway at sixty-five miles per hour with my little girl in control, I hoped, of the car. This was the youngster who loses library books, forgets to do homework and drops dishes with alarming regularity. She's also the person who rolled our Jeep two days after getting her driver's license. But she has learned a lot since then, I told myself.

I shut my eyes and began counting backward from one hundred. The car engine rpm increased. Again I opened one eye; the speedometer needle hovered at seventy-two.

"Did I mention that I will pay my speeding tickets and you will pay yours?"

"Oh, darn," she said, grinning. Confident. Happy. Totally lacking in my forty-plus years of reasons to worry.

She was also the young person who would be out in the world without her mother in a short time. I shut my eye, turned my face toward the door.

Another curve.

I opened both eyes, sat up. "I'm not really sleepy yet," I said, then added, "When I can clearly read the license plate of the car ahead, I assume I'm following too close."

Without speaking, she slowed.

I chewed the inside of my cheek. I couldn't spend three thousand miles correcting every aspect of her driving and expect to arrive in good humor. I talked about the scenery, the trip, hunger, as I practiced ignoring differences between her driving style and mine. Gradually, during my second driving shift the wearies replaced the worries. Besides, Cherie had repeatedly missed cars, trees and other obstacles. Cherie drove, and I began to doze.

My nap continued through St. Louis, where a maze of freeways, even in light traffic, always offers challenges. When I awoke I had trouble believing she had successfully navigated a strange city without my help. My daughter was growing up! Growing confident! Growing . . . away? Would she simply march off, out of my life?

"Are you okay, Mom?"

I realized that I had drifted out of the conversation about passing through St. Louis. I tried to laugh. "I can't believe we're through St. Louis."

She laughed.

"I'm a good mom," I blurted.

This time we laughed together.

A short time later, at a gas stop after St. Louis, we noticed a strange thumping in the front end when we turned the wheel hard to the right.

I crawled under the car but saw nothing loose or jammed. There was no noise or problem going straight or at higher speeds. Perhaps we had picked up a piece of gravel in the mechanism. We opted to continue, more slowly, until daylight and an open garage coincided.

We found both at eight in the morning in Kingdom City, Missouri. Bad tie-rod ends. Needs a new axle and new brakes. No one here to work on it. Needs to be towed back one hundred miles to St. Louis, where the service department won't be open until Monday.

After only nine hundred miles our trip seemed doomed.

This conclusion came after five hours of telephone calls to dealers, warranty agencies, garages and tow-truck operators. We killed time waiting for return calls at the truck-stop store and game room, where I beat Cherie at pinball three times in a row. By that, I knew she was tired.

Yet she offered no complaints, no crankiness. The endless demands—food, drink, bathroom, games, money—I associated with traveling with my children were absent. Eventually she wandered out to the car and curled up in the front seat for a nap. I watched her for a time. Her cheek reddened in the sun, her right arm clutched our Chihuahua to her chest. She looked five. She had been acting thirty. My daughter had become a changeling, someone not quite firm in my thought. We were on the edge of something, and I couldn't let it go.

I returned to the phone.

We had no options with the car. It was not drivable and it could not be repaired before next week. I chatted with the garage owner about other possibilities. The airport was only fifteen miles away. I considered the Chihuahua, the open boxes of childhood treasures I was taking to my son. A bus? Same problems. I called a car-rental agency. A car was available; the cost would be close to a thousand dollars, a ridiculous price to pay for a drive. But what if it was a last shot at a once-in-a-lifetime experience with my daughter? What was it worth? And, ultimately, what would it cost us, financially and emotionally, to stay in a hotel and eat in restaurants in St. Louis—not one of my favorite vacation haunts—until the car was fixed? It would be at least four nights, maybe more.

By three o'clock, we were driving a rented Ford Taurus into the sun. The day had taken its toll. Our adrenaline was down. We were tired. That may partly account for the speed at which Cherie was traveling through Nebraska when she passed the two semis, between which the highway patrol car was lurking. With the seventy-two-dollar ticket in the glove compartment, we continued our journey. Cherie muttered about the high cost of trying to recapture lost time.

As we traveled deeper into the West, our problems dissipated like water mirages on the highway. Both of us had cut our teeth on western landscapes. Born in Denver, I spent most of my childhood clambering among mountains and desert canyons; Cherie, born in Moab, Utah, cherishes spaces where buttes and jagged spires tower in red, violet, brown, gray and yellow. Now, as the sun set, light clipped distant hills into angular shapes, and cloud shadows skimmed across the landscape like the ghosts of ancient birds.

"I wish we could just move back here," I whispered.

"Remember how the horses loved running through sage?"

"Remember how James used to scare me about cougars in the backyard?"

"Remember when we sat on our parkas and slid down the snow fields on the La Sal Mountains?"

As our memories touched, again my daughter shifted slightly in my perception.

In Wyoming I was driving through low, rolling foothills when we hit our first bad weather. Snow flurries danced across the road, then off again, as powdery ghosts. Their dance increased in tempo as wind speed rose and temperature plummeted. I was grateful we were not on a route farther south, where the Rockies loomed, with their glaciated valleys and bleak tundra. It was early evening when I pulled over for gas in Laramie, between mountain ranges, and turned the wheel over to Cherie. I added a warning of more snow, maybe ice. Neither was a part of her driving experience.

Our next stop came much quicker than anticipated. We were on the entrance ramp to the freeway when I realized Cherie was continuing to gain speed on the diminishing-radius curve. "Cherie! Slow down!"

Maybe my warning came too late. Maybe if I had said nothing, she would have handled the wheel differently. Whatever might have happened didn't; she responded by slamming on the brake and cramping the wheel to the right, in the direction the road followed but not, unfortunately, the direction of our skid. We began a three-sixty, jarringly interrupted by one of the metal reflector poles along the side of the road. Silence, heavy, broken by Cherie's wail of dismay: "I can't do anything right!" Her cry telescoped all the emotional ups and downs, the fatigue gathered along our two-thousand-mile trip. The sound caught at my memories of parenthood—the midnight call to rise and release my baby girl from a nightmare.

Her self-denigration had little to do with the spin, a great deal to do with her age and its cycles of agony: low grades, a broken dating relationship, a wrecked car the year before, exhaustion. I held her, sitting on the deserted freeway ramp. The only light came from our headlights on the Wyoming road. "It's all right, it's all right"—the crooning nonsense sounds we all use.

I yearned for the wisdom parents are supposed to have to soothe childhood fear. Then I realized this was not a child, but a young woman with a mind and spirit of her own that understood what I could offer: a chance to talk. "Hey, a year ago you couldn't drive a standard transmission without leaping ten feet to start. You were terrified of a freeway. I knew you when you had to learn to walk, learn your own name."

She almost laughed.

"Each time we learn something, we forget how much we've accomplished. It's a good habit to break because we all go through this, always thinking we haven't accomplished enough just because we made one small error in the process." I thought back to my own trials in learning to be a good parent. "This has nothing to do with who you are, just what you're learning. You take for granted what you're capable of, but I see your growing confidence and ability and understanding, and you inspire me."

Finally her head came up off my shoulder, her jaw clenched, her eyes brightened. From somewhere within she was reshaping her emotions, winning control. "I'm doing okay, aren't I, Mom?"

"We both are," I said, and I felt some of my own doubts disappear in that truth.

Eventually I clambered out of the car to assess the damage. The pole was flattened. Miraculously, the rear end of the car showed no dents, no scrapes. "Well," I said, "I see no reason to go hunting for the state highway crew in order to own up to their damaged pole. Let's just go." I hesitated. Did I take over the driving, give her time to relax? Or was this one of those proverbial horses that needed to be ridden again? Although Mother is supposed to know best, it seemed a decision not mine to make. "Do you want me to drive?"

"No. I'm okay."

Her answer jarred me a little, but I climbed into the passenger seat and watched my daughter start the car, grip the wheel and guide us back on the road toward our next challenge—which came quickly. Within a few miles the snow began again, then patches of ice where a heavier snow had been beaten down by vehicles. Soon we were climbing a pass. Ice covered the road. As we approached the summit, we joined hundreds of trucks, bumper to bumper, slowly navigating the icy road. At the top, we stopped. Trucks had been lining up behind an accident for hours. Their tractor and trailer lights created a brilliant chain of orange and red, glittering on and off like fireflies. Ours was the only passenger car in sight. We remained suspended in that wintry landscape, surrounded by trucks, for about forty minutes, then began inching slowly forward. Cherie remained patient, never braking too hard, never swerving.

It was dawn before we had completely left the ice and the coldest weather behind. The sunrise, however, brought more than light. "It's so beautiful," Cherie whispered while we watched the light roll across the land like a flash flood, brightening sky and land at the same time, unlike a city sunrise which creeps from sky to sidewalk. As if it were an epiphany telling me my daughter was someone to learn to know all over again, the light made me blink in surprise.

That day brought a new confidence and a comfortable pattern to our routine. We each enjoyed our driving shifts and slept soundly during our breaks. We gorged ourselves on chocolate, doughnuts and fruit.

Evening found us climbing a hill that led into a long-lingering sunset that deepened, scarlet to purple, then flashed orange and red again. The colors filled the car, lit our faces, our eyes. We touched, a tap on the arm or shoulder, to draw attention to yet another colorful display; each touch seeped into the skin, lingered in a way that felt new. I felt memory growing in each of us, almost as I had been aware of Cherie's growth during pregnancy. But this was different, as though we were each mother and fetus at the same time.

We entered Washington, the last state on our journey, in a deep purple twilight. The remaining few hundred miles seemed insignificant, a minor journey, and we happily wended into mountains, through a spectacular thunderstorm, down into Seattle, then onto the ferry to the Olympic peninsula. Our energy remained high, charged by our accomplishment: three thousand miles, handled ably.

For us, however, the real journey had ended somewhere in that spectacular sunset, with a new awareness of one another. I acknowledged that journey with some sadness: my daughter had grown up. As her mother, I had somehow always thought I knew where her personal landscape began and ended; now I saw her as a western landscape always shifting, with no clear beginnings or endings. As I hugged my son and daughter-in-law, greeted my first grandson, laughed with my brother and his wife, my glances kept returning to my daughter, a shape-shifter: child, friend, stranger.

Of course parental nudging didn't stop; habit fails to start and end with reason. During our stay, on the uneventful return trip and continuing when we arrived home, I offered unwanted advice, reminded her of chores, urged caution when she went out for the evening. Today, Cherie wanders the globe, keeping in touch through email and short visits; regardless, my endless parenting rambles on. But sometimes the words catch in my throat when I realize they are ritual only. Confused for a moment, I meet her eyes and then it's as if that sunset re-fires in the space between us. We smile, reach out to touch, a lingering brush of fingertips reaching deeper than flesh, spiraling through all the connections of our lives.

I've come to see our routes as intertwined, growing from old roots. My own fears of being alone, of being "childless" have dropped away, have been replaced by all the pleasures echoed in that western landscape, wide open and changing with every curve.

mourning ropes

monifa a. love

On May 31, 1999, at 12:33 A.M., I made a vow to my newly deceased husband. Two hundred eighty words. The signed and dated paper rests in the drawer of my nightstand. I wrote down the words so he could read them when he returned. Two months after his death, I did not believe him dead, just gone somewhere. I folded the paper print-side out so he would have easy access. *I take your hand asking that you help me go on in this world. I take your hand with the belief that love never dies.* The vow made me take to the road. I am uncertain why.

Part of me has been pacing the highways. Another part has been searching for him. Another has been going this way and that, waiting for direction. Another has been looking for respite from the impossible questions his sudden departure engendered.

I cannot say exactly when I stopped reaching for my husband's hand and reached for God. I believe it was after crossing a bridge in Ohio, on my way back from Cincinnati and suicide.

I am not being coy. It has been a time of fluctuating clarity and truth telling. I may tell others that I drive because I am afraid of commercial airline travel or because there is no other practical way to do my research or interview assignments. These assertions are, at best, cover. The seemingly endless network of roads, the fleeting images and sounds, the going away and coming home is consoling and inscribing. I am out there, on the road, and I am steadied. I enjoy the anonymity, and I need to know copies of my itinerary are in the hands of friends. Although I have not felt lonely in my home, I have felt bound and defenseless.

Traveling even the most prosaic byways, grief and God speak through the landscape, architecture, clouds and insect life. They call me by the strum of tires on uneven pavement and the pattern of dotted and solid lines. I am connected to them through broken-down buses with their exposed passengers and baggage. Through flares and shattered glass. Through wreaths of flowers and harvested fields. Through the crushed and acquiescing bodies of fallen animals. Through small-town holiday decorations and cemeteries divided by highways.

I begin my long-distance forays as I begin my prayers: requesting recognition. I drive a bright blue Dodge Ram pickup. Talismans are tucked in its secret places. Tools to better my reception adorn the windshield and dashboard. My wedding ring hangs from the rearview mirror. I wear green and blue. I wrap my head in white cloth. I keep my headlights on. In an odd mixture of faith and doubt, I draw attention to myself so God can easily distinguish me.

As I drive, I pretend that what I'm about to experience is just for me—life projected in my private screening room. I begin my travel feeling both powerful and childlike—independent and self-seeking, and in need of care and protection. I pack my truck full of everything I could possibly need and much I will not. I dream of meeting any emergency or challenge. I do not expect all of what I will experience to be pleasant. I know it will all be instructive.

On a trip of innumerable sights and sounds, I am struck by some phenomena immediately. The poppies along I-85 in North Carolina. The tilt of their crowns toward the sunlight. The blinking red cross of a tractor trailer signaling through the soupy fog of the Smoky Mountains. The erratic flight of hatchlings across the causeway to St. George Island. The lightning over Macon hurtling horizontally and raising the hair on my arm. The song of an unseen mourning dove at a stoplight in Amherst.

Other occurrences take time to register and to change me. Sometimes I see and don't trust my eyes. An event can be too concentrated, metaphoric or conceptual to seem real. The lighthouse seen in my rearview mirror after I cross the Tappan Zee Bridge. The bison farm in Hadley. The cross burning in an Alabama field on a winter evening and the silent fire engine racing to the scene. Bob Marley's "Redemption Songs" coming from a white social club in Louisiana. These moments enter me slowly like dreams of making love after deeply moving sex.

On a trip of countless route variations, I am directed. Turn left. Get off this road. Follow this way. I travel through and stop in places I did not intend: Hamlet, North Carolina. Birmingham, Alabama. Mars, Pennsylvania. Courtland, Virginia. Franklin, Tennessee. I find treasures: Ocmulgee Mounds. Crystal River. John Coltrane's home. Swing Low Cemetery. Blackhead Signpost Road. Not all treasures are lovely.

I take notes in a green notebook smaller than my palm. The notes are scribble-scrabble. I can usually only make out some of the words— as if the writing is not my own. Occasionally, I pretend I'm writing automatically, or in unknown tongues. When I read my notes, I fill in what I can't decipher. Sometimes I am journalistic and try to remember exactly what I experienced. Sometimes I am a dreamer and fill in what comes to me when I close my eyes. Sometimes I put in any old thing, knowing in some way it is more than that. Sometimes I just put a question mark. They are field notes of my mourning. A grief journal that is an intentional tangle. The notes tell me I am going on. But this cannot be. How can I be going on and still be so anguished?

May 2000

Traveling to the Monuments of the Black Atlantic conference in Williamsburg, Virginia. Memorial Day weekend. I'm speaking about Ed's work. His life. What I can make of it. What I can say about it as widow-observer. Blues and the Abstract Truth. Brother Stewart will memorialize his mother this weekend. When he speaks of his loss before a gathering in California, I will be standing at a podium in Virginia telling mine. I wonder if his mother and Ed ride the same ark. Arc (?)

A traffic jam in Williamsburg. Two very beautiful black women appear to be identical twins (same features, same physique, same hairstyle and clothing). They sit on the trunk of a dark green MG. They begin to kiss passionately. They are parked next to the entrance of the Dunkin' Donuts. Their amorous activity creates a stir. One doughnut aficionado drops his box of assorted treats when he spies them. There is much pointing inside and outside of the shop. I understand. They are provocative. I want to get out of the car and observe them up close. I want them to be a lesson just for Pisces me, some fable about my two selves in deep accord. From this vantage, they are more spectacle than vision. I want to feel the light around them. The couple goes on kissing and embracing as if it is their last day, and they know it. A white man in the car next to me watches them as he speaks into his cell phone. He is smiling. I wonder if he is telling his listener what he sees. I wonder what he does see. I wonder how it differs from what I see. I want to call him from my car and ask him. I wish I had a little button on my console that would lower both of our windows so I could say, "Hey?" and raise my eyebrows and tilt my head toward the action in the doughnut-shop parking lot. Ask him without asking. Would he hear my unspoken question? They are still kissing. In my mix of feelings, I am happy for their stamina and their ardor. I envy their ability to hold on to one another. I like their car.

Homeward. South Carolina Welcome Center. I-95. I am parked two spaces away from a Lexus. A black woman unlocks the door. She is curvaceous. She looks to weigh 290–300 pounds. Every pound glamorous. She enters the passenger side. She waits only a moment or two before a slender, tall, bald and muscular black man strides across the parking lot to her. He opens her door and lights the cigarette that she held up as he was approaching the rear of the car. No words I can hear pass between them. They kiss lovingly. He buckles her seat belt, walks quickly to the driver's side, gets in, kisses her again and drives off.

A white couple pulls into the space next to me, after the black couple leaves. A woman is driving. A man is asleep. When they come to a complete stop, the man sits up, pulls down the vanity mirror and adjusts his crooked toupee. He licks his hands and smoothes the errant hairs. He gets out of the car. She rolls down the windows. He wears a blue undershirt, blue shorts, blue calf-high socks and loafers. He wears lots of gold. He leans in the car. To tell her he'll be right back (?) She says, "Whatever you say, my sexy man." She speaks loudly and smacks her lips.

North Carolina rest stop. An adolescent white couple sits at a picnic table. They share a banana. Each one eats from a different end of the banana, simultaneously.

Georgia rest stop. A couple pulls up on their Harley. They wear matching spandex red-white-and-blue spangled unitards. They are very fit. Both have gymnastic bodies. The driver gets off and removes her helmet. She looks to be seventy or so. She turns to the rider, takes off his helmet and kisses him all over his face, leaving lipstick marks. He appears to be a little older. They secure their gear. They hold hands as they walk to the women's bathroom, where he waits, leaning against the brick, until she returns. He escorts her to a picnic table. His arm drapes over her shoulder. Her arm rests along his waist. He leaves her for the vending machines. He brings her a drink and a snack. They do not share (?) His gaze is his meal (?) I wonder where he keeps his money.

It is often like that. A trip will have a theme. Did I notice these lovers because of my longing for my dead husband? Was I allowed to see them so I could recall the joy of loving and not the pain of it?

Themes always make me ask, What brought me to those sights and sounds? Who brought me?

I watched the lovers with envy. What a gift to know the face before you can actually be touched. And held. And kissed. To breathe in the singular smell of the beloved. To feel the electricity when your tongues connect and to follow the taste of salt and longing through the body.

I have become a voyeur. It is more than that. Sex is everywhere.

Driving down dirt roads in the country is erotic. It is best after a short and intense rain. The brush of leaves along the surface of the truck. The scent that comes from the broken twigs in sunlight. The dusty seduction. This brings my husband to me. I can pretend he has come home from the studio with the smell of metal and dirt in his beard. His damp clothes beneath my fingers. His body relaxed from the exertion of welding, grinding, hauling metal, thought. On the road, he has been everywhere and no place I can reach.

Seeing those women—flagrant in their expression and celebration of love—made me feel my fullness and my division. I wonder at their willingness to be seen and their total disregard. I should not wonder. I flirt with being an exhibit myself.

Driving can give me a sense of wholeness and power. Along the highway, I feel as if I own my selves. With my arm in the sunlight and my hand lightly touching the silver window frame, I feel united and something akin to being free. Free is not the right word. I do not know the right word.

Although I have been preoccupied with his passing, and longing to understand why we pretend we have guaranteed time, I have not begun my road travels listening for a fixed message or searching for specific footage to undo my grief. I do not expect to see his face or God's in the sky. Rather, I set out believing the grueling nature of driving will yield something of use. Those accustomed to being passengers may not understand how demanding driving can be. The nonstop input is taxing. It can be like getting high, or being toxic. I feel the influx in my blood. It makes me drowsy. My mind rebels against the constant duty. I find myself dreaming deeply and separating from the reality of a sixty-four-hundred-pound vehicle moving through space at seventy-five miles per hour. Time becomes transparent. I rest my eyes, my head drops and bobs. Too much input has made me want to let go of the wheel.

February 2000
I have worked it out. Cincinnati. I can cross the Ohio and be free. I am traveling my own underground railroad—seeking peace from the nightmares, from the replay of a heart stopped, lips so blue, a body that does not accept my breath as sufficient currency. As sufficient current (?) Corvettes abound. I follow SOOSWET, MYTOY, CRVET, VETRAN, CMESPD, YSNDEED. The shiny fiberglass bodies make me think of Oz and some wizard who could release me. One car looks like ruby slippers. There is the Corvette museum. Maybe there is a widow's place in Cincinnati. When I come to that exit, will it be backed up like this one? What will our license tags read? GN2LNG? NOEXT? GRF2GO? It is difficult to drive

thinking of suicide. I want to simply let go of the wheel. I don't want to bring anyone else grief. How cruel would that be? I hold on very tightly.

The valet parks my truck and I am glad to be released from responsibility.

I have come 692 miles to find a parking garage where I can place a rag into the exhaust pipe and go to sleep. I have told my friends and family I have come to a concert. I have never driven over one hundred miles to go to a concert. They must know this. I can't write more or I'll write myself out of it.

I do write myself out of it. A final message to a colleague is read and responded to. He writes back, clearly knowing my intent. He has lost a friend to suicide only days ago. He makes a bridge for me to cross.

The trip back home is long. My hands shake most of the way. I sleep in the car in the driveway.

Months later, I let go of the wheel on a deserted road. The terror of racing toward a stand of elm trees is sobering. I am glad to feel the terror.

July 1999

I am headed to Mississippi to pour libation into the Gulf of Mexico for Ed's people. Everyone I have told has said, "Mississippi?" the same way, with their chins jutting. When I said, "Yes, Mississippi," they all paused. I have not mentioned it to anyone who was born in Mississippi. I should. Even the people who live in the South act as if going to Mississippi is to enter the lair of the beast. Bloated bodies and burning crosses are in their eyes.

I follow the glitter of billboards to Biloxi and to the water that calls me. It is right for me to be here. I take a video through the windshield. Not looking through the lens, hoping something will come out to record this night.

The video is dark. My notes are the only testimony.

September 1999

Dallas. Montgomery first. Dexter Avenue. King's pulpit. I stand there. The Civil Rights Memorial. I touch the forty martyrs named in that black granite. I feel the water, passing over them and those words from the Book of Amos.

> *Fifty minutes to Birmingham. I think of walking with the fear of snipers. I think of my own righteousness moving like a mighty stream. Would I have taken those steps? Can I be that stream?*

It is like this. Going sixty-five, I can time travel. Fifty-five doesn't work. I am too conscious of doing the speed limit to become different. Going seventy, seventy-five, eighty . . . I can go back into a past I did not live. I can go forward into speculations about who I am, who I can be. On a plane, the speed does not compel me. On a plane, I don't want to think about anything except when I'll get where I'm going. In a car, going a little fast, I can leave myself.

February 2001

I have driven too far. It's too late. I keep saying I won't drive so late. Ed always told me, "Please stop before sunset." For some reason I never did stop before dusk. I don't want to be driving. I don't see well at dusk. There are phantoms in the air. Why didn't I stop? Why don't I stop?

> *Home is another ninety minutes away. At least. I am in that part of Alabama that makes me uneasy. I remember the night a cross was burning. It seemed twelve feet high. I rubbed my eyes to be sure I was seeing what I was seeing. I hate rubbing my eyes. It makes me feel like I'm in a movie. That night it was the movie about the little colored girl who floored her accelerator, zooming into the night. A fire engine passes me. None*

passed that night.

I have a moment's desire to go back and follow the truck to the fire.
A fleeting desire.

July 2002

I am trying to write going ninety. I want to remember this road, these
clouds, the Tennessee River. Maybe it's the speed. I should stop.

I am not safe.

I don't want to be safe anymore.

I don't want to hurt anyone. I do. I'm still angry. I won't. I still
believe in God. More than ever. More than grief.

The road and the river are flowing, opening up before me like a
display. I can see myself in the road, in the river. Finally unfurling like a
silk scarf in the breeze.

The Falling Rock sign slows me down. It does not slow the others
doing ninety. I know about things suddenly halting my progress. I pull
over. Now it is safe to write how much I need to be out here.

It is September. I have driven from Tallahassee to Amherst. I have been
too concerned with packed boxes and a twenty-four-foot U-Haul truck
to take notes. Now I can write what I have been hearing all around me.
What are the words? Where are the words? What is my vow?

messieurs monsters hit the road

alexandria madero

*J*anuary 25

I am sitting at my computer, battling Messieurs Monsters. They showed up earlier than usual and now stand at the edge of my desk, arguing. One has to tie up his horse, another has to hang up his wings. One has to polish his halo, another has to park his motorcycle. Where is the silver rag? Is today street cleaning? Can they tie the horse to me? Can they strap the wings to my back?

I ignore them and concentrate on the map I found on the Internet. I need out. I know these monsters are only a figment of my imagination, but they have been relentless recently and now I fear it is not just my attention they want, but my very soul. If I really want to write, I need to put some serious miles between me and these needy party crashers. I put Nina Simone on the stereo and look at the clock: time for tea. After that, I'll consult the map again and decide where I want to go.

Two of my monsters, Critic and Booze, follow me into the kitchen while Monsieur Make-up Sex sits in the corner picking fights with me. The doorbell sounds. Seems Monsieur Guilt has forgotten again that he already has the key and Lust, just in from the fire escape, is demanding a bath. Considering that I have been locked in my apartment for a week trying to write a book, forget my recent breakup and remember to change my clothes, I think a bath might be a good idea for me as well. I ponder joining Lust but hear Critic scanning the cupboards, asking, "Why do we never use the fancy cups?" Booze, shaking his martini, taunts Guilt, saying loudly, "He's wearing all of your rosaries again!"

I put the kettle on and chain-smoke, watching the blue streams draw toward the open window. I rise to shut it and Messieurs Monsters complain, the only thing they have agreed on today. I stare down at the traffic and watch my muse run down the street away from me. I don't blame her; if I could, I would run, too.

I muster defiance as I set the table and turn to face my monsters. "Oh, just shut up and drink your tea. Can't you see I am trying to have some quiet?" Messieurs Monsters hold their pinkies in the air while they sip and then they laugh, but not really at me: I think Booze got them all to spike their drinks. "Mortal," they say in unison, "will you be putting out the biscuits now?"

Later

Messieurs Monsters are napping on my bed, arms, legs, wings and halos askew; they are not so fierce when they are asleep. I shut the door and return to my desk. Now I will steal as much quiet time as I can and get some writing done. The map I found earlier still sits on my computer screen and I decide to look at that for a while first.

January 26

This is shaping up to be one of those days when not much gets done. I got up early and threw back the covers with a flourish to greet the dawn. I stumbled into the kitchen to make coffee, remembering too late that I broke my coffeemaker while doing dishes two months ago. I decided this was very writerly behavior and opted for tea instead.

Tea at the ready, fuzzy slippers and space heater on, I fire up the computer and immediately set to work. Only I am distracted by Napster, my new friend and the reason I have been rising at these obscene hours. I download random pieces and organize them by mood, creating a "to write to" playlist which, when played, doesn't inspire me to write, only makes me wistful. Like an old woman on New Year's Eve, watching the year disappear, I begin to mourn my youth, even though at last count I was only thirty-three.

On these days when I don't write, I make sure that I *appear* to write. Anyone looking into my living room from the sidewalk would see me at the computer, posing and staring. Seemingly caught up in the antics of my characters, I cradle my cup with both hands and take long, dramatic drags off of my cigarette.

After my private modeling assignment, Monsieur Critic comes to join me for my morning ritual. I study him for a moment; he reminds me of a fop you might find in a Jane Austen novel. I'd like to name him after an editor from the *New Yorker,* only I don't know who any of those people are.

"You're up early," I say, pouring him some juice. He reminds me that he is a dedicated monster, and I have to admit he is. Probably the most dedicated of all, considering he is the only one who shows up every day—though, to keep it interesting, never at the same time. I have actually been able to get an entire page written before he turns up to stop all activity. Most times, though, I am stopped before I have even begun. He whispers in my ear that now would be a great time to start playing solitaire on Yahoo! and the next thing I know it is time for bed and the only thing I have written during the day is a check to my therapist. She tells me I am a genius with words and I would like to believe her, but I worry that the only thing I am a genius at is procrastination.

I call my mother, who is always good for at least an hour's distraction. She is home but can't read the quiver in my voice and says she is late for her goddess-worshiping festival in the forest that abuts her farm. Despite her great efforts to graduate with the times and embrace Martha Stewart, a hippie she will always be. "Will you ladies be sampling peyote or magic mushrooms this time?" I ask her. She tells me it was somebody else's job to secure the "stuff" and she is just going to let it be a surprise. I laugh out loud and the sound calms me down.

January 27

It's two months today since the love of my life ran off with another woman, and I walked away from my career as an agent and all of the Hollywoodishly fabulous stuff that accompanied it. It was quite a day. Today, I almost went to the store to buy a new coffeemaker. I consider this progress and proof that I am on the mend. At first things were so bad I couldn't even be bothered to brush my teeth or cope with the work involved in turning out the lights before bed or separating my whites. Facing the totally uncertain world of trying to make a living as an artist, with gray hair coming in hand over fist and my heart broken, I was not feeling the way I thought I would. Rather than embracing all of my new freedoms with a smile and a tingling sense of expectation, I was acting as if every day was the day before the worst period I ever had.

I read the biographies of women I admired to a soundtrack of music by Bread, and lay awake at night wondering why *their* friends seemed so much more loyal, why they didn't care about *their* mustaches and why *their* love affairs seemed so much sweeter, their heartbreaks so much less damaging. I knew if I didn't do something drastic, I would die. Literally die, right there in my bed. The coroner would say, "Broken heart and unfulfilled dreams is what killed her in the end. Don't mean to sound trite, but she was a frustrated artist, and as we all know, artists still die from these sorts of things."

January 28

I am happy. This news is a bit shocking and for a while, I didn't actually trust that it was true, but here it is. I have decided to make the open road my partner. I have settled on a road trip through the Southwest and have been making hotel reservations all morning. I'll go first to my mom's farm in Mendocino, then to a riverboat casino/hotel in Laughlin, Nevada, on to the Grand Canyon, followed by Mexican Hat in Utah, Durango, Colorado, and a few days in Taos, New Mexico.

I will be a pioneer and do the things I read about in all of those biographies. I will strike out on my own and learn to paint like Georgia O'Keeffe. I will read brave, original poetry at open-mike nights around the country like Carolyn Kizer. I will wear rings on every finger like Frida Kahlo and I will learn to be caustic like Dorothy Parker. I fantasize that I will have a stream of sexual exploits, real bodice-ripping, tortured affairs. I will fuck women, I will fuck men; I'll even look at pets differently. I will be insatiable and mysterious. I imagine local sheriffs imposing curfews in their small towns, trolling the streets with bullhorns saying, "Hide your sons and daughters, we just heard from Amarillo that she is headed this way!" Old ladies and young mothers will hurry inside, turning off lights and closing storm shutters. "That's right, Mrs. Johnson," they'll bellow, "get Fido in the house. We have no idea what she is capable of."

January 29

I am on the phone with my therapist and she tells me that I have to take my "inner child" with me on the road trip. I tell her that this just won't be possible because I accidentally, while drinking with Booze, let it slide that I was planning a road trip, and I have had a sneaking suspicion ever since that Messieurs Monsters are planning to come along. Things have been a little too quiet over here and I can smell that something is up. I explain that there will just be too much interior dialogue going on as it is and the last thing I need is a kid slowing me down.

She tells me it will be easy. "Find a photograph of yourself as a child and then every night light a candle, look at the photo and say, 'I love you.'"

I groan and feel put upon. "Honey," I say loudly, like someone giving directions to a foreigner, "I am tired. Really, really tired, and after the last few months *I* think that what *I* need most is to be free of responsibilities. I want to be independent, ya know, just do those things that appeal to me and not worry about anyone else's agenda."

"First we have to give her a name," she says, waxing over what I have just said. "What were you called when you were little? Did you have a nickname?"

I see her hustle from a mile away. Despite my pleas, she wants me to use this time on the road as "an exciting opportunity" to take my healing to a new level and, shiver me timbers, she expects me to grow from it as well. I am on to her, but say anyway, "The Italian side called me Happy, my mother called me Shmoolee, but the cutest is probably what my little sister Justine used to say. She is three years younger than me and couldn't say Alex, so she just started calling me Ax."

I am instantly transported back to Canada, where we lived on a commune for four years during my childhood. I can see Justine, maybe two or three years old and craving my attention, chasing after me through the trees on the way down to the river, where I was going to meet friends my own age. "Wait Ax," I can hear her yelling plaintively, "you run too fast for me." I remember ignoring her and whispering to myself, "Go home." Already, I had grown weary of looking after Justine because our "family" of adults were too busy getting high and quoting Sartre. Because of therapy and age, I understand now that I had too much responsibility at too young an age and that it was totally appropriate for me to want to hang out with my friends and not take care of Justine. But all I see is her little face, scared that she is alone in the woods and incapable of understanding why I would leave her there.

My sniffles begin to give me away. I wipe the tears away with my sleeve and know why I am upset about the assignment—I don't want to go back. I have been running from all of that for years and now, even in the safety of my own home, twenty-five years later, I start squiggling in my chair and biting my fingernails. Sometimes the memories of my early life are so sad, even when they are so sweet, that they remind me of an after-school special, only without the bit at the end where everyone comes together with frozen smiles, their problem resolved in thirty minutes, forgotten.

I tell this to my therapist and she says, "Well, you have tried it the other way and that hasn't worked, so let's just experiment with this, and we'll see. You never know, could be fun!" I hang up on her and stare out the window. I ponder what she has told me and find the photograph needed to begin the assignment. I look at it for a while and have to admit, I was pretty cute.

In the photo I am six years old and standing on a snowdrift at our old farmhouse in Quebec, at the edge of a grouping of birch trees. I am bundled up in an outfit that would make Mr. Blackwell cry in public, and I wonder if my mom dressed me that way as a sort of "fuck you" to her years as a model and a part of the New York fashion establishment. I call her and she tells me that I always insisted on dressing myself. "I know the outfit you are talking about," she giggles. "Yes, we were always bravely mixing our plaids and squeezing as much color into the day, weren't we?" I hang up on her and study the photo, looking for clues.

I'm wearing three different patterns in hideously contrasting shades, sweater tucked into wool ski pants à la Ed Grimley. My hands appear so large in the adult-size hand-me-down mittens that, on first glance, I think, If my hands were really that disproportionate, I could get work at a carnival and dispense with all of this art business. I look at the ridiculous outfit a little longer and know it makes sense. I look around my apartment, look at what I am currently wearing. It makes sense. So . . . I like color and texture and, I get it: I have been myself since I have been myself. It is a good moment; I feel oddly relaxed and not so afraid to bring Ax with me. I call my therapist back and tell her this. She claps her hands together and says, "Excellent!"

January 30

It is late. I am packed already and all of my maps and driving directions and hotel confirmation numbers are in a folder. I am ready to go. I am thrilled to be going and am a bit restless, too. I feel as though I can't get out fast enough. Today, my ex drove by my house and her new girl-friend walked by with her dog. I know that they live in this neighbor-hood, too, and have every right to come and go as they please; it just seems kind of gross that they pick my block to showcase their happiness. I have managed to keep myself sane only with research about the trip and Napster.

I am labeling tapes when I hear music coming in through the fire escape. It is unseasonably hot and balmy tonight, so all of the windows are open. I go to investigate and find Lust playing "Moon River" on a ukulele in perfect Holly Golightly drag. "Nice outfit," I say, taking a seat on the sill. I start to hum along to the music. He's really good; I guess he'd have to be in order to seduce all those people. I wonder if he is the one who does the cooking as well, but get kind of dreamy in the heat and don't ask. He finishes the song and I say, "Where have you all been lately? I was starting to get a little worried."

"Packing," he says lustily. "We've been packing for the trip." I knew it. I knew Booze couldn't keep a secret.

February 1

I arrived yesterday at my mom's farm. I'm letting her take care of me and tell me that I am okay. These days when I visit my mom, I find that I study her more and more. Most of the time, I just sit and stare at her in awe. When I was growing up, she was such a serious woman. She was such a poet. I remember her rising early, cuddling up to her notepad with coffee and cigarettes and writing beautiful words. I always liked the romance of my mother, wrapped up in some llama wool throw with her feet peeking out beneath the blanket, always warm. Staring out the window aside her huge Colette poster, waiting for inspiration to strike, ruing her life choices, ruing her kids, always looking for a pen with ink. Hair hanging beautifully in her face, lit by candles, she was a born-too-late-for-her-sensibilities sort of gal.

I sit at her feet, trying to soak up every bit of her mystery, trying so hard not to repeat her mistakes, waiting for her to notice me and hand me down all of her good stuff. Ax and I get comfortable on the floor and, as I have done for years, I say, "C'mon, Scheherezade, one more story."

February 2

I was starting to believe I was okay, until *they* showed up. I heard them coming up the garden path and, after jumping out of bed and running to the living room window, I saw them: Guilt, Lust, Booze and that asshole, Critic. I let out a groan and told my mother that she should set extra places at the table because my monsters had found me. As she reached into the cupboard for plates, she said, "Useless to run dear, they *always* find you. Trust me."

Looks like I'll manage only to write the Advance Praise section of my book today, knowing full well it is the only part of the book I do not write. It makes me feel better, though, imagining what Anne Lamott, Fran Lebowitz and David Sedaris would have to say about my "important work." I head back into the main house and find Ax sitting on the couch, bored out of her mind, and the monsters waxing philosophical about what I expect to find out on the road if I'm just staying hidden at my mother's. Then Mom comes in with two slices of pie à la mode in place of breakfast and suggests a jigsaw puzzle. Ax perks right up and the monsters seem sated by the pie as Mom and I start turning over the pieces.

February 3

I drove from Mendocino to Laughlin, Nevada, in nine hours. Now that I have arrived, I've realized there isn't much to do but gamble and people-watch. I lose seventy dollars at video poker while making up stories about the lives that belong to the bulbous and sunburnt thighs I see all around me. I finally pull myself away and upstairs to watch television and congratulate myself on taking this trip. I know something is going to happen, I just can't wait to see what it is.

After having driven on the interstate all day, I decide to take smaller roads from now on. Our anthems are always promising beautiful country but God knows I didn't see any of that today, just gray roads and gray hills and gray people working at gray gas stations. I think about getting a gun or at least some pepper spray because I don't think I will have cell range on my mobile and if I get stuck somewhere, I will be screwed. I'm trying not to freak myself out too badly though; if I am smart and don't drive at night, I am sure I will be fine. Anyway, what's my option, go back home? That I won't do; there is just no *there* there. As I'm falling asleep I remember my mom's sendoff at the farm. I had pieced together an ensemble that I thought would suggest that I'm a sophisticated, been-there-done-that woman of the world. If for some reason I was accidentally photographed by, say, Bruce Weber or Herb Ritts, I would be ready. She laughed at my cowboy hat, motorcycle boots, Mexican blouse, California Highway Patrol sunglasses, myriad rings and necklaces and said, "Honey, it doesn't matter if you look the part of a traveler, it's just important that you know you are. Keep your eyes open."

February 4

I wake up and head to the bathroom, but Ax wants to jump on the bed. I can almost see her and wonder if I might be going crazy. I have been doing the photo thing for a week now and have been surprisingly enchanted by this precocious kid, so I say, "Okay, but just for a minute. We are having another adventure today!"

Showered and ready to head out, I make my way through the football-sized casino that runs between my room and the parking lot. It is nine in the morning and the waitresses from last night are still waddling around, asses high in the air, like ducks, only with lace, not feathers, ruffling behind them. They carry their trays high above their heads, and even though they are smiling, their voices are weary. "Cocktails? Cocktails?" I look around to see who might be taking them up on the offer and wonder what a life looks like when it wakes up to alcohol.

Continuing through this never-ending room, I sometimes look over my shoulder to make sure that Ax is still with me. I really have to wonder how far I am supposed to take this assignment. I pass by a blackjack table and see both Critic and Lust playing twenty-one. They are winning, of course, with huge stacks of chips in front of them. Critic is sipping tea and pretending he is British, but I don't think the dealer is buying it. Lust plays with one hand on his chips and the other up the skirt of the southern waitress who is clearing up his empties. I am horrified and shield Ax's eyes. "Get in the car," I say through gritted teeth to both of them. "Move!"

As Messieurs Monsters follow me to the car, Critic bends over to pick up Ax and carry her the rest of the way. I think to say, "Don't you touch her!" But I realize it has been a long walk and she is pooped, so I say, "You can carry her, just don't say a word to her. Not one single word. She's too young to understand you." I must say it is a strange little unit, but somehow we are a family and today we are headed to the Grand Canyon, just like millions of other families.

Later

Passing through Arizona toward Williams and the turnoff for the Grand Canyon, it is an awesome scene. All sorts of red mountains, heaps of snow, cactuses that are still green and small pink flowers are all huddled together under dense, gray clouds that move across the sky. Like supermodels, they stand still long enough to be photographed or at least remembered, and I know I will remember. Every day on this trip so far has been a chance to sift through the slide show of my life and, like a finicky curator with only days to go before the big show, I am learning to pick only the moments I wish to keep. Monsters and inner child are asleep, cradled in my chest, which is heaving with gratitude. I think to wake them so they can see what I am seeing, so I can tell them, "See, this is why we got scared and left—so we could see something beautiful." But the air is so still and I recognize it as the first of many payoffs I will receive for the bravery I had to find just to plan this trip, and so I just sit and appreciate it as long as I can.

February 5

I wake at dawn to see what the canyon, sky and sun do when forced to get out of bed like the rest of us. The sun hasn't broken through yet; it's just flirting with the edge of the canyon and teasing all of us. We are standing on the precipice, tourists from all over the world, lined up single file and staring into the abyss. We snake along the rim of the canyon for miles and look like some bizarre Greek chorus outfitted by Eddie Bauer. I look across the line, studying the faces of these strangers and trying to find some way to connect. It is only my third day away from the farm, but I feel a little bit lonely with only my screwy thinking as company. I need to make eye contact.

I am reminded, as we all stand here with one purpose in mind, of how we motorists pull over to the right automatically when an ambulance passes. It is in those moments that I feel most connected to humanity. It's the only time I can imagine that nuns and serial killers are doing the same thing.

I decide to go inside. It is snowing and cold and, with no one to hold my hand or call my name, I feel a little too vulnerable standing so close to the edge. The hotel has huge picture windows that frame the view of the canyon. I think I will have some coffee and watch the action from there. It'll be like TV, which is what I am used to. I need the glass. I need the barrier.

Later

Navajo- and Hopi-owned roadside stands dot the landscape on the way out of the Grand Canyon. I am looking for a turquoise bracelet, a big one that looks like a cuff—something I think will add some authenticity to my driving costume. I finally find one at a stall owned by a Navajo man named Mike. Aside from short exchanges with bellhops and waiters, I have not used my voice in so long that at this first opportunity for conversation I just start talking. I tell him I am one thirty-second Cherokee and because of that, maybe I can understand his plight and the plight of his people. He is very sweet with me, but the whole time I can see that he is just thinking, Do you want the bracelet or not, paleface?

February 6
I can't be sure of exactly where I am. Because of these back highways I insist on taking, I am rarely, if ever, notified when I enter a new state. The signs are just too small and I never know when to look for them. I am ascending a very large mountain range, and I roll down the windows because through my windshield I can literally see how clean and powerful the air is. This turns out to be a mistake. First, I realize that it is freezing outside and all forms of monsters and little Ax start grumbling about the cold. Second, I decide to take huge gulps of this visible air and hold it in my lungs, trying in vain to wash away twenty years of smoking. I start to pass out. I pull over to the side of the road and stop the car—I am going to faint. Here. Alone. I realize that I should have known: I don't get much oxygen in my daily life, not in L.A. I have been a sea-level girl my whole life. And now, after years of sampling from the pu-pu platter of drugs that has always been available to me, I have my first actual overdose. Only it's oxygen. This is very unsettling and not at all romantic in the manner of Jimi Hendrix or Janis Joplin. My eyes go fluttery and my heart starts to race. I close my eyes and lean my head back and think of the store I passed in Utah this morning: a repair shop that was closed for repairs. It made me wildly nervous.

I wait until I have my bearings back and slowly continue up the mountain road. Monsieur Judgment reminds me that it was a stupid move to be that risky. I am horrified and stare at Booze. "So, what's the gist here, did you tell *everybody?* I haven't seen Judgment for weeks. How the hell did he know about this trip?" Booze shrugs his shoulders and changes the CD.

Later

Just passed a small sign that said Leaving Rocky Mountains. What? I just drove over the Rocky fucking Mountains! I am thrilled, but wonder if I would've appreciated them more if I had actually *known* they were important mountains while I was driving through them. Then I think of how, when I pulled over at a rest stop, Ax went tearing through the knee-deep snow, making snow angels and admiring how the sun reflected off the ground, making the white seem like gold, and I know that the moment couldn't have been more reverential.

February 7

I have been navigating by the lights of the twenty-four-hour Dairy Queens I pass every few hours. I can hear the collective groan of nutritionists around the world as I pull into my second drive-through of the day. The words "dangerously thin" have never been used anywhere near my name, but despite my penchant for cheeseburgers and chocolate shakes, I am actually on the lean side these days. I realize that the breakup, betrayal and career change have had a pleasing effect on my stomach. I can tell I am getting a little bit better every day because at least I can recognize that every crap thing that happens has a plus side.

Pulling back onto the highway I see a forest of birch trees. I think of the photo of Ax and say, "Look, honey, trees." She is excited and we decide to pull over and take a walk. Tromping through the snow, I notice a sign hanging in the branches of the tallest tree: Jesus Loves You. I am stopped in my tracks and can only stare up at it as if my single act of staying frozen and holding my breath will somehow absolve me of a lifetime of sin. I wonder about my sins, the real ones, not the kind that the Catholic Church is always trying to pin on me.

It is Guilt's finest hour as he kneels at the base of the tree that holds the sign, dressed in an outfit that says, "Every day is a funeral." He clutches my rosary, looking very much like the old Italian woman he is at heart. I realize this place is a church. Ax runs in the dappled sunlight, eating snow. I smile at Guilt and, jealous at first of his undying faith in miracles and God's love, I remember that it is my faith, too, and kneel beside him to pray.

February 8

This is a lonely-stretch-of-road sort of pain. A Tammy-Wynette-song-that-I-play-over-and-over-on-the-roadhouse-jukebox sort of pain. It's a can't-get-out-of-bed, can't-fall-asleep sort of pain. It's the kind of pain I have been thinking I will never recover from, and yet today I saw a snow mound in Durango with a lone blue jay standing proudly on top and thought, If a blue jay can get up early on a Saturday to protect this mound of snow, I can get up early on a Saturday to protect myself. Don't ask me why this correlation is working, just trust that it is and that it's come just in time.

Today I'm concentrating on tears—mine and those of my monsters. We are all a mess. It is not often that something happens that affects all the monsters at once. They are usually divided; one takes the morning and another the middle of the night. This is when we do our quiet talk; this is when, like a child, each crawls up to get special attention that separates him from the rest. The millennium version of "quality time." Today, though, the virus of heartbreak has spread out and left no stone unturned: we all weep. Every one of us is in the sadness outfit: robe with cigarette hole, hair like a bird's nest, T-shirt with two-year-old coffee stain and sweat pants stretched at the knee.

We are all disfigured, and I cannot pay attention to them today, have no care to provide. We will just have to be the sick house, quarantined until I stop feeling hurt and remember that the sun is shining and that Rollerblades can be rented at the seashore.

I hate my ex and I hate her girlfriend. I have been fantasizing all morning that something terrible will befall them. Not too bad, not death or disfigurement (although, wouldn't that be nice?)—more just that someday they will understand what they did to me and then, I don't know . . . maybe they will be able to come up with an apology I can accept.

February 9

I am listening to Sarah McLachlan, really letting myself go. The music is sadder than hell and I sing at the top of my lungs while tears well up and stream down my face. I am not really aware that I am crying. Messieurs Monsters and Ax all sit uncomfortably around me, the way my sister, brother and I would when Mom was still drinking and looking for an excuse to be angry. I look at Ax and my heart breaks. I think I am raising her with all the same mistakes she got the first time around, and I am embarrassed.

My cell phone rings out of nowhere—literally, we are in the middle of nowhere—and I practically break my neck lunging under the seat for it. It's my friend Constance. She hears the music in the background and groans. "Baby," she says too sweetly, "where you at?" I cry and cry and tell her that I don't know if I am going to find what I need out on a highway and that I don't think I am ever going to be better. She tells me she loves me, and I kiss her through the phone. I think she does the same for me because I feel something new.

I realize that there is a *there* there. I can go home any time I want because I do have people in my life who love me as much as they love themselves, and who don't care what happens to me on this trip, as long as I come home safe and sound. I decide to stop worrying about what will happen and just drive and keep my eyes open. I begin to take off my ridiculous accessories—the glasses, the silly necklaces, the hat—and when I am done I feel cleaner. I leave the Indian bracelet on and channel all of the courage of the moment into it. It is my Wonder Woman weapon—I feel strong with it on. No matter what anyone throws at me, I will be protected now.

I look at Ax and apologize. Smoothing out her hair, I say, "Look at that beautiful sunset, honey." She presses her entire face against the window, just staring at the colors as I change the music.

the grapevine passport

moe bowstern

*i*t was early when I woke up in the Anchorage airport. My flight from Portland had arrived in the middle of the previous night, so when I got off the plane I made my way down to my favorite spot under the windows behind the polar bear case, where I slept peacefully until airport activity increased enough to convince me it was time to rise and shine.

It was late May, and I was heading up to Kodiak Island for another summer of salmon fishing. I had a ferry to catch in Homer in three days' time, a phone number of a woman I had never met who had agreed to be my host and guide in Soldotna (en route to Homer), a huge backpack and my fiddle. My plan was to hitchhike from Anchorage down to Soldotna, where I would meet and stay a few nights with Ana Helena Garcia, then somehow make it to Homer and catch my ferry to Kodiak.

The janitor at the airport politely ignored me as I packed up my sleeping bag and strapped my fiddle and my fishing boots to my pack. I gave a nod to the polar bears and mountain goats in their glass cases, and lurched off to the departure terminal to find a ride. I approached wary drivers at the terminal and finally got a ride from a reluctant and skeptical man who warmed up a little when I talked about fishing. He dropped me off a few blocks from the highway. As I cut across a Burger King parking lot, an old coot in a wired-together pickup truck stopped to chat. "You look like you're going a long way."

"Well, if you call Kodiak a long way," I said, thinking of my friends who had dropped me off the night before in Portland, of how far I had already come. "Gotta get to Soldotna today."

"I sure wish I was goin' that way," he said, all wistful-like. I smiled and started walking, trying not to stagger under my load. I had walked half a block when the old guy stopped his rusty orange pickup in the middle of the street. He leaned out the window at me. "You had anything to eat this morning?"

"Naw."

"Well, get on in. I'll take you to the highway. There's a box of burgers in there in the back. I got a friend works at Burger King. They just throw 'em out. Perfectly good burgers. Grab yourself a couple."

"Thanks." I clambered in the back and we drove a few hundred feet to an on-ramp.

"I guess this is as good as any," he said, as he stopped the truck. "Did you get some burgers? Take some!"

I stuffed a few in my bag so as not to offend. "Thanks," I said again. I climbed out and dug a paintbrush and some ink from my pack, took out a piece of cardboard I had scored somewhere along the way and used his truck bed as a table to make a bold and legible sign: SOLDOTNA. As I painted the big black letters, my new friend began talking about loneliness, a subject many Alaskan bachelors are quick to discuss with traveling single ladies. Least with me, anyways.

"What I do to keep from being lonely," he began, "see, look at this." He reached inside the cab of the truck and brought out a robust, long-haired black Chihuahua. "This here's Mama," he said, like a husband, like a papa. Mama was proud and calm, confident of her place at the exact center of the universe. She allowed me to pet her. Her coat had hard, yellow blobs stuck to it. "Insulation foam," the old guy chuckled. "Baby's in the truck." And there indeed was Baby, a smaller, orange version of the dog in the old man's arms. Both dogs were silent as I thanked them all again and bid them good day.

I stood for a while on the on-ramp but soon began walking out of boredom. Of course, once I was on the highway no one stopped. After my arms began to go numb from the weight of my pack, I realized my folly. But I was committed, at least until the next ramp.

I had never hitchhiked outside of Kodiak before, and usually skipped the "all about my hitchhiking adventure" parts in zines and books because they were, I thought, boring. "Well, I waited here for a long time, and then I waited there. Finally I got a ride . . . " Now here I was on a highway, alone except for my various belongings dangling from my pack, wishing I knew a little more about what I was doing. I suddenly understood the difference between reading a sentence like, "I spent the night in the pouring rain," and actually being out in the pissing-down rain with no protection for eight or nine hours, starting to sneeze after three or four. Those boring hitchhiking sections of the books and zines were instructions! Who was I, to think I would never need what I now saw was valuable information? Hitching? Not me, I always said. No, I fish in the summer. Hitching season is over by the time I finish my boat jobs.

I knew my summer would involve lots of brute labor, so I resigned myself to my vertebrae-squishing walk and sang a few songs—the ones with the most verses—to the dusty road as I tramped. Hitchhiking itself would, I figured, teach me what I needed to know.

I made it to the next ramp and climbed over the guardrail and down the hill to wait in a forest of fast-food franchises and Wal-Mart-style stores. Lots of women drove by in family-mobiles—vans, minivans and Suburbans packed with kids and car seats. The kids all stared at me; the moms all stared resolutely ahead. Finally a woman pulled over in a small four-door.

"This is a real bad spot," she said. "These rich people won't pick you up, too scared. I'll take you to a good spot." She cleared out the back seat for my gear and I climbed in. "I've got Honey's car," she said. "Lots of room." She talked a lot, and quickly. "I have a friend who hitchhikes all the time, he figured out the best spot to get a ride. I'll take you there." Raindrops began to hit the window and I felt deep gratitude at being on the dry side of the windshield.

My driver was in her forties, very friendly, a bartender, she said. "It's a good job for a single mom, and I get to meet a lot of people. Flexible hours." She talked about her two kids, and Honey's daughter. "Poor little rich girl," she said, raised her eyebrows and tilted up her nose. "Thinks work is no fun. Me and my kids, we turn up the tunes, smoke a bowl and clean the house. It's a good time!"

She dropped me off at her friend's spot, a pullout just past the wetlands park on the highway out Turnagain Arm. I waved goodbye as she zoomed back toward Anchorage. The rain had stopped. I carried my pack to where I estimated a car might stop and stepped back out to the road. Barely had I flashed my sign when a hell-bent teenager in a beat-up car pulled up.

"What's that say, Soldotna? Great! I been calling all day to find someone to drive to Soldotna with me. Gotta go for a job interview." The whole time she was talking to me she was shoving crap out of the back seat to make room for my pack. I slid in the front seat as raindrops hit the window, and we were off. A large green bud rolled back and forth on the dashboard as my driver attacked the many twists and turns of the Seward Highway, a breathtaking and treacherous two-lane blacktop that runs next to one of the wildest waters in the world, with thirty-foot tides and five-foot tidal bores.

My driver set me to work immediately, handing me a small pipe to load. After nearly swerving off the road a few times we simultaneously agreed that perhaps we should pull off the road to smoke. That done, we returned to our rapid trip to Soldotna. My driver was in a hurry to make a noon interview three hours away, and it was a little past nine.

She was a slim nineteen-year-old with long blond hair pulled back into a barrette. She talked faster than my last ride and drove faster yet. She had a few close calls that made me nervous. "Whoa," she said under her breath after each maneuver. I could tell by the way she handled her beat-up trusty car that this girl loved to drive. She was a little wild, but she was confident and had a good feel for the car. She'd zoom up to a line of cars and we'd be stuck a while behind them. The two-lane road was often hard to pass on—lots of blind hills and curves, some oncoming traffic. She would hang, impatient, behind someone's back bumper until a hole opened up. "Yesssss!" she'd hiss, triumphant, and we'd pass them all, one, two, three, four. I hadn't realized until then how staid, how stodgy, how sensible I'd become on the road. I used to drive like that in a beat-up car on all the back roads of my small-town teenagerhood. Nothing else to do.

My driver talked and talked, and won my heart with a fishing story, American-girl-style dream come true. She went to a king salmon derby on the Kenai River with her boyfriend Josh—he's so cool. She hooked a big one, and bets against her landing the fish started going around.

"There were, like, three hundred people there and I was the only girl! It took a long time and nobody helped me. I brought that fish in all by myself and it was the biggest one anybody'd caught that day! Then I went around collecting the beer from everyone who bet I'd lose it. I had, like, a case and a half! I don't drink though. I gave it to Josh, he's so cool."

As she talked I appreciated her more and more, how tough and raw and emphatic she was. "Goddamn, girl, you rock, you kick ass!"

That stopped her briefly. "Yeah?"

"Fuck, yeah! What's your name?"

"Jenny," she said.

"I'm proud to meet you, Jenny, and grateful for this ride. My name's Moe."

"Yeah, nice to meetcha, Moe."

There's a moment, as I move toward my various destinations, when a person turns from being my ride or my seat partner on the bus—from a stranger—into a character. Sometimes it is prompted by an unusual kindness, like on the Christmas Day I found myself on a jam-packed bus and, as the last passenger, could see no place to put my bags. I was standing slightly dismayed in the aisle when my seat partner, a young musician, leaped up and stowed my bags and instrument in his own storage areas. Sometimes it's food shared, or a rich, unexpected conversation. This Jenny was a firecracker. I didn't figure she'd remember my name for longer than it took me to say it, but I wanted her name. I like that place where I say, Well, I'm Moe, good to know you.

Jenny went on to tell me that her dad was a roughneck down on the oil rigs in Texas, and moved with the oil to Alaska, then to Norway, where he now lived with the rest of Jenny's family, which left Jenny somewhat lonely. She lived with Josh, her twenty-five-year-old boyfriend who drives a Harley—so does she. She met him at a bluegrass festival.

We lapsed into a comfortable stoned silence.

Outside of Girdwood ("Me and Josh go skiing there, it's so cool") we passed a shooting range. I was staring out the window, wondering about my next move once we got to Soldotna, when Jenny turned to me.

"You like shootin'?" she asked me.

"Huh?" No one had ever asked me that before.

"You like shootin'?" she asked again. "There's a range, we could go shootin' if you want. I got a .357 in the trunk, Josh gave it to me, it's fun."

"Uhh . . . " I didn't know what to say. I didn't think I liked shooting, mostly I just wanted to get to Soldotna. I played various scenarios in my head: I refuse to go to the range and she pulls over and shoots me; we go to the range in the middle of the Alaskan wilderness and she shoots me . . . All the reasons not to hitchhike started to echo in my ears like an after-school special. "Don't you have a job interview to get to?" I finally said.

"Oh, right," Jenny said, and we sped on.

When we got to Soldotna I didn't really know where to go, so we pulled into a place called Mykel's Soldotna Inn. Jenny brushed her hair in the parking lot and adjusted her barrette. When I came back from the bathroom, she was checking herself out in the rearview mirror. I dug a copy of my zine out of my pack and gave it to her. "I get around a lot," I said. "Drop me a postcard if you ever need anything."

She took it, surprised. "Cool, thanks!"

"Good luck with the job," I said. "Have fun with Josh." I struggled into the inn with my load.

The Soldotna Inn was dark and blue. There was a busy luncheon that reminded me of a Rotary or Lions Club meeting, but the sunlit bar was blissfully empty. The bartender busied herself with dusting the mirrored glass shelves behind the bar, adjusting things. I watched her reposition a tiny glass ornament three times before she was satisfied enough to move on. I wondered what her house looked like. I wondered what she'd think of stoned, bedraggled me, with airport sleep hanging off me like my fiddle hung off my pack.

"What can I get you?" Within three minutes she set me up with hot coffee, a free phone, conversation and assurance that, yes, I could wait as long as I needed for my friend-of-a-friend to come pick me up. The bartender was a pro: She chatted me up and left me be. Like the fairy godmother who'd dropped me off earlier at Turnagain Arm, she talked about the sensibleness of bartending as a career choice for her as a single mom, about her boyfriend and her love of travel. Another customer came in, and I relocated from the bar to a corner table and settled in to wait for a while.

Ana Helena Garcia and I had been playing phone tag for a few days, and I had finally spoken with her at the airport the night before. She was calling from a jail, she was there for her work, she would explain later, she only had three minutes to talk. I had been calling her for days and when I finally found her, she slipped through the wires. I stared at the faded carpet and tried to list the kinds of jobs that would require a person to spend a night in jail.

The same friends I had pestered for hitchhiking advice gave me Ana Helena's phone number and recommended I stay with her in Soldotna while I waited for my ferry to Kodiak. When I asked my friends who she was, what she did, how I would know her, they smiled and shook their heads. "Ana is Ana," they said. "She'll take care of you. You'll see. She'll find you."

When we talked, Ana Helena gave me a message number and told me to call her in Soldotna with a phone number and location and she would pick me up whenever I arrived. It was okay, she assured me, she would recognize me. Our Portland friends had vouched for me.

The grapevine passport is a powerful ticket. The more you punch it, the more you can use it. My friends' house in Portland was a way station for all kinds of folks, and one of their perks was calling in favors. If I needed a place to stay in any U.S., Canadian or even European city, I had it. In addition to just plain being a friend, I delivered Alaskan salmon to them every fall and kept an open hearth of my own for any wandering folk waiting for a train, a plane, a ferry. As long as I kept my name clean and was a respectful and reciprocating houseguest, my passport would never expire.

I made my call to the message service and reported my coordinates. I was comfortable enough to wait for an hour or three, but I hadn't hit the halfway mark on my cheap coffee when a small, fortyish woman in shorts and a tank top with a big blond hairdo (puffy in the front and tightly curled all over) walked quickly into the bar, paused and headed right for me with a big smile. Could this be the Ana Helena Garcia I had heard about from my friends? Somehow I had assumed she was my age. Well, I knew what they say about assumptions, so I left them at the table as I stood up to her generous and welcoming embrace. "Moe?"

"Yep, that's me," I said, grinning. It's not often I get the chance to tower over someone.

"I'm Annie, Ana's mom." She called her Ann-uh, not Ah-na. Interesting. "Her car's broke down."

Annie had her friend Shelley along, and the two of them chatted with the bartender—an acquaintance, it turned out—as I took my stuff out to the car. "Well, that's Soldotna for you!" Annie said as she skipped out to the car. "Everybody knows everybody."

Annie's outfit impressed me. I was comfortable in my sweater, jacket and long pants, and here she was in a terry cloth tank top—no, it wasn't even a tank top, it was an elasticized thingie, no sleeves or straps. Her plump bronze shoulders shone in the noontime sun.

We left the Soldotna Inn and drove to a parking lot where another short woman waited in overalls, a big flannel and a knit cap. That,

I said to myself, is Ana Helena Garcia, whom I seek. And so, real and true, it was the woman herself, approaching the car, talkingtalkingtalking a mile a minute, greeting me with a big smile, directing her mom to drive us to her house, telling us all about having two cars break down in a week, and on and on. I was wrapped in a blanket of conversation punctuated with squeals and guffaws, sideways talk about lovers and drugs and plenty of expert curses directed at unreliable men and automobiles. I had arrived, in four hours, in Soldotna.

For the two days I was there I never did know where I was or where I was going. I didn't feel the need to, either, because everyone else did and I was not about to challenge anyone's itinerary. I was saving my strength for fishing season. I was like the out-of-town cousin who always sits in the back seat, and whose name no one ever remembers, but whom everyone likes. I never seemed to be in the same car twice and for all the driving around we did, everything looked strangely the same—tin-sided square buildings, no sidewalks, lots of dust and gravel. Everyone else had ideas about what and where and when—for me, it was enough that I had found Ana Helena. I believed my friends, that she would take care of me. I had a few days to get to Homer, and I was happy to pass those days secure in the belief that she would get me there.

Ana Helena was delighted to have company and was hungry for news of our friends in Portland. It had been a long winter. I told her stories of meals shared and dogs walked and gave her freshly made art. She told me that she would come with me to Homer, it was her day off. All we had to do, she said, was find a car.

The first part of finding a car seemed to involve some sort of bureaucratic hoop-jumping on the part of Ana Helena. Annie picked up Rick—Ana's soon-to-be-ex-boyfriend—Ana and me at noon, thus concluding our morning of passing a Baggie of cereal back and forth in their empty living room. (Ana and Rick were moving out of this shack by the water after only three weeks because their lease evidently included an insane and unreliable substance-abusing postpunk landlord. We had all slept out on the bluff behind the shack because the locks on the doors didn't work.)

We climbed into the car, Annie and Ana talking at each other the whole time. Annie drove us from office to office and back again. All the offices seemed to be adjacent to or across the street from each other, but in the spirit of the modern Alaskan we drove every inch. Ana Helena would go in while Rick and I waited in the car with Annie. Rick was a troubled soul, struggling to end nine years of substance abuse in a land of folks on and off the various wagons. He and I would listen to Annie as she talked over her shoulder about Ana Helena, Honey (did all Alaskan ladies call their live-in boyfriends Honey?) and the garage sale she was holding at three—she had to be home right at three and Honey didn't approve of the sale so she had to do everything with no help. Rick and I would nod, uh-huh, then Ana Helena would approach the car with a stormy face, get in and give an indignant account of her treatment at the hands of this or that office worker in the automotive or licensing or insurance department. She'd order Annie to the next office and we'd do it all again.

At some point we went to a car repair yard full of wandering filthy dogs where a bearded mechanic informed Ana Helena that her car, while beautiful, was unfixable. This took a little more outrage and indignant arm waving on the part of Ana Helena before it was absorbed. Then it was back into Annie's car and Ana took us all out to lunch, where I surprised myself by correctly guessing both Honey's astrological sign, Virgo, and Rick's, Pisces gone bad.

Annie made it home in time for the garage sale, and set it all up in no time, with some help from us. Honey called Annie three times from his work—he was a cook at a barbecue pit—while Annie directed us, placated him and ran for the Xanax. Ana Helena wheedled the car out of her mom, who allowed us to borrow it after we promised to return it before Honey got off work at 9 P.M. Honey made the insurance payments on the car, so no one but Annie was allowed to drive it. Every time we drove past the barbecue pit that night we held our breath like high-school kids and laughed, then turned up the radio when we were in the clear.

Our first two tries for a getaway car were strikes. Ana Helena's convenience-store friend needed her car that day, and Annie said no way. No way.

We tried some friends of Ana Helena's from work. Ana worked in social services. She was changing jobs from working at the emergency shelter, which took desperate kids for two months, to the long-term community base, where she would be with the same kids for two years. Darby and Gretchen, Ana Helena's friends, no longer worked there. Both left, they said, because of staff politics. "When I worked there I was pissed off all the time," Darby said. He had previously quit drinking and doing drugs for twenty-three months, but after six months at the job, he fell off the wagon—got so drunk on New Year's Eve he lost four days.

Kids were medicated, they said. The most common drugs were Zoloft, Prozac, Ritalin and Trazodone. Kids were sent in for arson, huffing, theft, vandalism, gang activity, drugs and grand theft auto. In the latter, it was often a parent's car that was "stolen" and wrecked. Kids were abusers and abuse survivors. All of them, strangely enough, had attention deficit disorder or attention deficit hyperactivity disorder. Ana Helena lived around-the-clock with them for three days, then had four days off.

After a long discussion about work over wine and smoke, Ana Helena offered Darby thirty dollars to rent his car to take me to Homer. Darby agreed immediately, but said he'd have to start it for us because it was having some trouble. Ana Helena and I flashed each other triumphant grins, finished our drinks and headed out to the driveway to check out our ride—a big, black, badass pickup truck.

Darby tried starting it. The engine caught and died several times. We hooked up battery cables. No luck. After half an hour I began assuring Ana that it was okay, I could hitchhike to Homer. But Darby was a man possessed. He began pouring gas directly into the carburetor, where it burst into flame inches from his face. The first time this happened we were all a little spooked, but Darby was unfazed. He continued to pour the gas, motion for Gretchen to turn it over, jump back from the flames, beat out the fire with an oily rag and do it all over again. At one point he poured gas into the carburetor while leaning over the engine with a cigarette hanging out of his mouth. I felt like I was trapped in a Raymond Carver story. Gretchen waved sadly at us when we finally left. Darby was still under the hood, concentrating too hard to wave. Ana Helena told me eight months later that Darby had shot himself dead, and Gretchen and their little girl were managing.

We drove away in a doleful silence. "What about Kenny?" Rick said, as we turned to avoid passing the barbecue pit. We drove to Kenny's trailer, which was parked in a dusty empty lot Kenny's boss owned. Kenny was home, hosing the trailer clean. Tomorrow his nineteen-year-old fiancée and her daughter were moving in with him.

"Kenny, wanna go to Homer?" Ana Helena started in. I got out of the car and we double-teamed him.

"Thirty bucks to rent your car," I offered with a swagger and a smile, ignoring the fact that this guy had never seen me before in his life.

"Plus gas?" Kenny shot back.

"A full tank," Ana assured him. "I'm buying breakfast, too."

Kenny looked from me to Ana several times fast, like a bird. He had a crazy grin, wolf teeth pointing out the sides of his mouth and big horse choppers in the front. He kind of stuck his chin out when he smiled. Ana Helena continued, "We gotta be back by noon so I can get to work."

Kenny turned abruptly and began coiling up the garden hose. "Okay," he said.

"Great!" said Ana Helena. "Come get us at my mom's."

"Be right there," Kenny said, tossing a sleeping bag in his car. Ana, Rick and I drove off, ducking as we passed the barbecue pit.

It all came together. Rick, Ana and I helped Annie pack up the garage sale and unloaded my stuff from Annie's car. Kenny showed up in a smashed-up hot rod with one of the tiniest back seats I've ever had the pleasure to endure, and we loaded his car and left without my ever having met the phantom tyrannical Honey.

Soldotna was a lot more like hard-luck Hudson, New York, where my cousins live, than the Alaska I knew as a seasoned fisherwoman. Maybe that's what the rest of Alaska is like, outside of Kodiak, I don't know. There was a lot of hopelessness there. When I observed the shittiness of Ana's social-work job, of her friend's convenience-store job, Ana Helena shook her head.

"Oh, you don't know what it's like, to be jobless, so broke and desperate all winter. I was so happy to get that job; I'm still happy. It's not like Portland here, it's hard." If she'd had a cigarette, that's where she would have exhaled.

We reached Homer during the few hours of summer darkness. Kenny slept in the car; Ana Helena and I camped illegally on the spit. In the morning Ana bought us both breakfast—good food, grumpy waitress. It was sunny and rainy in Homer, and the funny weather infected us: One minute we were all laughing, the next I was overwhelmed and Ana and Kenny were arguing about nothing.

Ana Helena and Kenny returned to Soldotna soon after breakfast. I bought a one-day camping permit and walked around. The tent city on the Homer Spit had the same rough edge as the one at Gibson's Cove in Kodiak—lots of boys, not much money, people losing job leads by sharing tips with friends, people getting drunk and robbed. I got caught in an afternoon downpour and walked to the fancy hotel by the ferry dock at the end of the spit, on the hunch that there would be comfy chairs and free coffee. I was right, there were both and I passed a comfortable afternoon drying out, reading, writing and jacking-up on the bean. The rain subsided with the evening and I had a solitary time, happy to be in Homer, happier still to be leaving on the morning ferry. The only person who spoke to me was a Czech guy who dished out classic Eastern European–guy come-ons. I was trying to find out about the Old Country and all I could get from him was, "Zo, all ze pritty garls go to Ko-dyak, hmm?"

Back at my camp I built a fire and cooked a few yams and a flower of garlic I'd brought from Soldotna. For entertainment, I played some fiddle, avoided the geeky didjeridoo player who wandered from fire to fire looking for friends, and read Vine Deloria, Jr.'s *Custer Died for Your Sins* until I went to sleep on the rocks, while the boys walked, Saturday-night drunk, back and forth past my tent.

In the morning I ate my cold garlic yams, packed my stuff and toted it down to the ferry terminal, where I left it, muttering a prayer to the protector of musical instruments that my fiddle not get stolen. The hotel had more of the ever-flowing coffee and I sat and drank until the ferry office opened. I bought my ticket, sixty bucks one-way, solarium passenger, fourteen hours to Kodiak.

The ferry finally showed up, the Tustumena. Everyone I know calls her the Tusty, the rusty Tusty, though she's definitely one of the fancier boats I've had the pleasure to board. She's got a wicked roll, bad for the uncertain stomach, good for romance. In the summer months she's so full of counterculture adventure/job seekers that the folks in

Kodiak call her the hippie canoe, but it was early in the season yet, and there were only a few of us. In the bright sun of the early evening we arrived at the familiar port of Kodiak.

Before I even disembarked, the family I would fish for and with all summer had spotted me. I was home. My strange traveling limbo was over, at least until September, when I would repeat my migration pattern in reverse. When I stepped onto the dock, I would jettison for a time my passive traveler self, who drifts with strangers in circumstance, who knows that the number of ways to the journey's end is uncountable. Four months of hard work was all that separated her from me. The Tusty blew her horn. I picked up my bags one more time and left her behind as I went to join my crew.

bridging the waters

karen sbrockey

*t*he Ohio River cuts through the undulating green hills between Ohio and West Virginia, defining the border. For several hundred miles, a series of bridges arcs over the water, like stitches closing a wound.

The accident occurred on the Ohio side, October 4, 1970. The ambulance took us across the bridge to a Parkersburg, West Virginia, hospital. Twenty-seven years later, while visiting my mother, I drive south along the river to remember the accident. I was raised on the Ohio side, so I cross the bridge near Dilles Bottom and head down through Captina, Proctor, Sistersville, Friendly and Raven Rock, each town a handful of little houses and a store tattooed with faded signs.

Parkersburg is a city. It takes a while to find the hospital, a high-rise at the end of a busy street. Suddenly an ambulance with siren screaming and lights flashing comes up fast behind me. I pull over as it speeds by. I cross myself. This surprises me. I am not Catholic. But someone must have prayed for me that day long ago. I pass it on.

What I remember about the accident is riding in the back seat of a yellow VW Bug, falling asleep and waking up in the hospital. I never again saw any of the other people involved. I learned the facts from my parents and my sister Mary Ann.

Here's what else I remember: lying on the ground, the world tumbling and urgent, feet rushing, fear, someone screaming and screaming, "Get away! Get away from here!" But what I really know lives in the space between the inhale and the exhale. It is bone marrow memory, dreams, twinges, wispy images and a fluid, shimmering awareness borne by a body composed mainly of water.

Fifteen years after the accident, I used it as an example for a teaching lesson: write a letter you will not send, to someone you cannot communicate with, to say what never got said. I was teaching in the adolescent psych ward of a Denver hospital. Emotionally disturbed teenagers throbbing with anger.

As a model, I read the letter I'd written the night before, to the driver who'd hit the yellow Bug I was riding in with three other college students.

Dear James (They told me his name and I remembered it):
You do not know me. I survived, that day you smashed into our car.

I read aloud to the slouching teenagers, from my notebook full of loopy, scrawled writing.

We never met and we never will. I wonder if you ever think about that Sunday afternoon, the lives you destroyed.

My voice was clear and even.

I wonder if you have children. I wonder if you still drink.

My heart opened like a trapped bird sprung free, and tears came. The kids softened, the anger dissipated, the air released a big sigh.

Do you ever travel that road? How does it feel when you go around the bend? Do you ever think of us, in that yellow VW Bug? I wish I could say that I forgive you. Sometimes I do. Other times, I hate you. And the confusion is always there. I wonder how it is for you.

The teenagers wrote earnestly. I told them their letters did not have to be shared.

Going around the room, checking everyone's progress, my heart shriveled back into teacher mode. One girl vibrated with anxiety and mistrust, yet she tried to be present. I asked to see not what she had written, but that the paper had words on it. She crumpled her letter and fled the room. And this is what stays with me: that split second, a seed of hope crushed.

James had no insurance. He had no job. My parents' insurance company, and that of the VW's driver, covered expenses and damages. Some years after the accident, I received notice, as one of his creditors, that James was filing for bankruptcy. I threw away the letter, thinking I had nothing to claim.

My sister Mary Ann has carried a different story all these years. She told me recently that James was not drunk. He was driving home from work and fell asleep at the wheel, veering left of center into our car. I know she is wrong about the job, but if he hadn't been drinking, it changes everything.

The accident happened right before homecoming, my senior year of college at Ohio University. Three Dog Night was coming to campus, Richard Nixon was going into Cambodia.

I woke up in the hospital with a concussion, a broken cheekbone, facial paralysis, a collapsed sinus cavity. My parents told me that everyone else was fine. My friend Charlotte came to the hospital and asked about the homecoming tickets. I said I thought I could make it. I spent six weeks in the hospital, didn't go to homecoming, and everyone else was not fine.

It was the fall after the spring of Kent State—May 4, 1970. Four Dead in Ohio. Shot to death for protesting the Vietnam War. Or, for some of those killed and wounded, no reason. They just happened to be walking to or from class at the exact moment that a bullet intersected their path. Shot by other people their age, in the National Guard, a contingent of twenty-eight ordered to drop to one knee and fire. In thirteen seconds, four students were dead, one permanently paralyzed and eight others wounded. The closest student wounded was thirty yards away from the Guard, the farthest was nearly 250 yards.

My boyfriend John, a student at Kent State, was at the university commons that Monday. He'd visited me at OU that weekend and hitchhiked back to Kent early Monday morning. The weather had turned cold. I gave him a sweatshirt to keep warm on the road. Three hours later, he wrapped it around the legs of the boy who would be paralyzed for life.

That spring of Kent State, Four Dead in Ohio, my father asked me, "Do you read those books that tell you to kill your parents?"

No. But I did abide by the adage, "Don't trust anyone over thirty." And all my professors seemed to want to be twenty-nine.

A bunch of earnest grapplers in the student union, we diverted ourselves with endless bantering, trying to corral Truth into a ring of cigarette smoke.

Think about time, man. Here's what it is. Time gets worn out at the seams and splits open. Like, there are weak spots at random junctures, like that's how they split the atom . . .

You're fulla shit.

No, listen. Like the war. Whoever happens to be there in that weak moment gets zapped.

Bertrand Russell. Logical positivism.

Who wants a burger? I'm hungry.

As if God gives a shit whether you live or die.

God is dead—napalmed.

I think a split second is wide enough to drive a truck through. It's waiting eternally for you, and only you, to step forward.

Yeah, like "Desiderata," man.

Let's go get a burger.

I graduated from high school in 1967. Salutatorian in a class of two hundred fourteen, I gave the proper commencement speech about goals and dreams and hard work, before Don McLean sang bye-bye to all that. I thought Elvis was vulgar and had never heard of marijuana.

Two years later, I was riding the wave of a frenzied fantasy of invincibility, as the world exploded, the psyche expanded, the naked body went public and liquid music, acid-laced, curled down the double helixes.

And I was happy to be there.

The truth is, I was marginally political. My sister Mary Ann, a year older and writing for the college newspaper, made me send a telegram protesting our invasion of the Gulf of Tonkin. I barely knew what it was about. When all hell broke loose on campus, my friend Charlotte and I teased our hair, applied mascara and walked up to the green to see what was happening. The ROTC kids in uniform with their rifles, the local police with tear gas, the frizzy-haired radicals with microphones. We looked for our friends, and left before tear gas was lobbed and clubs were swung. As Richard Nixon said much later, in the passive voice, about Watergate, "Mistakes were made."

We all look back and tell stories about that time. My friend Dean was demonstrating at another college with a group of longhairs, poet-philosophers draped in American flags. They got into it with the ROTC guys, Dean says, and were dared, Come over here and say that! Dean strode forward into the middle of the green with his limp flag, looked back and saw that no one had followed.

Now, it has the aura of kids' games, like Red Rover Red Rover and Capture the Flag. Back then, everything was absurd, but nothing was funny.

The whole world was watching the pinko commies, "effete snobs" and "outside agitators" stirring things up. Radical speakers were cancelled at OU, no reason given. My sociology professor held class in his apartment and passed a joint around. The college president asked the governor for permission to send in the state highway patrol instead of the National Guard, to keep things calm. Permission denied. Ohio University closed on May 15, and no graduation ceremonies were held for the class of 1970.

I watched the news. Americans with bayonet-tipped rifles stalking through the jungle. Phnom Penh, Da Nang, Phan Si Pang. Weird-sounding names of villages destroyed in order to save them. Guys going over, guys running to Canada. I did not have the patience to sort it all out, but I knew we could not win, should not be there. Some things you just know.

Now Vietnam is a tourist destination, the Generation of Love is a target market, and Truth still eludes me. The Vietnamese woman who runs my local laundromat told me recently, in her broken, tonal English, that she left her country against her father's wishes. She had seen how it was in Saigon. She left with two pairs of pants, two shirts and a sweater. Everything had to be black, for safety. Her family, the villagers, no one—she waves her arms to make this clear—no one knew who were Vietcong among them. "How could Americans know?"

That October of my senior year in college, 1970, I saw the ad on the ride board at BBF, the local burger joint commonly called Barfburgers: RIDER NEEDED TO KENT STATE. CALL LINDA M.

The shootings were history. Fall, a new school year. Maybe *normal* was a place we could still go back to. I decided to visit John before homecoming. I called Linda M. and became her rider, along with her friend Teresa. We drove to Kent in Linda's yellow VW Bug. I sat in the back, and paid half the gas.

Linda drove north along the river a short way, before turning inland. Three young women on the road, testing newfound freedom. Time was endless, a weekend was forever. Linda and Teresa were childhood friends, going home to Kent. Both were pretty and lighthearted. Linda, with brown hair, majored in education. Teresa, blond, studied sociology. We didn't talk politics. I didn't wedge myself into their space. I was simply the rider in the back seat. The car hummed with anticipation. They talked excitedly about friends they'd see, places they'd go, while I daydreamed and watched the landscape pass.

My hometown, Bellaire, was not far off our route, but was light-years away from my new life in college. The poet James Wright grew up just north of Bellaire in Martins Ferry. Our towns were archrivals in football. Wright's poems helped me reclaim this valley, long after we'd both left it. Several years after the accident I discovered his poem, "In Response to a Rumor that the Oldest Whorehouse in Wheeling, West Virginia, Has Been Condemned."

. . . Swinging their purses, the women
Poured down the long street to the river
And into the river.

I do not know how it was
They could drown every evening.

. . . For the river at Wheeling, West Virginia,
Has only two shores:
The one in hell, the other
In Bridgeport, Ohio.

And nobody would commit suicide, only
To find beyond death
Bridgeport, Ohio.

Many years later, when the unnamed yearnings of unfinished business pulled me back, I visited Martins Ferry to learn about Wright. A
woman in the newspaper office remembered him from high school and
dismissed the Pulitzer Prize winner as "just a big sissy." I don't know
what bridge carried Wright out of there, but I imagine that, for a long
time, his pen kept him tethered above the muddy Ohio.

Mary Ann was the bridge for me, when I was in the hospital
after the accident. I remember being lost in a foggy gray space, a nether
region of the permanently wounded. Suddenly, her hand came toward
me, open and strong, an offering. Then other objects took shape. I felt
the flat surface beneath me, the mattress, the sheet. I saw the chrome
sidebar. I reached up and took Mary's hand. She pulled me back into
this world, where people believe their bodies are solid. When I clasped
her hand, I joined them, and knew that I would recover. Mary Ann
does not remember this. It doesn't matter; I do.

Linda drove me to John's apartment and unloaded my suitcase from the
trunk under the VW's hood. We all smiled, waved goodbye. I spent

Friday and Saturday pushing the envelope in ways I am thankful to have survived without too much emotional scarring or brain damage. On Sunday afternoon, Linda and Teresa arrived at two.

I sat in the back again, behind Linda. She and Teresa asked me perfunctory questions, but were engrossed in their own conversation, which was fine with me. About halfway to OU, we saw a hitchhiker. A tall, skinny guy who looked decent, clearly a student.

These are crucial details, fragments I sift through. Who saw him first? Who suggested we pick him up? Linda pulled the car over. It felt like a group decision, or a non-decision. Perhaps we had no choice but to enter that big, wide, breathing, split second in a yellow car.

I noticed the guy had long legs and Linda had her seat up farther than Teresa. I scooted to the other side. Another split second, not really conscious, just courtesy. He climbed over me and sat behind the driver, where he could stretch his legs.

The scene was now set for the accident. Everyone was in place. The timing was on schedule for collision with the big Impala, down the road.

We talked a while. Bill Sullivan was a farm boy. Soft-spoken, lanky, nice looking. His head came close to the roof of the Bug. He clasped his hands loosely in his lap and looked quickly at me, then away, saying he'd been home for the weekend to visit his folks. His hair was almost shoulder-length. I wondered how his father felt about it. He was majoring in business, but wasn't happy with college. Then he smiled apologetically.

"All I really want to do is farm."

When you walk the hills in southeastern Ohio, you understand. The earth is sweet and green, moist and soft. Your feet knead the undulating body of the world and, no matter what the weather, you are soothed. I didn't know this back then, of course. The only place I wanted to be was away.

Soon Bill and I had said everything there was to say. I leaned my head against the window. The little motor hummed. The world outside grew dark. Linda and Teresa talked and laughed up front. I fell asleep.

Six weeks later, out of the hospital, the story I have carried with me, what I thought I heard. A drunk. Driving too fast. Speeding around the curve, veering over the center line, smashing head-on into our little Bug.

If the man was not drunk, I'll have to reopen this wound from the opposite shore, where there is no target of blame, where the fallible human condition accounts for mistakes made. But right now, I'm on the Bridgeport side of the river. The man was careless and negligent. He made a terrible mistake.

The force of impact tore the car in half. Linda and Bill were killed. Teresa had her seat belt on and received only minor injuries. I think she got the worst of it: she remembers. I called her several times when I got out of the hospital, but she never returned my calls. Linda's mother, whose husband had just died the year before, also did not want to talk.

And then there are the details of death. Linda was decapitated. We, the living, consider this especially horrific. The head, our cache of sensory jewels: the sight of a full moon, the taste of chocolate, the scent of gardenias, the sound of Pavarotti. The head is the body's treasure trove. Linda was decapitated, but Bill is no less dead.

My father went to the jail in Parkersburg to see the man who'd hit us, to talk to him. But unlike in the Bob Dylan song, *Any day now, any day now, I shall be released,* James already was. After thirty days in jail and a hundred-dollar fine, he was free.

Later, Dad took me to the junkyard to see the remains of the yellow VW Bug, a frail pile of crumbled metal, caved in on the driver's side like a fist to the mouth.

Mistakes. Blame. Choices. Alternative scenarios: Linda ignores the hitchhiker. We wave, shrug, mouth, "Sorry! No room." Comment that he's cute and buzz on by. He drops his arm, mutters, "Damn," and he's still alive, moving Black Angus from one pasture to another.

Without Bill, we zip on down the road thirty seconds sooner, and meet the Impala at another point on the curve. In that moment, James is clearheaded, having just sneezed, blown his nose, taken a sip of hot coffee. The light is better. The curve is wider. He sees us. He keeps his hands tight on the wheel. We pass by, unshaken in our belief that life is seamless, a solid breathing container, like this car, like our bodies; and that life is generally fair, for the young and good-hearted. And Linda is planning lessons for her third graders in Cleveland Heights.

Or maybe James does veer dangerously close to us. Linda hits the brakes, drives onto the shoulder. "Idiot!" She blasts the horn, gives him the finger. But close isn't bloody. It's just a sly goosing. We get a burst of anger, a shiver up the spine, a hyper-vigilant moment. Time wraps its gauzy fabric up tight again, and death goes sashaying on down the road.

And the possibility that haunts me most: we stop for Bill, Teresa opens the door, we all say "Hi." He gets in and sits behind Teresa. I don't move. I stay behind Linda, the driver, because I don't feel like moving. And anyway, it would be a hassle, his climbing over me. So he scrunches up, his big legs folded like a grasshopper's. I ignore his discomfort. After all, he's lucky to get a ride. But I do not sleep, edgy with his awkward frame shifting around. We head for our rendezvous with the Impala, around the curve, gunning for us, cream-colored metal, shiny chrome, grinning death in our face. Eyes wide and horrified, gasp. Screaming! Bam! Thudding blow. Searing pain. Metal. Blood, Linda's head flying. My bones crunch and mangle. Something strikes my chest and every- thing goes black.

My spirit rises out of the car, floating toward Linda's. We hold hands in the airless world, looking down on the rushing, terrorized, torn humans. Lights flash. Cars stop. Paramedics extract broken bodies from the yellow wound. Teresa rages, hitting people. "Get away! Get away from here!" James staggers, head in hands, numb, uncomprehending. We give our blessing, Linda and I.

Bill heals in the hospital. It is my parents who mourn their loss, not his. Bill quits school, goes back to the farm, marries his high-school sweetheart, has kids. He thinks about the accident every so often, while threshing wheat, smelling rain in the air, but never tells his children.

Teresa finishes school. She keeps to herself for a long time, goes to work as a rehab counselor and finds a gentle man who loves her. She has three sweet children whom she keeps a close eye on. For many years, she binges and purges and does not dream at night.

James blocks it all out until he gets into a twelve-step program. He tries to recapture our names and the vital information, but he gives up easily. He hits on a woman in the AA meeting and dates her for a few years, then goes back to drinking.

But I did not die. I finished college with dreams and goals veering out of reach. Instead of participating in graduation, I decided to go to a rock festival in New Orleans.

My mother was livid. "At some point," she said, "you have to be responsible."

"What does that mean?"

Whatever her answer, it wasn't enough. I hitchhiked to New Orleans.

Now, returning from Parkersburg to my mother's house, I am ready to sort through old boxes. I set aside the letters, ribbons, photographs and other childhood paraphernalia. I pull out the file on the accident and open it like a prayer book, carefully handling each hospital bill, each doctor's report.

Wrapped in plastic is the *Parkersburg Sentinel,* October 5, 1970, the morning after. Front page, right column, "Two Killed, Five Hurt in Route 50 Accident." Above it, "Eggs Are Tossed at Nixon's Car." Below it, with a picture, "Janis Joplin, Pop Singer, Found Dead in Apartment." It is the first time I am aware that she died the same day. Such a long day it really was then, the day the music died.

Next is a form filled out in my father's neat printing, requesting a copy of the accident report from the Ohio State Highway Patrol. He filled in one blank with "$3" to show he was enclosing the fee to obtain the details, to get the real story. My father died in 1992. His clear, careful writing, as familiar as his face, makes me cry.

I read the accident report and learn that two other cars behind the VW were also hit. My parents probably told me, but memory chooses its own threads, weaving a fabric one can live with.

And then, I read the investigator's report, complete with diagrams, submitted by Patrolman J. A. May.

The driver of the Impala, James Hansen, had a chauffeur's license. He was unemployed. Under "Driver Condition" is a list with tiny boxes. What is checked: had not been drinking. Fatigued. Apparently asleep.

And now, I begin the process of changing my story. It is like prying open a tight fist one finger at a time, releasing James, and myself, from blame.

The accident lives in my body as an occasional, deep, subtle ache in my upper left arm, where I probably slammed into the front seat. But what I really know, beyond the mind, is that Bill grabbed my arm when he saw what was coming. He seared a terrible warning into my flesh.

I feel that ache when I do yoga. It hits me, between the inhale and the exhale. And then I curl into Child's Pose, spine bridging the body, forehead to the ground, breathing.

an adventure's tale

lorraine caputo

*a*n adventure is made up of many tales—some can be told, and others cannot. This is not a tale of sacred secrets, nor mysteries. It is a tale of what I can tell.

I can feel the stone-mosaicked earth beneath my tennis shoes as I walk from the nearest village to the campsite. I stop for a moment, seeing the Pyramid of the Sun swirled in the low clouds of this morning, and think of how this adventure began. Months ago Alejandro, one of the head shamans of the Strength and Harmony Journey,* passed through my village in the north. With him came a growing number of runners from the four directions. He asked me to come with them to Teotihuacán, to witness the ceremonies marking five hundred years of conquest of the indigenous peoples of

*All names have been changed to respect those involved.

Turtle Island—North America. I refused. I did not want to face its spirit portals again—I feared its power. Still he told me he would see me here. Just before the ceremonies, I moved to Austin with some friends. Even before stepping into our new home, I told them I would return in a few weeks. The wind carrying the rains from the north carried me south, south of the border, south to the Valley of Mexico. I will never understand the *why* of this tale.

I near the gate of the site, shifting the weight of my old knapsack on my back. The air is sharp with the scent of wood fires and of sweet, cinnamoned coffee. Colorful bundles and worn packs are shoved into car trunks. Polyglot goodbyes are shouted. Already car after car is leaving for the north again, carrying home the hundreds who ran from their homes throughout Turtle Island to this valley. Soon this mud will hold only our footprints.

I move toward the murmured voices, the warmth of the kitchen fire. Sara hands me a metal cup full of coffee. It nearly burns my chilled hands. I let the steam bathe my face. We talk softly of our trip home. She and her family can give me a ride as far as Guadalajara.

Our quiet conversation is interrupted by the deep, accented voice of Alejandro. "Lorena." He puts a firm hand on my shoulder. The morning mist pearls on his silvery black hair, pulled back in a braid. With a nod to him, Sara walks away to help her husband finish packing their car. Alejandro looks me in the eye. "There's a guy who wants to take one of the vehicles that has been donated to the Journey back to the States. It isn't in the best of shape." He points to a blue Jeep Cherokee rusting into the earth. "He doesn't know any Spanish. It would be best if someone could accompany him."

Sara's husband calls to me that they are almost ready to go. I wipe a rain-dampened strand of hair back into its place. "It'll have to cross at Juárez, no?" I ask the shaman.

He is beckoning to a long-haired man, waving his hand down at the wrist as Latin Americans do. "Yes, to go through customs there. The Journey has to prove all the vehicles brought into the country return—or else the bond on them will be lost."

Ciudad Juárez is on the other side of the Río Bravo from El Paso. "That's a damn long ways from Austin. It'll cost me a bundle to get home from there."

"No, he'll pay for the gas," Alejandro says as the man approaches. Yes, an obvious gringo, down to the grin and ratty cowboy hat. "Isn't that right—uh, what's your name?"

"Michael." His grin grows. He pushes his hat back. His dishwater-blond hair is thinning at the temples.

"She'll go with you, Michael. You pay for the gas, okay?"

Ay, Alejandro once more is presenting me with a new adventure. What can I say? This Michael is a stranger in a strange land—and Alejandro is calling me into service for the Journey. I feel I cannot refuse his request.

"Lorena," Sara calls. *"Tenemos que irnos.* We've gotta go. Are you coming?"

I look quickly over to her. Alejandro crosses his arms and raises a brow. I toss the last of the coffee toward the fire. Her car horn blows. I shake my head and wave them on. They leave in a spin of loose stones.

Alejandro leads us over to a tailgate where several others are studying a map. We'll take Highway 57 through Querétaro to San Luis Potosí. From there 49 goes to Fresnillo and El Paso. We'll convoy with four others traveling to Juárez.

Shouts and slamming doors. This convoy is about to roll.

"Oyen, ¿hay lugar?"

"No, no hay. Tal vez con ellos. Tienen un carro grande."

Two Mexican shamans stroll toward our Cherokee. One is tall and thin, the other portly. Their bundles-in-hand bump against their legs. *"Perdone, ¿pero podemos viajar con ustedes?"*

Michael calls over to me, stowing things in the passenger seat. "What did they say?"

The mud oozes beneath my feet as I walk to the other side. *"Muy buenas, señores. ¿Qué quieren?"* I turn to Michael. "They want to know if they can hitch a ride with us. They're going to Guadalajara. They say we can drop them in Querétaro."

The back door slams once the last of their baggage is stowed. We are four in this tale of adventure, Michael and one shaman in front, me and the other in back. Shouts bounce through the aging morning: *"Vámonos."* "Hold on, I'm coming." *"Vengo, vengo."*

The starter whines with each turn of the key. "Damn," Michael mutters. "This damn engine."

"You want me to give it a try?" I lean over the back of the front seat.

"No, it's a pretty sticky car. Ah, there it goes." The motor spews bluish smoke into the low-cloud day.

"Well, I can help drive later on, if you need. It's an automatic, no?" I offer.

"Yeah," he says, looking over his shoulder to me, grinning. "But it's a bear to drive 'cuz it always wants to conk out. Gotta drive it two-footed." He revs the engine, his other foot on the brake.

"Vámonos." The first car of our convoy leaves the camp, its passengers leaning out the windows. *"¡Adiós!"*

"Well, here goes." Michael shifts into drive and joins the line of vehicles heading out.

Thump, thump, thump—"¡Pare!"

"What the heck!" Michael suddenly brakes. The engine moans in deathly tones.

I lean out my window. It's Alejandro, pounding on our fender. *"¿Qué hay?"*

A stocky woman runs up. Her brown hair brushes her shoulders. "Can I catch a ride with you?" Her English is accented.

A second car has pulled out of the site. "Sure, but get in fast," Michael tells her. The shaman from the passenger seat throws her knapsack in back, and sits with me. She gets in front.

We join our place in the departing convoy, hitting bottom as we leave the ruins on the high mountain plateau of the Valley of Mexico. A squeak of springs, the crush of rocky desert beneath worn tires. The *humph* of an old motor hissing steam into the dry air. The *cru-u-unch* of the underside as we sway precariously over a rather large stone.

And here we are—Michael from Philadelphia and I—with our passengers: two Mexican shamans from Jalisco State, one named Jesús and the other with a Nahuatl name that translates to something like "Jaguar Breath," and Nadia from Slovenia. Michael and Nadia speak no Spanish; Jesús and Jaguar Breath no English.

The hours and the kilometers pass, and with each our engine coughs and sputters. The tarred road sizzles beneath the nearly bald tires. Long ago the last member of the convoy passed from our sight. We are alone on this highway, north of Mexico City, heading north. The warming air of October blows through the Jeep's open windows. Michael hums as he drives. We others stare out at the desert whizzing by. I nod off to the tires' drone and the wind's roar, sandwiched between Jesús and Jaguar Breath.

Clang. Rattle. Scra-a-atch. Boom. The car swerves a bit into the other lane as Michael tries to bring it to a stop on the narrow shoulder. The unmistakable flapping of a blown tire. But what is that metal-on-pavement scraping?

We all get out. The sun is beginning to sear the late-afternoon clouds. "Well, the right back tire is gone," Michael declares. We can see chunks of its rubber littering the shimmering highway.

Jesús crawls under the car from the passenger side. His voice echoes up: *"Es la flecha. Se quebró."*

"Huh?" Michael asks me.

I shrug and pull myself beneath. Stones bite through my shirt. One end of the drive shaft lies fractured on the ground. "It's the drive shaft. It broke."

We settle into the stale heat inside the Jeep and share the bit of bread and fruit we have. The road is barren of traffic. We are someplace, but who knows where? A long way back from the road is a chainlink fence that meanders for miles and miles. Razor wire atop captures the rays of the now-setting sun. Further back is a low, broad building. "A prison?" I ask the Mexicans. They shrug in unison.

With a pocketknife, Jesús peels an apple. The thin ribbons fall between his fine-boned fingers to the floor. He offers pieces to Jaguar Breath and me.

"So, you all are from Guadalajara?" I bite into the firm flesh.

Jaguar Breath spits a seed into his broad palm. "No, from little villages near there."

"What do you do there?"

"Oh, I work on the railroad," he responds.

"And I have a stall in the market with my wife." Jesús passes another chunk to me.

We pass the time talking of their families, their children. Yes, Jesús already has grandchildren. The last tints of the sunset are fading into the gray of dusk.

A battered pickup pulls onto the shoulder ahead of us. I get out with Michael, the shamans following behind. Two men approach us.

The older one introduces himself as a mechanic. With a flashlight, he examines the drive shaft. "Sure, I can fix it for you. It'll be three hundred thousand pesos."

Whew, one hundred dollars. We four go into a huddle.

"This man is not a Green Angel," Michael says, referring to Mexican mechanics authorized to assist motorists stranded on the highways. "The guidebooks all say travelers should only trust Green Angels to help them out. How do we know . . . ?" He beats his yankee sombrero against one leg. He wrinkles the thin skin of his forehead, sunburned to his hat-line.

"Look," Jesús says, "we've been here now how long?"

Jaguar Breath kicks at a pebble, "Well, we can see if he can drop the price a bit, no? Three hundred thousand pesos is quite a bit."

We approach the man again. We let Jaguar Breath and Jesús negotiate. "Well, since you are coming from ceremonies, I could . . . How about 120,000? Including the tire," the mechanic offers.

Soon we are left alone again, the mechanic and his son gone with the shaft. The hours pass with only an occasional tire-sizzle, the sporadic *whoosh* of a truck going by. The stars begin to spin thickly through the sky.

"So, Nadia, where are you from?" Michael says, breaking the silence.

"Slovenia." She reaches into a plastic bag of bread. "It feels great to have the freedom to travel. We couldn't before, under the former government."

Michael takes the bag she now offers him. "And where are you traveling to?"

"Oh, to Real de Catorce." She breaks a piece off and smears some peanut butter on it.

Real de Catorce. I've heard of this place from many other foreigners, and from my readings about the indigenous people of Mexico. It's an old mining community near San Luís Potosí. There is only one reason why she would be going. I translate what she said for Jesús and Jaguar Breath. Jesús grunts. "Why, Nadia?"

"Oh," she wipes her knife off, "because I want to have a spiritual journey. I understand I can do so there."

"That's where the Huichol go on pilgrimage to have their peyote ceremonies, no?" I say in English and Spanish. The two shamans nod.

"Yes, and I'm so excited."

Jesús shifts in his place, his elbow hitting my side as he crosses his arms across his lean chest. "Peyote is a sacred herb, a gift from the Creator," I translate for him as he speaks. "It has its own ceremonies that must be followed."

"Well, of course I won't just take it. I understand there are men there who will give it to you."

"Who will sell it to you. But they do not follow the ceremonies."

Nadia sighs a laugh. "What ceremonies?"

Jesús turns his hard eyes to her. "The Spirit of Peyote is strong. One must pay him respect or one will not have a good journey."

I hear Nadia's sigh again in the dark.

"Uno tiene que cultivarlo de pequeño para cultivar una buena relación con él. Así lo muestra respecto," I repeat to Nadia, forgetting to translate. It's been so long a day. "One has to cultivate it from when it is small, in order to cultivate a good relationship with it. In this way one shows it respect."

Jesús nods at me, then continues, "But before taking it, one must purify oneself. One must go away to a quiet place, and fast and meditate for two weeks . . . "

Nadia cringes. "What?"

"Then one must sing the songs to him, and say the prayers before asking for the journey. One must pay much respect to him, or one will not have a good journey and may get lost."

The lights of a passing car silhouette Nadia's shaking head. "Ah, that's all just superstition."

"Actually not," I say. "There are several herbs that are considered sacred by the indigenous peoples of the Americas, and they must be taken with great care and proper guidance." Jesús nods. "Another one is called jimsonweed. It, too, is very strong. Many years ago I knew a guy who took some. He's still in a mental hospital. They say his mind is just gone."

"But I've known many people who have taken it without problems."

"And what luck they are still here to say so," counters the shaman, settling back into his seat.

Nadia turns away, peering into the darkness.

The mantle of midnight has spread over the desert. Someplace a bird calls. I pull my blue jean jacket closer around me as I sink beneath my sleeping bag, unzipped to accommodate the three of us in the back seat. Just as I begin to drift, standing on the edge of the dream world, we hear the crunch of gravel in front of us. The battered pickup has returned. We hurriedly get out.

He's got bad news. He has no electricity. He doesn't know how long it will be out. Yes, he promises, he'll get to work repairing our drive shaft as soon as he can. He's sorry.

What can we do? We get back in; I take the seat behind Michael now. Fatigued by the days gone by, and by this day gone by, we settle into the night, hoping for some sleep.

I am drifting. I am . . . someplace, I don't know where. I am . . . half-awake, feeling a tongue licking the ridges of my right ear, teeth gently gnawing it. I shift under the sleeping bag, chilled by the air seeping through the car. I am . . . more awake, aware of a cat's breath on my neck, his tongue, his teeth. I am . . . totally awake.

"*Híjole, cabrón,*" I mutter sharply, shoving my elbow into Jaguar Breath's meaty ribs. "Didn't you say you've got a wife and kids back home?" I pull the bag around me tighter, moving closer to the door.

And I drift back, standing again on the edge of the dream world.

A crunch of gravel in front of us. The sky is beginning to lighten with pale magenta. The battered pickup has not returned. No, this is a black Mercedes. The shamans are already awake. I tap Michael on the shoulder. A uniformed man walks around to the rear passenger door. A well-dressed man gets out. We slowly tumble into the morning.

He is the owner of the local factory. He waves out yonder, to that place a long way back from the road where a low, broad building hunkers into the earth and a chainlink fence meanders for miles and miles. Its razor wire is reflecting the rays of the rising sun. His guards called him last night, reporting our presence. If we like, while we wait for the mechanic to return, we may come in to have some breakfast and to freshen up. Just tell the guards at the gate, and they'll let us in.

He waves a short goodbye, the sun glinting off his gold watch. The chauffeur closes the car's door. Nadia stumbles out of the Cherokee, her blanket tangled around her legs. "Who was that?" she asks as we watch them pull into a turnoff a few hundred meters up the highway. The earth billows behind them, settling momentarily as they await a gate's opening. The Mercedes shines in the growing light.

While Nadia and Jaguar Breath are away at breakfast, the battered pickup returns. Yes, his electricity finally did come back on, early this morning. By the time our traveling companions return with some food for us, the mechanic and his son are packing away their tools. One hundred twenty thousand pesos and a new tire later, we are ready to roll.

Once again the hours and the kilometers pass, and with each one our engine still coughs and sputters. The road sizzles. We are alone on this highway, north of who-knows-where, heading toward Querétaro, Fresnillo, El Paso. The warming air of the day blows through our open windows. Michael is humming. The rest of us stare out at the desert. I watch a roadrunner dart toward the shade of a cactus.

Clang. Rattle. Scra-a-atch. The car swerves a bit into the other lane as Michael brings it to a stop on the narrow shoulder. Metal on pavement. Could it be?

Jesús looks under the car from the passenger side. He stands up, wiping the sand from his hands. *"Pos, es la flecha. Se quebró."*

"Huh?" Michael asks me.

I look into Jesús's brown eyes. *"¿De veras?"* A smile cracks his face, he shrugs and turns away to Jaguar Breath. "Ah, Michael," I wince, "it's the drive shaft."

Jaguar Breath crawls beneath and shoves the shaft out one side. "It must have just fallen off," I translate. "It appears not to have been the right size."

"Shit," Michael kicks the side of the vehicle. A chunk of rust falls to the ground. The customary hissing from under the hood begins erupting into a geyser. Michael throws his hat onto the ground. "Damn piece of shit. I should never have offered to take this back. I should have listened. It's worthless."

We share the last remnants of bread we have. The road is barren of traffic. We are someplace, I don't know where. There are no signs, no markings of where we are. Just endless desert stretching to either horizon, speckled now and again with *nopales* and frail trees. The sun moves higher into today's clear sky, its white light glaring off the blacktop. Nadia shakes a now-dry water bottle.

A battered pickup pulls onto the shoulder ahead of us. No, this is a different battered pickup truck. The shamans get out of our Jeep, with Michael and me following behind. Two men approach us. The older one introduces himself as a mechanic. He looks at the drive shaft lying on the shoulder of the road.

"Well, what do we do now?" asks Michael, rubbing the many-days-old stubble on his chin. We form a loose huddle.

Jesús shakes his head. Sweat pearls on his close-cropped silvery-black hair. Jaguar Breath throws his hands to the sky.

"Look, why don't we strike a deal with them?" I suggest.

And strike a deal we do: a free tow to their garage, a letter to Mexican customs explaining why we had to abandon the vehicle and a free ride to the nearest town.

In the limp shade of a small copse of trees I am rolling up Michael's clothes, packing them into a large duffel bag. I promised Alejandro—and Michael—that I would make sure this gringo arrives safely in the States. I shake my head, single braid swaying. I cannot believe that this man decided to bring this much stuff with him for a three-month running journey. Before I began this task, I asked him if, indeed, all this were his. I suspected it might be castoffs of the other runners. Michael only shrugged and nodded, then turned away.

I look over to him. He is sitting in the open door of the passenger seat, looking at some papers.

"What you got there?" I ask.

"Some of my kids' drawings." He looks up at me as I approach him, shuffling them in his hand. "I guess I won't be able to take them."

"We'll see what we can do." I pull some more clothing out of the back of the Jeep Cherokee and resume packing the bag. "Look, here are some bookbags. Perhaps you can sandwich the pictures between some of those books you've got, eh?"

He nods absently. His hat shades his gray eyes.

"So, Michael, how many kids do you have?" I push the contents of the duffel down harder, to get a few more things in.

"Two. They're nine and seven. My wife . . . my ex-wife has custody of them." He places the drawings in a large book about Teotihuacán. "We got divorced just about four months ago." His flat voice is spiked with pain. "I figure I can try to start anew once I get to Las Cruces. Perhaps get a job teaching science."

The human silence of these afternoon hours drifts on insect songs. Jaguar Breath and Jesús are sitting on some rocks under one tree. Nadia is by herself, reading.

All I can think is to do my best, salvage as much as possible for him. The duffel is full. Two big bookbags, and now a third, are packed tight. "I can help you carry some of this, but I don't know how much more we can take on the buses and trains, Michael."

I see the mechanic leave his brick-block office, a piece of paper in hand. Michael shuts the driver's door quietly, and gives the keys to the mechanic. "Well, perhaps the tent and my sleeping bag, too?"

"Okay." I look at the receipt the mechanic has written. Jesús and Jaguar Breath read over my shoulder: broken drive shaft; engine in bad repair; carburetor needs rebuilding; leaking radiator; threadbare tires. Is there anything else?

"No," I tell him. "I guess we'll be ready to go."

The man motions to his sons to load our stuff into the back of his pickup. Nadia climbs up and sits on a wheel well.

I see Michael looking at the stuff we have to leave behind. "Are you sure there's nothing else you want. We can find a way . . . "

"No, it's okay. You all can have it," he waves to the several coolers, the milk crate of books, the god-knows-what-else piled to one side. Jaguar Breath grabs one of the ice chests and tosses it in the back as he gets in.

Hours ago that battered pickup abandoned us at the small bus office in San Juan del Río. Together, we five—Jesús, Jaguar Breath, Nadia, Michael and I—caught a bus for here, Querétaro. The shamans assured us they'd be fine, and blessed our journey. They caught the first bus for Guadalajara and home. Nadia left without a goodbye and headed for San Luís Potosí. The sun has long since set, and the chill of the night desert is beginning to creep into this steel and glass station.

Michael is looking at one of his children's drawings. I prop my feet up on my knapsack and lean back in my orange plastic chair, marking my place in my journal with its red binding cord.

mapping home

deborah gitlitz

$\mathcal{W}$e are lumbering through the suburbs, peering into the desert dusk for the house number Osprey gave us on the phone. The adobe houses all look the same to me, a series of faded buttes along the rim of the street's shallow canyon. I imagine how our dusty, blocky van must appear from someone's kitchen window: an errant mesa, escaped from its moorings, towering uncertainly down the narrow, winding street.

There it is, 1512: Osprey's house. From behind a stuccoed arch the porch light shines on a fat cat blinking at moths. We're home.

Whenever we land somewhere for a day or a week, I like to say that I live there. For instance, we have lived in New Mexico for a couple of weeks now, and before that we lived in Arizona, Nevada, Utah and much of America's north and west. To think of myself as just passing through makes me tired. I am not a vacationer; I have lived in this van for months now. The van is as home as it gets.

This is what happened: we quit our jobs, my lover Val and I, and bought a big Ford van and drove away, out into the world. We have no "real" home to go back to. Outside the van's oblong windows the world rolls by, while inside I wash the dishes, brush my teeth, lay my head on my favorite pillow. Wherever we park is home.

We have driven all over the country, our wheels turning across thousands of miles, through states I had never seen before. We have parked our van in campgrounds, neighborhoods, hospital parking lots, rest stops, the driveways of friends. Our backyard is a Wal-Mart; our front yard is a Gulf Coast estuary. We cook in the van, sleep in the van, pee in the van. We orbit the earth like a tiny, erratic, rectangular moon, driving in and out of seasons. We gaze at the land spreading out seamlessly in all directions.

Now we have landed in the street in front of Osprey's house. Now we live in Santa Fe.

We have cactuses in our front yard.

I lived for a number of years in Olympia, Washington, where dark trees grow tall to meet the rain that falls continually from the generous skies. All winter long, from October till June, long, taut kite strings of rain anchor the flying clouds above that wet little town. Each spongy day soaks up the rain and dribbles into the next; a chain of puddles makes a week.

To resist the rain, I found it necessary to keep busy. I chinked my days with projects, from mentoring teens to gardening. My library job imposed an insistent structure on the soggy days: there was a morning scramble and there was work and lunch was from twelve-thirty to one-thirty and people expected things. It was very stimulating and distracting. Moments left unplanned might mildew.

I began to miss myself.

An escape seemed more and more imperative. Val and I conspired to quit our jobs, give away our things and drive away from the city of rain.

Thus was Camp Runamok born.

This is what I wanted: to (re)discover myself, my lover and the world. Isn't that the road-trip promise? More specifically, my desire was to take off my raincoat and let the world wash through me. I wanted to make room in my overscheduled life for new, unpredicted events to occur. I wanted to see the fabled sunsets of the Southwest and meet weird people in dented cafés. I wanted to trace the contours of my homeland, to bring conscious meaning to being American. I wanted to shut up so I could hear myself thinking. I wanted to stay up late talking with Val. I wanted to reconfigure myself, unleash my full potential, speak my true desires. I wanted to peer into lighted windows at dusk, to see how other people invent their lives.

I wake up every day in this playhouse of a van. It is a brown and tan van, chunky and square, as long as two cars and nearly nine feet high. We can stand up inside. The carpeting curls up to the ceiling, which we have adorned with glow-in-the-dark stars in personal constellations. All along the sides of the van are cabinets and cubbies, cozily reminiscent of a preschool coatroom.

We have a whole miniature household in here: sink, stove, fridge, a set of drawers, a small wardrobe. In the back of the van is a queen-size bed, with storage beneath. This bed can be converted into two benches, but usually we leave it in bed form, with pillows and books scattered around. There is something startlingly humane in being able to pull over anywhere, anytime and crawl into bed for a nap.

Most pleasing of all the furniture is the van's Porta-Potty: sturdy, bumper-stickered, squat, indispensable. It never stinks; its seat is sweetly curved; it is always there for us, waiting at the hitching post, loyal and conveniently close at hand. Furthermore, the van is so compact that one can pee and stir-fry dinner at the same time; so you see, we are having adventures.

Photographs of friends line the incurving walls. They remind us that we are known. It would be easy to forget that the van is not the only world we have lived in. It would be easy to drift off along the dusty highways of America until we were nothing but a speck in somebody's distance, a speck that belonged nowhere in particular. Sometimes it feels like, if nobody knows our names, we could vanish.

So we orient our drifting around visits to scattered family and friends. It is reassuring to observe ourselves from time to time in other people's eyes, to be reminded of who we are to them. It is soothing to borrow the easy comforts of someone else's home: the shower, the TV, the telephone; the entitlement to park in this driveway, in front of this house.

Osprey's house is of rough peach adobe and inside it are two dogs, one cat and Osprey. She and Val were housemates once in Anchorage, and now she is here, in this dry, windy, light-filled land, studying acupuncture. Osprey is impatient and smart and she is at the top of her class. I've just met her but I want her to put her needles in me. I imagine the needles will slide in like I am butter. It won't hurt because the needles will slide *between* my molecules and into the heart of me. Once the needles pass through my skin they will emerge into my internal chambers, shining in the dark, and my electric syrup streams will divide around their definitive points and flow off in new and interrupted and more serene directions.

It seems likely to work. There is plenty of time in the van to observe all sorts of arcane workings of my body, including my permeabil-
ity. Light enters my eyes and makes pictures in my head describing the
valleys we drive through. The voices of people we meet spiral into my
ears, carrying patchwork stories of life in a collapsed oil town. The night
air seeps through the van windows in a lonely campground and passes
through me somehow, raising my hackles and sending shivers through
my dreams. It even seems sometimes, as we drive along these cracked
back roads, that the world itself washes through me in waves, bits of
sunlight and sand, now interspersed with the molecules of me.

Every day somebody asks, "So what's it like, living in a van, driving
around the country, having adventures? God, you must be having an
amazing time. I'll bet it's fantastic. I'll bet you just love it." You will
notice that this is a question that answers itself. This is what people
want to hear: that we are, indeed, living the great American myth. That
life on the road is revealing and mystical, adventuresome and pure, that
there is freedom on the road to find yourself and have a grand time
while you do. People want to believe that we have broken through to
another place: the road-trip dream, a place they keep in the back of
their minds, hoarding it for its potential to save them should they ever
need it.

    It's all true. I'll tell you that right now. The Great American Road
Trip is everything I needed it to be. Things happen, things I didn't even
know to ask for. Things like getting enough sleep, every single night.
Like pulling off the road to chase armadillos because it turns out they
can jump straight up in the air, and it's the funniest thing I've ever seen,
and we don't have to be anywhere, so we can chase as many armadillos
as we can find. Things like meeting my dead grandmother's best friends
in Tuscaloosa, Alabama, and hearing stories about her beer brewing,

ballroom dancing and giant concrete art. The world is full of surprising invitations and gifts, and it's easier than I thought to make room for them.

But let me tell you something else.

Sometimes we get lost out here.

It turns out that when you drive away from everything you know, you leave behind the mirrors that tell you who you are.

Like this: in Olympia I knew I was smart and capable because people said so at my job. I helped people find answers and books to love at the library. These were accomplishments I could recognize and tally. I knew I was likable because my friends called me up, and funny because I could make them laugh. I was the kind of person who helped my neighbors. Girls flirted with me in cafés, because I'm queer and in the Northwest people recognize queer in the street.

I miss being recognized.

It irritates me to admit this, and it frightens me a little. Out in the middle of this big country people don't know who I am. They don't see the things I thought were obvious: that I'm a good girl; that I'm queer; that I'm a grown woman, and inclined toward friendliness. They don't hear Val's endearing giggle or see the kindness in her brown eyes. These things don't translate without the proper contextual signifiers. Two women pass through town in a van, and nobody sees us as we are. As I think we are.

I thought, when I started, that on the road I could look at the bigness of the world—I could look at the unfamiliar ways other people enact their human lives—and find the freedom to make myself up in some creative, better, more expansive way. But instead, in all this un-charted space, I seem to be disintegrating.

Val says it is happening to her, too: she is getting fuzzy around the edges, losing track of who she thinks she is. Sometimes I think this must be the beginning of our magical transformation into bold and limitless creatures. We will stop reading the script society tries to hand out—in which we work full-time at our careers, keep off the grass, please, and don't sing on the bus—and we will expand our ideas of how it's possible to be. But as soon as I start to lose track of my idea of myself, I get scared. I retreat to my three-quarter-ton shell and shut it tight around me: holding myself in, holding myself together.

We lose ourselves, and we hide in the van. And then, we are lost in the van. We have gone from resisting the rain in Olympia to resisting the atmosphere everywhere, afraid that if we expose ourselves to the air, to conversation, to life in a small town, there will be a chemical reaction with our environment that will change us beyond recognition. The eggshell of the van contains our increasingly shapeless selves and protects us from alteration. But isn't alteration what we were after?

I'd always thought a road trip was comprised of adventures. A string of bright, attractive adventures, comical and scary, neatly tied up into a loop that brings you home at the end to tell your stories. Val and I have collected our share: stories of Baptist Bible study in west Texas, of mud boggin' in Elko, Georgia.

If adventures don't seem to befall you, with a little hard work and an outgoing personality you can manifest some. Soon the trip will be over, so live to the limit—you can rest back at home. But what if you aren't going home? What if you're just going?

Month upon month on the road simply becomes life. Adventures aren't meant to happen every day. We feel as though we're letting you down, you in your house with your running water and your stationary backyard garden that shows you a sweet small new leaf every morning. Whenever we call, you ask us, And then what? What happened then? But listen, my friends, I'm tired of being plot-driven. Val is tired of stir-fry dinners and we're both sick of acrid Southern water. I want to spend a day baking. Val misses her motorcycle. I'm tired of making and breaking camp; I'd like to leave the dishes sitting unwashed in some other room. I am preoccupied with finding a place to sleep, again, tonight, and a grocery store open on Sundays. We need to fill up on propane again. We need to dump the potty. Val's worried about that skritching the van has started to make.

The van is the frame for our days. We spend a lot of time thinking about it, coddling it, repairing it and cocking our heads to the side, saying to one another, "There! There it is again. Is that coming from your side or mine?" The van is our home, our mobility, our one familiar refuge. If something happens to the van, we will be both homeless and stranded. We learn to read its vital signs just as habitually as we attend to our own bodies, and a malfunction in either distracts us from all else. The van is an extension of us, and life in the van, rather than adventures out of it, makes up the texture of our days. The adventure is in living so uncertainly, and in gathering our stores around us to be comfortable despite everything, despite feeling lost and cold and dependent on a cantankerous old Ford van.

We awaken in the Southwest one morning, unsure of our surroundings, because it is winter and although we stopped early the night before, it was already dark when we pulled in. Maybe we are staying at an RV park, in which case we are plugged in and the refrigerator is humming, causing the coffeepot, ready on the stove, to rattle and dance. Or maybe we parked in a quiet residential neighborhood, hoping to be taken for someone else's visiting cousins. In this case we get up quietly and leave early, often in the dark, before our lights and toothpaste dribbles give us away. Or wait, are those the sounds of the graveyard shift at Wal-Mart, and the light seeping through the curtains isn't dawn but the incandescence of the moon-white parking lot lights? No, it's the best kind of morning: a state park morning, quiet and cold and sweet smelling.

The van is freezing cold and some time in the night I seem to have pulled on my wool hat. Having finally adjusted the flannel sheets and down comforters to make a tolerably snug cocoon, I can't imagine emerging before spring. I open one eye to watch my warm breath condensing over the bed and shredding away like dreams. Valerie, on the other hand, is a motivated morning person. Her chemical desires propel her from bed, gasping and swearing, and into her frost-stiff clothing, so that she can get that coffee going and have her first smoke of the day. We have left the propane turned on and the coffeepot ready for her morning fumbles, and since I am still under the covers she can move unhindered in our tiny "kitchen." The small two-burner stove heats the upper half of the van quickly, and Val, kind soul, pours some hot water over a washcloth and hands it to me so I can take my morning bath right there in bed.

Steam from the coffeepot condenses on the faux-wood paneling. I notice the corners of the wallpaper are beginning to curl. Val cracks the shell of our egghome to step out for a smoke and a gander at the day from our front stoop. I have taken to laying out my clothes (on top of the toaster-oven) at night, so in the morning I can heat them under the covers in the warm spot Val has just vacated. When she vanishes into the unknown morning, I unfold myself from the sleeping pod, finish my washcloth bath with the last of the stove-heated water and hurriedly dress.

Except for the innermost layer, I am wearing the same clothes I've worn all week, consisting of nearly every warm garment I possess. The mirror is fogged over but I've stopped looking at myself anyway, mostly because I don't think to. I seem to be shedding my vanity and simultaneously forgetting what I look like. It doesn't matter what face I show this town since I won't be here tomorrow. As for Val, I'm not sure how she sees me anymore. Our unremitting proximity in the van makes us act more like littermates than lovers. Certainly the world sees me very differently than it has for the last four years. The professional librarian (frequently addressed as ma'am) seems to have disappeared along with the coifed hair and the grown-up wardrobe. Now I am a study in evident happy-go-lucky scruffiness in a 1985 Econoline van. These components add up to "hippie" or "college student," implying "young" and "free of responsibilities." I am thirty but frequently mistaken for twenty.

Bundled into sweaters and polar fleece, my chilblained fingers already cold, I open the van's side door and duck out into the world. The scenery changes daily but it is time to find out where this new home keeps its water pump.

In October, before we set out on this trip, we kept a large United States map in the living room, where we could look at it as we strode back and forth carrying boxes. The map was pinned to a rectangle of cardboard, its creased wings permanently spread in a glorious display of road-trip possibility.

The moving-out process was endless and painful. We wanted to be gone. We wanted to get straight pins with colorful ball tops and mark up the map with the evidence of our intentions. We looked at places called Sweetwater, Texas, and Tuba City, Arizona, and wanted to hold them down with pins until we could get there.

Then we realized that a map full of pins and braced with a big slab of cardboard would never fit in the glove box, would have to be left behind. We bought a box of shiny star stickers instead and covered the map with star-destinations until it looked like every state in the Union had four capitals. On November first we unpinned the map from the cardboard so it could spread its wrinkled wings and lead us into the world.

Now I sit in this coffeepot of a van these long, cold, dreamy afternoons, listening to my self percolating along, mysterious and steamy and anything but pinned down. I'd like to relocate the elements that define me. If I spend my days and nights gathering food, shoring up my shelter and watching the vast land unroll around me, how do I know I am more than a creature? How can I pinpoint the source of my identity, now that I've stripped away the mirrors of job, house, friends? The location of my "self" is elusive, trackless, though it seems to reside in this body somehow. This warm and tangible body, taking up space in the passenger seat, is all that I can be sure of.

This is why acupuncture intrigues me: I want to go spelunking, to find the meaning at the heart of the body/creature. I want to poke a hole and let a little of the mystery leak out and take shape in front of me.

And so I am titillated and alarmed when, on the third evening of our Santa Fe stay, Val tells Osprey about the odd pain I have in my back. It is a kind of kink in the muscles on the right side of my spine. I feel it under my ribs too, as though a button in my upholstery has been pushed too tightly in, dimpling my muscles front and back.

Osprey points to the guest futon and commands me to lie down on my stomach and get comfortable. She sits by my head on the floor, and from a small vial pulls out a needle for me to inspect, grasping it by its square blue plastic hilt. Its blade is about an inch and a half long and very fine, like the needles used to string tiny beads. Osprey tells me it is solid, and that "most of the needles you probably won't even feel."

I ask how many she plans to put in me.

She says, Six.

Oh, I say. All right.

I remember the star-crowded map as I lie on the futon with blue-handled needles protruding from my skin. Four in my back, one in my foot, one in my hand; all marking, according to Osprey, critical *qi* crossroads of my body. I don't feel the needles, except as a small pressure when she moves them, and the one in my hand that tugs at me like a faint but persistent pinch from inside.

Val comes in to observe my acupunctured skin. I think I must look like a crossroads after the survey team has come through, leaving their small wire flags to mark the locations of hidden cables and pipes. I am tempted to hire Osprey for a full survey; she is very confident in pinpointing my mysterious underground conduits.

Val and I have a joke about this trip, this mind-bending time in our test tube of a van: we call it "experimentation on animals."

Craning my neck, I glance down at the needle in my hand. At least we're ethical, I think. We experiment only on volunteers.

After twenty minutes or so, Osprey returns to un-needle me gently. Grateful, I cuddle back into my sweater, then lie for a few minutes, stretching my neck and trying to tell if I have been altered. My whole body feels noodly, the way it does after sex or a hard climb. When I join the others on the couch, the tickling inside my wobbly knees makes me giggle. I grin at everyone.

"Oh," says Osprey, looking me over. "I forgot to tell you. Especially since this is your first time. You'll probably feel funny for a while. We call it 'acu-stoned.'"

I giggle again.

The delightful sensation of being acu-stoned lasts about two hours. My whole body feels relaxed and boneless, filled with whipped cream, and I am dreamy and swimming with delight and goodwill. I have been altered, it appears, although it isn't anything I can put my finger on. Just another foray into the unfamiliar world of this body I call home.

The mysterious part is the map. When I look at myself in a mirror, what I see is skin, with skeleton and muscles implied beneath. Osprey, though, has an acupuncturist's map: a small plastic model of a human figure, tattooed like a subway map with a grid of colored dots and lines. When Osprey looks at my skin, she sees beneath it to a map of my moods and misfortunes, all the interconnected systems of my body. I am less guided than she. Mapless, I experience myself randomly. My old guideposts to self have turned puckish and unreliable. I remind myself of someone I used to know, but the essence of me refuses to be pinned down.

What good is a map for a wanderer, anyway? A map is for navigation, for finding the way to a destination. Perhaps, to recognize myself, or even to remake myself, I need to find my way home. To pick a home, and plant myself there. To make friends, and help neighbors, and watch lives unfold daily around me. To hang up some mirrors and to look, now and then, into the reflection of my own eyes.

But for now, we're making a lot of it up: this trip, our selves. Now and then we consult the map in the glove box, but more often we just try to remember what it looked like, where the stars were, and invent from there. The map is about as relevant as the frying pan. We use them both, we put them both away; neither one tells us quite what we're doing. We live on the road, in a van. We have left everything behind except some treehouse necessities and our bodies, our selves, however you contain that notion. The world fills the windows and falls into the van with us as dust, light, water, sounds. We take these things in and we are altered. It's all so strange, so hard to explain, and yet the ride is easy.

The more I ride along, the more comfortable I get. I haven't reached any destination and I haven't reached any conclusions. I am in my body in the van in the world. It's all made of the same stuff, the same elements, I mean: water and dust and electrical thought. Everything is permeable to everything else, one way or another. A little disintegration around my edges lets me mingle more freely with other elements of the world. To lose myself, though disconcerting, is not such a fatal thing. To be lost is to visit somewhere unexplored. As I relax my anxious grip on the self I have been, I am freer to unfurl in unexplored directions, mapping myself as I go.

inheritances

jeffe kennedy

Some stories become parables; they are repeated in a family to avert bad luck, to hold disaster at bay. This is ours.

The first day of October 1969, it rained in North Carolina—far from unusual weather for autumn in the South. My mom wondered if the rain and gloom would delay the afternoon's flight exercise. She had no special premonition; her days and love had simply formed a pattern of idle worry over when the fighters would fly, and when they would return.

My mother, barely a woman at nineteen, married an Air Force Academy cadet and left her birthplace in the Rocky Mountains to live near the Okefenokee swamp in the foreign South. In the wedding pictures, crossed sabers reflect the searing sky and scatter light on the Peter Pan bride in ice blue, holding the arm of her Officer Knight as they descend the white chapel stairs. Though the photographs are curiously blurred, as a little girl I could always see the brilliance of the day; no thunderclouds loom in the background.

Hatted and gloved, she attended the Officers' Wives Clubs in Georgia, Alabama, Florida and finally, North Carolina. She sipped too-sweet sherry and discussed flight schedules over luncheon, she and the other ladies sifting international news for information the husbands couldn't give. The men were always gone, mysteriously stationed overseas for weeks and months, leaving the base manned by homemakers and babies. Gossiping over back fences while their children played, the ladies talked earnestly of the weather. "Meteorology says the deployment may be delayed by the offshore front." "I heard the TAC squadrons are grounded until the pressure front shifts." "Can they fly in this?"

On this particular rainy day my father, Ted, already in his flight suit, ate the lunch my mother prepared. Perhaps he kissed her. He grasped his bike by the handlebars and rode back to the squadron house. My mom bundled me up to run errands.

The memories are my mother's, so my perspective shades toward the lover and husband. Ted never spoke much, she says. The rare times he was stationed at home were like a honeymoon. After eight years of marriage and less than a full year physically together, they still courted, spending Sundays in bed with the newspaper and each other. I build these images in my head from photographs. In one Christmas picture my father drapes his arm along the mantle, one hand dangling down. From this I know my hands are his. I grew up with my hand—his hand—on my mother's heart, feeling for her hurt and worry, anxious to bring her happiness.

When my mom spotted a purple bike on sale that afternoon—complete with training wheels and handlebar streamers—she knew it would be perfect for me. But because I had left my tricycle in the neighbors' driveway where they backed over it, my dad thought my carelessness should not be rewarded with a new bike. My mom felt a three-year-old shouldn't be punished too long. Torn, my mom called the flight shack from the store to persuade my dad.

"Sorry, Kathy," the duty officer answered. "He just left on that mission. Want me to have him call you when he gets back?"

Now when I travel, my mom never telephones on the day I plan to leave, in case the call meets with empty air.

Twenty-five years later, we planned the "excellent adventure," as my mom dubbed it. An antique teacart with my name on it awaited me at Grandmother Mize's in North Carolina. Grandmother refused to ship it and worried that she would pass on before I claimed my inheritance: a cherry-wood teacart I first saw when I turned twelve and my mom finally sent me to visit my southern family—she had waited for me to grow up enough to look past their racial hatreds.

"Jeffe, this is yours. I got it from Aunt Stella Mize Turner, who brought it from Emporia, Virginia, in her Hudson when I married Pop, and I was to give it to my oldest granddaughter at her wedding. She got it from your great-granddaddy John Vardey when she married. She voted for FDR, you know," she drawled on. "I'll keep it for you until you marry."

The inheritance thrilled me. The dark wood inspired visions of generations of gracious women passing the treasured piece to their daughters, dressed in princess gowns for Cinderella weddings. Every summer visit, I would examine the teacart and imagine my own home and daughters.

At twenty-eight, a year older than my mother when she was widowed, I remained unmarried. But with Granddad gone, Grandmother's health worsened relentlessly. She had already lost one leg to bacon grease, buttered grits, tomato-and-mayo sandwiches on Wonder Bread, and Crisco frosting on the wedding cakes she made; she could go to her maker any day. And I did have a house of my own. I had to drive from Wyoming to get the teacart. Soon.

My mom had visited her husband's family only once, a year after the funeral. Even once was unbearable. She described the shrine Grandmother had kept, with flowers, Ted's picture and candles burning. "Oh, it was just awful. Mom Mize cried all day, kissing the pictures. I was drowned in everything I had managed to put behind me. I never could go back after that."

Now Mom was ready to see the old house again, where I was conceived on a Thanksgiving leave. We would visit Grandmother, Uncle Rocky, Aunt Beth and the boys. With the teacart safely ensconced in the back seat, we would go see Seymour Johnson Air Force Base in Goldsboro—the base she lived on for three years, but couldn't remember. And from there to the site of the plane crash, on the South Carolina border.

I spent the night in Denver, and Leo, my stepfather, loaded the freshly washed car with every emergency supply we might need. We left as first light opened over the flat eastern edge of the city. We plunged on through Kansas, through St. Louis, gradually leaving the sky behind. On the topographic maps, you can see the descent—from my sere sagebrush plain in Wyoming down to the High Plains, down to the Great Plains, drop to the Mississippi valley, go deeper and greener over the hump of the Blue Ridge Mountains, and roll down the gentle slope of North Carolina to the sea. As the trees, heat and thick air closed in over us, my mother became quieter, more withdrawn. We slept, tired, cranky and behind schedule in Asheville. But in the morning light, Mom could see the Smokies, rounded, old and misty, just as she remembered. I remembered being twelve and laughing at Grandmother and Granddad for calling them "mountains."

We called my Uncle Rocky from the cell phone, so he could meet us at Grandmother's in Statesville and let us in. With several crack houses in the old neighborhood, he didn't want us waiting outside. My mother shook and cried hard to see Grandmother Mize again. I'd never seen her as a mother-in-law, though I knew the stories: how she would sneak me out of bed to play after my parents went out, how she slipped me candy, how Ted would take my mom to Hardee's on the sly because she couldn't bear the canned creamed corn and fried liver mush at every meal. These two women, unconnected but for me and a man long gone, sat together, weeping and laughing over old visions. "You're still so beautiful," Grandmother Mize told her. "I can't believe the house looks exactly the same," my mother answered.

We stayed the day with Grandmother and the night with my uncle's family. And then we pressed on to find the spot where my father actually died. Planning had mainly involved finding records of the crash site—no mean feat. No one ever told my mom where the two planes went down; or if they did, she has no memory of it. The history of that day is chronicled in the stark and lucid bits she does remember.

She did buy the bike, but didn't unpack the carton in case we had to return it. Instead, she put me on the back of hers and rode down to the path by the Officers' Club, where my dad would ride home. As was her habit, she waited for him; but he didn't come. We went home. As my mom drove me through the close green tunnel of the highway so many years later, she gave me a new piece of the story. I understood why Mom had never told me before of the near relief she felt to see the base commander's car pull into the driveway. It was an unmistakable icon. In the language of the base wives, the message resounded clearly. Her neighbor ducked in the back door and took me, without a word, to play with her children. My mother greeted the men—the

chaplain, wing commander and squadron commander came, too—
and waited for the words she had dreaded since her wedding day. The
waiting was over.

"I hope you don't think that's bad of me." My mom intently
watched the highway, gracefully changing lanes while wiping wet mascara from under her eye. "I think I always knew it was coming. But I
still wasn't ready when it came. I wonder what happened to his bike?
You don't think they just left it there waiting in the bike rack at the
flight line?"

Military protocol today is cumbersome at best; in 1969 it was
unassailable. To prevent other wives from realizing their husbands'
mortality, my mom and I were put on a plane for Denver less than
twenty-four hours later. Everything, the furniture, the dog, the dishes
and my bicycle—still in the carton—was packed for us and shipped on
the train. Psychological jargon today refers to this as a "lack of closure."
It means that my mom has recurring dreams that Ted is living, wild and
without memory, in the dense North Carolina woods. Or off somewhere with another family he loves better. No closure means she
couldn't have his class ring because they couldn't find it. It means all
they buried at the Colorado Springs cemetery was his uniform.

The quest for the accident records was my introduction to military meth-
ods. Apparently I could have gotten very good records had I asked six
months earlier. After twenty-five years, the records are destroyed to save
space. The military offered a guided tour of Seymour Johnson and some
edited classified documents. *How* had the accident occurred? *Where*
exactly? Classified—not because the information is still sensitive, but
because those are the rules.

Mom jumped at the guided tour. It took some time to find the
base entrance, since we arrived by an interstate that hadn't existed in

'69—Goldsboro wore a different, modern face. It frightened her, confirming how little she remembered, but once we wended into the older part of town, she unerringly directed me to the base. A young officer, fresh from the Academy, greeted us at the gate. I tried to impose Ted's face over his, but I couldn't picture him so gangly and bashful.

"We were never that young," my mom whispered to me.

As he drove us about, Mom scanned the buildings, trees, runways intensely. I knew she searched for some image that seemed familiar. She thoughtfully peered at the planes, recalling the "elephant walks," trial emergencies with bombers and fighters marching up and down—but those happened on every base. Our old house she picked out because she knew the address still. She frowned at it, willing it to seem like a place she had lived. I drank in everything—it was so much lovelier than I had pictured. Even the brick housing seemed softer than the poorly colored photographs showed. I memorized the driveway, pictured the crushed tricycle, saw the commander's car pulling up, me in the backyard. We eventually left the base behind, my mom resigned to her blank memories, me full of new images to color in the old stories.

Old newspapers, not the military, revealed our ultimate destination, leading us to Lumberton, North Carolina. The newspaper articles shook my mom up. They didn't describe a midair explosion that instantly vaporized bodies and class rings, as she'd been told. She'd known about the air show. She'd even known they were demonstrating airborne refueling. But how the planes clipped off treetops, breaking into flames as first one, then the other, skipped into the ground . . . The edited official reports seemed even worse. Autopsy evidence revealed no alcohol or drug use.

"How could they autopsy, if they didn't recover his body?" my mom asked, her eyes begging me to change the path of her thoughts. I had to look away, thinking of the military's careful maps of the crash site, marking the location of engine parts, body parts.

"I guess they checked the parts they did find."

As we entered Lumberton, I only hoped we would find someone who could point us to where it all happened. If we could go to the actual place, we could hold one piece of truth for ourselves.

In the county seat, the sixty-year-old reporter I looked up remembered covering the crash near Rowland. We followed township maps to the rural road described in the articles about flaming F-4s. Finally we found the retired sheriff who directed us to the right crossroads. The crater was still visible, he assured us. His wife thought they still had photos somewhere. Everyone knew where those jets crashed.

The teacart squeaked and rattled in the back seat as we bumped down the dirt road. Corn and trees and kudzu surrounded our silence; perhaps, like me, my mom was picturing rain and smoking jets clipping treetops. How would his face have looked? Sometimes I think of the 737 crash in Colorado Springs, how witnesses said they could see passengers screaming and pounding on the windows. But maybe my dad would have been concentrating too closely to even glance up, his blue-green-gray eyes that I inherited seeing only the instrument readouts and not trees appearing from the fog. A military pilot friend who read the reports told me that, flying on instrumentation as they were, the wingman would have followed the lead plane anywhere—even straight into the ground.

We pulled over at the deserted crossroads by the oak tree landmark. Three live oaks stood tall from the volunteer corn field, another was shorn halfway down, seared and broken where one jet had hit. My mom and I waited a moment, changed shoes and stepped from the air conditioning into the place we never knew to dream about. Our own expectations, or the presence of ghosts, hummed against our skin. Wandering in different directions, we searched through the corn.

The crater was not obvious to the nonlocal. I climbed the angle of the broken tree to get a better perspective. My mom's protests reminded me that this was the place where a loved one had been lost and it was my responsibility to stay alive.

As the late afternoon light slanted through the thick air and the August corn, I finally relinquished logical searching and allowed myself to be drawn by blood to the place. Or I stumbled upon it, depending on what you believe about these things. It was no crater, but a wide low place, no bigger than my front porch, where the ground showed shiny and hard through the sparse, dry plants. I reached down, pried a large piece of rusted metal plate from the ground and called my mom.

We stood in that spot, pouring sweat and old sorrows. Only the corn spoke, and maybe there were other spirits present. We decided to rebury the metal. I suggested we could put up a memorial. "I don't think we need that," my mom answered softly. "I think he's glad we came here, though, don't you?"

Driving away into the dimming evening, sweat drying in the air conditioning, my mom told me how she wished she was like me. "I should have made them tell me where he was back then. I should have demanded they bring me here. You would have," she explained slowly. "If I had been strong like you are, I would have been here already."

I watched the wall of green hiding the sky and told her that she was strong, that no one could have fought that battle against the rules that kept the wives at home in their hats and gloves, sipping sherry they hated. We can't really regret how the years have been shaped. Ted was gone from us, but the military death benefits and insurance had brought a wealth the Air Force never would have. The money had sent me to a private college. My mom had become involved in politics, art and her own career. Most of all, we had grown up together. Any strength I possess comes from this life we shared, and the man we lost.

As best friends we traveled on our adventure. Most women I know can't talk on the phone to their mothers without flipping out, but my mom and I, with our cooler of wine, beer, cheese and apples, drove along the ocean from Myrtle Beach to Charleston. We ate lunch overlooking the surf, visited plantation houses, read Anne Rice aloud and talked as we always have. We phoned home to our men and laughed about how they warned us to watch out for hurricanes. Cruising the tree-smothered landscape, one of us would yell, "Look, a hurricane— duck!"

We understood how they worried for us. Yet, traveling down those roads together, we couldn't be bound by fear. My mom and I have learned our lesson: sometimes people don't come home. Of course, we still practice our small spells—no travel on October 1, don't watch for someone to arrive, never call and try to catch them before they leave. But from that silent slanting afternoon, we created a new parable: one of traveling back and moving on, of grace in a silent corn field.

good for the long haul

alice evans

*i*n the summer of 1975, I zoomed into Oregon on the back of a BMW motorcycle, leaving behind everything and everyone I knew in southern Indiana. My sister's ex-husband had come through Bloomington to sign papers finalizing their divorce, and when he saw me, he took pity. By my own estimation I looked like a cat who'd just been through the wringer, not once but half a dozen times, my sad, woebegone appearance the result of a year in which I'd dropped out of graduate school after dropping acid and grieved two broken love affairs. To Bill, I was a damsel in distress, and he the white knight, his BMW a silver charger on which he would carry me away to adventure and freedom and perhaps romance. "Whatever happened to your friend Jon?" I'd asked just before we left Bloomington. "Oh, Jonny," he'd answered knowingly. "Jonny's in southern Oregon, and he's taking applications for girlfriends." I could feel my face redden as I realized I was speeding Jon's way over twenty-five hundred miles of open road.

The refuge Bill delivered me to—a circle of trees and falling-down cabins at a broken-down mineral spa in the hippie country outside Ashland—was as lovely and damaged as I was. There to greet us were two people—Bill's girlfriend, Sally, and his longtime best friend, Jon. Jon stood firmly planted on the gravel, his stoned-out ear-to-ear grin as enigmatic and seductive as the grin of the Cheshire Cat. He wore black baggy jeans cut off six inches above his ankles—tree-planter fashion—and a canary-yellow T-shirt taut over hard muscles. "Welcome to Hashland," he said. I'd been traveling through rain for two days, and Jon was the first sign of sun I'd seen in Oregon, his yellow shirt warm and bright as his grin, his arms something I knew right away I'd like to sink into.

Jon looked as cute as I remembered him from four years before, when I'd stayed with him and Bill in Washington, D.C., just after Bill and my sister Cat separated. Cat and I had joined a busload of protesters headed to D.C. for an antiwar march. It was May 1971 and a toothless wildman dubbed the Red Devil danced with Hare Krishnas on the lawn of the Washington Monument. Cat and I slept on the floor of Jon's apartment—along with the rats.

When the bus pulled out of D.C., I blushingly told my sister, "I'd like to make love with that man." Four years later, my body, heart and spirit still remembered the feeling. Within two weeks of my arrival in Ashland, Jon moved out of the High House, and together we moved into a brand-new apartment overlooking the sere Ashland hills.

A month earlier, Jon had bought himself a new car, a 1975 Datsun B-210 the color of Douglas fir needles. His luck had changed, he told me. First an inheritance, then a brand-new car and now—a woman.

Life was auspicious. I had never lived with a man before. Jon had never lived with a woman. Brand-new love and a brand-new car. We named that car the Green Cave, because it was snug and comfy and had front seats that laid back and made it possible to sleep or catnap, a feature we quickly made use of on a drive to Eugene to visit the University of Oregon. Jon was considering reentering school to study subjects as diverse as Spanish, which UO offered, and auto mechanics, which it did not.

I don't know when I had the first of my dreams about the clutch going out. All those mountains to cross, seems like we had clutch problems right from the beginning. The clutch emerged as a metaphor for my life back then—a tendency toward failure in the clutch. I had stepped off the path, dropped out of graduate school, left my family and given up control of my life to some force I couldn't comprehend. God? The devil? Or simply life itself?

My dreams say I was never driving. It was always someone else. Sometimes a man I couldn't see. Sometimes Jon. I had surrendered the wheel and we were speeding down the mountain, out of control around the curve. When the clutch gave out, we sailed off the mountain's edge and into space, the Green Cave floating down easy as a mallard, delivering us like supplicants into the shallow waters of the mountain lake, while all around us red-robed Hare Krishnas sang and swayed to the beat of drums and the tinkle of finger cymbals. *Red Devil, Red Devil, a toothless wildman dancing in the sun.*

Or we would be on a one-lane road in the high mountains, heading somewhere uncertain, suspended on a bridge that had no center, and we would have to get out and piece it back together with whatever we could find—old mattresses, springs, a rusted-out car—and with the clutch breaking off in my hand.

Sometimes the clutch really did break. Failed to engage. Or froze in second position. Refused to go into reverse. Indeed, it was the worst of the Green Cave's mechanical weaknesses. We replaced the clutch—once, twice, three times. I'd learned to drive on a standard shift, so the problem wasn't with me—I knew how to shift gears. Something metaphysical was happening, something extraordinary. I was sure of it. But sometimes I wondered if the problem originated with Jon. After all, he often seemed to think he was a racecar driver, driving right on the edge of his ability to control the wheel. And I, I was just hanging out in the passenger seat, in full surrender, seeing what would happen next.

One of the things that always seemed to happen next was a road trip. Twenty years after Kerouac and we were always on the road, me and Jon and the Green Cave. Not long after we became a threesome, we headed north toward the Canadian border, camping out in an open field under the stars. The Perseid meteor showers were in full bloom, and I lay back on my sleeping bag for the longest while, watching brilliant bursts of light streaking across the sky, so exceptionally vivid the stars seemed closer than they'd ever been, but so far away there was no hope of ever taking it all in, no hope of ever comprehending the eternal vastness.

Heading toward our families, we drove east through Canada, pitching our tent in campgrounds, or sleeping alongside the road in the car. After five days and nights on the road, we found ourselves approaching Jon's home state, New Jersey. Windows down, we sped through the midnight air along the Garden State Parkway toward Jon's mother, Mary. She awaited us, all but glowing, full moon to Jon's sun, her total love for Jon evident the moment we walked through the door.

Mary loved me right away, too. With a mother's heart, she knew I was right for her youngest child. As it turned out, Jon and I were just right for one another. After years of bad choices, I'd found a man-boy who matched me in spirit, heart and mind. Jon the outdoorsman, the pilot, the guitarist, the clown. To go with Alice the tomboy, woodswoman, folksinger, activist. I could match Jon hill for hill, song for song. Maybe I was a little slower on the upbeat, but I'd get there after a while. Jon, the birthright Quaker who had worked for Christian missions in Ghana and Lesotho, to go with Alice, who'd just come off a four-year mission to save the Earth. And now Jon had taken me all the way across the country to meet his mother. Not that he didn't spell trouble, but it was always small trouble. Bad-boy trouble. Trouble that could be dealt with lovingly.

Driving back, we spent several days in Indiana with my family. My parents and two youngest brothers, still living in the knob region where I'd grown up, welcomed us with fried chicken, okra, a fresh array of other garden produce and a display of owl pellets, the burgeoning science project of one of my brothers. My grandparents, bearing pies and cigars, drove fifty miles across the river from Kentucky. We exchanged kisses, hugs, photographs and stories. I had already regaled Jon with tales about Aggie, my grandmother. He knew her as the central spiritual figure of my life, ranked right up there with Jesus in terms of goodness, the family saint as well as the hub of the wheel that was family. Jon understood that Aggie kept in touch with every member of the family, all the way from fifth cousins to potential mother-in-laws of granddaughters. She had, in fact, already been in touch with Jon's mother, who was a friend of my sister's ex-mother-in-law. Aggie made it clear to Jon that she wanted to see me happily married, the sooner the better. Holding one of my hands and one of Jon's, Aggie begged us not to sleep together, gazed into our eyes and pleaded with us, saying, "It's not right in the eyes of the Lord." But we'd already been sleeping together for weeks, and we weren't about to stop.

When we headed home to Oregon, the engine started "missing." As used by Jon, the term alarmed me.

"What's it doing?" I asked when I first heard the strange hesitation in the engine.

"It's missing," said Jon.

"Missing what?" I asked.

"It's the points," said Jon. "I think they're burned."

We were somewhere in the vast stretch of nowhere that comprises the Great Basin. We had made it through the Rockies, we had seen the Great Salt Lake and we were out there, somewhere beyond the salt flats, driving through Nevada toward the Oregon border. Jon, a history buff, was talking about the Donners, though we were north of their route. "This is the way they should have gone," he told me.

I was beginning to fear that I was missing the point, or maybe, after all, I had only just discovered the point. That's how confused I felt back then. The year before, after reading Carlos Castaneda, Aldous Huxley, John Lilly and Ram Dass, I'd culminated my quest for closer union with God by taking hallucinogens. But I had discovered very quickly there are no shortcuts. I'd promptly lost God again. So I took more hallucinogens. God came and went, as did my comprehension. Anything could have been its opposite. I was sliding back and forth between complete understanding of the universe and no understanding at all.

We "missed" all the way to Ashland, sputtering down the Green Springs Highway from Klamath Falls. Backfiring and belching exhaust, we pulled our Cave into the parking lot of our apartment building, where it died altogether. "Good timing," we said. "What a heart."

Jon consulted my ex-brother-in-law, a master mechanic, then bought new points. Over the years, we went through a dozen or more sets of pitted points on that car, finally concluding the B-210 was made primarily for flatland travel, not mountain climbing. I proved myself to be a little like that car, better on the straightaway than the steep pull, good for the long haul once I'd managed to plod my way to the top, but sputtering all the way up, fighting for air.

After a year and a half of rambling along logging roads in southern Oregon's Siskiyou Mountains and bumping along Forest Service roads in the Cascades, I persuaded Jon to return with me to Indiana so that I could go back to graduate school. Not only had my brain settled down again, but so had my whole being, and I was ready to start driving the car myself, ready to reengage the clutch, ready to get to the point.

We had settled in Klamath Falls so that Jon could study auto mechanics, but he had realized rather quickly that auto mechanics was neither his calling nor his gift. Jon was ready to let cars go and move on to something more intellectual, like the burgeoning new field of computer science. In Klamath Falls I had practiced yoga, watched birds and worked as a typist for the local school system. I had also studied for the law school entry exam, thinking that I might reenter the battle for saving the Earth armed with a lawyer's sword, but after days and weeks and months spent hiking, dreaming, reflecting and writing in my journal, I had decided I'd rather become a writer.

Jon and I flew to Indiana to get married at my parents' house— with our entire families gathered around us—then flew back to Oregon. We loaded the Green Cave with all our goods—not much—and took off for a three-month honeymoon in the Southwest.

Inexplicably, we began the honeymoon by driving north to Washington, where we picked Golden Delicious apples in Lake Chelan for a week. Jon had worked the orchards for years when he'd first come to Oregon in '71, and he needed me to prove something to him, I guess. Or maybe I needed to prove something to myself. I stayed with him all the way, climbing the ladders, filling and refilling the bag that hung around my neck with forty pounds or more of perfect golden fruit, each full bag more than a third my own weight. A man with a strong back was asking a lot from a woman of slender build, I thought. I ended the week with the back of each calf one solid bruise from knee to ankle, where I'd leaned against the ladder for support. Yet I'd made enough to pay back an overdue college loan. Still, I held mixed feelings about the opening days of our marriage. Our honeymoon had begun with a question mark, each of us eyeing the other, wondering, Are you good for the long haul?

Then, zoom, south to Oregon again, traveling long stretches of blue highway, moving southeast through pronghorn country and into the desert of Nevada. Holed up at a state park, we played Scrabble in the sun, white rock spires like cathedral towers rising all around. Kangaroo rats stole silver gum wrappers. Red ants bit bare toes.

Home was the Green Cave for three months. We lay back in the seats and listened to the Cincinnati Reds slam-bang their way past the Yankees in a four-game World Series.

Or, home was the L.L. Bean orange backpacking tent dubbed the Orange Reality for the days we stayed trapped in the rain at Big Bend, near a waterhole that sported peccary tracks and mountain lion paw prints.

Either way, home was some pretty cramped quarters, but it got us where we wanted to go and kept us dry. Home was the whole vast American landscape, ours to enjoy with minimal human company in the off-season fall.

Zion National Park had Angel's Landing, where Jon stood on his head near the edge of a steep drop-off. He'd done a headstand on Mt. Shasta a few months earlier, and one on every peak we'd hit in the Siskiyous or Cascades. I was starting to get used to this behavior.

When we reached Grand Canyon National Park, the north entrance was closed for the season. Faced with a decision of entering as outlaws, or driving another half-day around to the south entrance, we chose to be outlaws. We hiked to the bottom and on the advice of a fellow camper, lay low, avoiding the ranger for two days until we packed out again, through eons of time, dusted by snow in the final mile.

By now, we'd learned the Green Cave's idiosyncrasies. We knew to listen for "missing" and to watch for pitted points. To reset the carburetor depending on altitude. To burn high-test gasoline every third refill. To always ride gently on the clutch. "Beware of downshifting," we reminded one another. "Not a race car—sixty-five miles per hour, tops."

In Santa Fe, on the night before Halloween, something went wrong in my abdomen. I spent the night in agony, wondering, What? Toward morning, the pain subsided, and I called home to wish my mother a happy birthday. My grandmother Aggie had been operated on the day before for cancer in her ovaries, my mother told me. I was stunned. My life had been largely untouched by death until this moment. My beloved grandmother lay dying. Somehow, my body had known and kept vigil, sharing her pain.

In the Guadalupe Mountains we camped in a grove of trees. Great horned owls hooted all through a bitter night of subfreezing cold. I couldn't sleep. Aggie was on my mind—would she live? At daybreak, we chatted with the ranger who lived there with his wife. "Watch for mountain lion tracks by the next watering hole," he said. The ranger warned us to be careful on the steep descent from the park—a packhorse had slipped to its death the previous week. On the way out we spotted the horse, rotting far below the path in a deep gully. Death, a promise, passively awaited our one small mistake.

Or death, a tawny predator, actively stalked us from behind thick trees. I thought of the sorcerer, Don Juan, who advised Carlos Castaneda, "Let death be your advisor." My grandmother lay dying, and one day I'd die, too. There were no *if*s, *and*s or *but*s. There was simply *when*.

Usually, we don't know when. On a visit to Padre Island two years earlier, just after I'd dropped out of graduate school, I'd almost been killed in a car crash. That was almost a *when.* And now, again at Padre Island, on what would turn out to be the final wilderness experience of our honeymoon, I came within one stride of stepping on a coiled rattlesnake of legendary size, as big around as a strong man's arm, a good six feet in length. Walking a strong pace among interior dunes, I'd seen the snake just in time to wheel and miss it. The sidestep—an instant choice. But I could just as easily have stepped forward one step too many. Surely, death was stalking me, advising me of something. *Pay attention, pay attention,* death said, shaking a shaman's rattle, dancing a dance of seduction, a grinning madman on the lawn of the Washington Monument. *Red Devil. Red Devil.*

As Jon and I walked back toward our tent in the balmy heat, an icy wind suddenly struck. Struggling against the wind, we reached our tent, but it had collapsed in the blast. One moment—balmy heat. The next moment—icy wind. We packed the Orange Reality, fought our way along the beach to the parking lot, forced our way into the Green Cave against the amazing wind and left Padre Island, driving over the bridge just moments before an ice storm closed it down.

We arrived in Corpus Christi at Thanksgiving, and it was time to give up the honeymoon, the weather said. Jon and I spent the next two days driving from Texas to southern Indiana, where we visited my family, then drove on to what I'd dreamed about all through the honeymoon: a place to settle into married life, a small house we'd rented on the edge of a square mile of state forest just north of Bloomington. I reestablished my Indiana residency, reapplied to graduate school and again accepted an offer of an all-expenses-paid trip through a master's program, this time in journalism instead of public and environmental affairs. Associate Instructor. Good deal.

Aggie went into remission, and Jon and I drove to Frankfort to visit her and Granddad as often as we could. We also drove to south Jersey to visit Jon's family.

In graduate school, I worked hard and took back the wheel of my car. Jon put the Green Cave in my name and bought himself a small, red truck.

That was the year of the blizzard. Snow came and went in great blasts of arctic air. Freezing, thawing, we took the car in for bodywork when spring arrived—road salts had kept winter roads safe for travel, but they'd also eroded the bottom of the Green Cave.

By the following fall I was back on the road, covering a nuclear power plant protest for a reporting class. I bedded down in the Green Cave, watched oil barrel campfires under the apple trees. I didn't join the campers singing protest songs, even though a few years back I had taken the early lead in fighting the utility company now building the plant. A hellcat environmentalist in my undergraduate years, I was now a palimpsest, a different version of myself superimposed over the earlier version. And I wasn't sure I liked the new version better.

The next day I panicked while taking photos of the protestors. I wanted to carry a sign, not a camera. I was wearing the wrong skin, an aggressive photojournalist, getting in everyone's way, lumbering awkwardly ahead of the surging protestors, trying to frame their movement just right. Inside their jail cell later, I looked for a good angle. The light was poor. Why was I free to leave, when they weren't? I judged myself harshly. I who had believed in civil disobedience. Why didn't I have the courage to be arrested? What had happened to the younger me?

I hunched my way back to the Green Cave, my neurons misfiring all the way. Who was I kidding? Me, a journalist? As I began the long drive home, the car commenced to belch and buck. I was in Nowheresville on a Sunday afternoon in rural Indiana. Everything closed.

Through sheer willpower, I made it back to Bloomington. Me and my sick car. Bucking and whinnying. Turned out the Green Cave had a cracked distributor cap.

I had more dreams, my mind interlocking with the car. Whatever went wrong with me went wrong with the car, in the dream or outside it. When I couldn't see things clearly, the headlights burned out. When I didn't know who I was, the car suffered an identity crisis, belched smoke, bucked and whinnied.

Eventually I went to work for the town's daily newspaper— general assignment reporter, weekend police beat. The Green Cave took me where I wanted to go. If I didn't really want to go, the car refused to start. When we were assigned to cover a story about a rural dump being used for toxic wastes, neither I nor my car could muster a spark of life.

Death was advising me again. My grandfather had died the summer before, and as I made my way to his funeral, hailstones the size of onions pounded my windshield. *Pay attention. Pay attention.* Sick again with cancer, Aggie went to live with my parents under my mother's watchful, loving care. Aggie died the next summer, and soon after, doctors discovered cancer in Jon's mother, Mary, and she died the following spring.

My parents moved to Arkansas, and with my parents and brothers gone, my grandparents and Jon's mother dead, there seemed little reason to stay in the Midwest. I was ready to leave the newspaper world, and now that Jon, too, had finished graduate school, he declared there was no way he was going to stay in Indiana, which had no mountains to climb and, apparently, no jobs. We considered our options. Oregon was all Jon could see in his future—Oregon, and me. He wanted to go back to Oregon, he said, but he would stay in Indiana if that were the only way he could keep me. I loved Jon, Jon loved me, we both loved wilderness, and our family members were scattered far and wide across the country, or they were dead. I would go, I said. Oregon had nurtured me before, renewed my soul with rainwater, ocean spray and vast stretches of wilderness. I could make a home there again, I said, with my husband beside me.

Jon drove the moving van. I drove the Green Cave, which ran like a dream—a good one—all the way back to Oregon. Three golden eagles dipped wings in a fast circle just above and beyond my windshield in western Wyoming. I could hardly believe my eyes, but indeed, I wasn't hallucinating. I was being welcomed back to the West—by golden eagles. Welcomed into a spiritual realm that would allow me to discover who I was, and what I really wanted in my life. Graduate school had given me new skills, and I had said goodbye to a place and some people I loved. But now, Jon and I were heading toward a future we could only imagine ourselves into. Oregon was a land that had enough room for us to grow. I'd had a sense of weaving forward before when I was in Oregon, weaving forward into who God intended me to be. And Jon already knew that Oregon was where he belonged—he just wanted me with him.

The Green Cave didn't start acting up again until I lost my way in Oregon—no job, a moody bottomland of recession, 1981. Nothing to do but drive. When Jon paid to have the engine rebuilt, her green heart throbbed as good as new. She carried me unfailingly back and forth on the 150-mile round trip to Eugene each week, from the Coast Range hills outside of Dallas to a fiction-writing class at the University of Oregon.

By now, Jon was working as a systems analyst. I wasn't bringing in a paycheck, but at the moment, something else seemed more important to both of us. I spent my days cooking or sitting at the typewriter writing stories while I looked out over the pond on the property we had rented. I watched mallards and mergansers landing on the water, or deer grazing in the field. The bullfrogs could never keep still, and neither could the red-winged blackbirds. I felt remarkably fertile. In a dream one night, Aggie whispered to me, "It's time to have a baby." By now, Jon and I had taken one another's measure.

In pregnancy, I sold the Green Cave. She'd been the car of my youth—my chariot—transport of my inner self. When I fragmented, she fragmented right along with me. When I failed in the clutch, so did she. I'd been eight years at the wheel, or not at the wheel. We'd crisscrossed the country together more times than I could figure. Back and forth between Oregon and Indiana, Indiana and New Jersey, Indiana and Kentucky, and finally, back to Oregon. We were about to turn over one hundred thousand miles of mutual distance traveled. Now, with a dog to carry and a child on the way, Jon and I looked for another car good for the long haul, a car with an extra gear. One that could pull the steep western mountains with ease, differently equipped for our changing needs.

cruising in my caddy

kari j. bodnarchuk

*i*t's late afternoon on a sixty-five-degree Monday when I slip into the front seat of my car, point my headlights southwest and roll out of Boston. My car takes me down I-95 along the Northeast's multi-multilane highways. I pass through Harlem, which isn't nearly as intimidating as the media suggests, even at 10 P.M. at a gas station, where I wait for a fresh pot of coffee and pore over my maps.

I have gone six inches so far. This is my first day of a twenty-one-day drive, during which I plan to steer my way down the East Coast, from Massachusetts to South Carolina, shoot over to Louisiana and then cut across to Texas. And back again. One coffee and an inch later, I'm driving through Newark, New Jersey, which at night looks like it's been blanketed in fiery debris from an exploded star—it's an endless city of dazzling lights. The glow fades once I'm beyond Trenton and Philadelphia and soon the blacktop lanes along the New Jersey Turnpike are so dark and unlit, I can barely see where the road ends and the grass median begins. The only visually interesting features that grace the landscape here are tollbooths, and really, I could do without those.

I've been looking forward to this trip for a while now. The last time I took to the open road—and I mean really *drove*—was the summer after college graduation, when I was crammed into a Subaru station wagon with an old boyfriend and two girlfriends. They were from England, a country that can be driven in a day, which is why they couldn't imagine that crossing the United States, from Boston to San Francisco and back in four weeks, would require some overnight drives, a lot of patience and the keen ability to sightsee at seventy-five miles per hour. With four sets of itineraries, it would also require a lot of compromise. Our main aim was to see as many sites as possible, from Niagara Falls to Alcatraz, the Big Apple to the Badlands. We camped out in national parks or slept in the car at truck stops—two people, head to toe, on the back seat and two people up front, sleeping at diagonal angles with the driver spooning the steering wheel or the gear shaft.

I'm leaving Boston again, but heading for Austin this time—alone—in a car so big I can stretch out and sleep in the back seat without developing chronic cricks and creaks. There is only one itinerary and complete freedom to stop and start at will. I'll also have plenty of mental space to think and daydream, and a chance to crank up the tunes and sing. Music is to my driver's mind what drugs are to an addict. It's my brain food and I am willing to go to extremes to get it. I spent two hours packing for this trip and six hours choosing CDs to bring. I have a compact disk player and an adapter for the tape deck, and yesterday, I spent four hundred dollars to fix the car's air conditioner, just so I can hear myself sing. It's useless if your words, along with your thoughts, get blown out the window.

On this trip, besides daydreaming and singing, I am planning to visit relatives I haven't seen in years—a decade, in some cases. Plus, it's been four years since I've owned my own car and had the freedom to drive wherever I please. Living in a city, I've relied on foot and bike power or public transportation to get around. Then my dad gave me a car and it wasn't long before I began thinking "road trip." So here I am, driving halfway across the country.

Originally, I had intended to visit my grandmother, my dad's mom, on my way out of Massachusetts, but I decided to skip that stop. I was afraid she'd recognize my new car, or rather, her old car—a 1990 Cadillac DeVille, a real cream puff that has led a garaged life and mainly been used for two-mile trips to church or the supermarket. Dad gave the car to me, unbeknownst to Gram, two and a half months ago because Grandma would drive to Geissler's Supermarket and forget the way home. Now, her Alzheimer's is so bad she can no longer remember the details of my life when we chat or that she's moved into a nursing home. Still, I'm afraid the car may click.

Who could mistake it? It's a virtual living room on wheels, a silver-colored, gas-guzzling, don't-mess-with-me, eight-cylinder beast. It has heated side-view mirrors, inside-outside temperature gauges, an electric trunk, thick armrests—remember those?—plus pockets, pouches, drawers and dials everywhere. An indicator on the Fuel Data Center tells me how many miles and gallons I can go until I hit empty. And another feature, called Twilight Sentinel, automatically turns on the headlights whenever it gets dark enough, like when I enter a tunnel or when I drive up close to the car ahead of me, thereby blocking out all signs of daylight from the sensors.

Best of all, the Caddy is super safe. Consider this: it weighs 3,546 pounds and its airbag can withstand several tons of force. So if I hit a stationary object while driving at, say, eighty-five miles per hour, the force of impact may cause me to quite literally kiss my ass, but the rear bumper will remain intact. If this scenario were repeated with a Geo Metro—same year, same color—it would be a different story. The Metro, in the end, would look like the wax seal on an envelope, or a postage stamp.

The Cadillac is also equipped with something called a Supplemental Inflatable Restraint system, or SIR. According to a sticker on the driver's side visor, just above the mirror with dual lights, the SIR deploys during "certain" frontal collisions. Certain? I have never owned a car with a SIR or, rather, a D'SIR, since it's only on the driver's side. There's about fifteen square feet of extra passenger space in the front seat, yet there isn't a SIR on the passenger side. I suspect that's because it would be called a P'SIR, short for Passenger Side Inflatable Restraint system. And let's face it, that's not really good PR. Imagine the ad: "1990 Cadillac DeVille, front-wheel drive, with D'SIR and P'SIR on board."

Now, just so you can picture it, the Caddy measures just over seventeen feet in length and is six feet wide. The hood, alone, is about five feet by five-nine—bigger than my bathroom, by more than a foot or two in each direction. The car stands four and a half feet high, and has more than three feet of head room, three and a half feet of leg room, four and a half feet of hip room (thank goodness), and nearly five feet of shoulder room. I'd rather not meet the person who needs five feet of shoulder room. The Caddy seats six people, or else a cooler, daypack, box of maps, bag of food and a big crate of CDs on the front passenger side, and a bike on the floor of the back seat. Meanwhile, its trunk comfortably fits a nightstand, end table and guitar, which I'm delivering to friends in Dallas, plus a box of books, two suitcases, a tent, tripod, laptop, Rollerblades, six pairs of shoes and two cameras, with plenty of room to spare. But its most attractive feature is the vertical emblem attached to the nose of the hood, which looks like an

Olympic wreath with a regal medallion in the center. It's like the sighting device on a gun and I just shoot for where it's pointing. Right now, it's pointing south.

I am not heading anywhere in particular tonight—just south. I spend several more hours struggling to see the edge of the road. Finally, I decide to pull off, and spend an hour driving around Havre de Grace, a small town in Maryland that has plenty of corn fields and red barns with big silos. My map indicates that there's a state park for camping, but when I finally find this remote spot, I decide it's too creepy to sleep out in the woods in an unfamiliar place, on a dead-end road, off-season. I am pleased with myself for recognizing the inherent dangers in this and for coming to a very responsible, adult conclusion. I sleep in the car, instead. I feel safe in the parking lot of the Church of Jesus Christ of Latter-day Saints, where I pull up next to a dumpster, lock the doors and crawl over my bike into the back seat. The Caddy's thick, cushiony back seat is almost two feet deep and perfectly suits my five-four frame. I stretch out, prop my alarm clock on the armrest and read by flashlight for a few minutes, then sleep soundly for six hours, with my hand accidentally resting on the bike chain. Besides that greasy mishap, I am in car-camping heaven. I have never known such backseat luxury.

In the past thirteen years, I have owned four cars: a Mazda RX-7 and a variety of Subarus. The two-seater Mazda was nine years old when I bought it and its wheel wells had rust holes big enough to fit my head. Everything else about it was small. It had room for one small-to-medium-sized friend and not more than a few bags of groceries. One winter, the Mazda broke down eight weekends in a row—and I only drove it on Saturdays and Sundays. But it was my first car, so I loved and pampered it. I replaced every knob and handle on its dashboard and doors, bathed it in Armor All twice a month and even replaced the engine—not once, but twice—after it seized due to oil and radiator leaks. My Subarus included a small beige sedan that I regularly tuned up myself; a low-riding, silver sports coupe, which I fell for because it had headlights that popped out of the hood with the flick of a switch; and a maroon station wagon that had so little power I was once passed by a jogger on a steep incline, but it still managed to take me and my English friends across the country and back.

What all these vehicles have in common, however, is that they can each fit nicely in the glove compartment of the Caddy.

Luckily, church parking lots are sleepy places at seven o'clock on Tuesday mornings, so my car is the only one around when I wake up. I crawl back over my bike into the driver's seat and then head to a local Havre de Grace spot, called the Bridge Diner, where I am the only female patron and suddenly feel very self-conscious about this fact. I order a bagel "to go" and retreat to my car, which is beginning to feel like my safe haven as I cut through unfamiliar territory. In another sense, it is also becoming a friend, and after driving 470 miles I have gotten to know it better—what types of bumps it can handle, how fast I can drive without causing the steering wheel to vibrate, how to turn on the radio without looking and, most importantly, how to work the cruise control (that took about three hundred miles).

I considered selling the Cadillac as soon as I got it, figuring I could unload it for a nice price and buy a more reasonable car—like a Subaru. For now, though, I'm enjoying the feel of cruising down the road in my luxurious living room on wheels.

My maternal grandma lives in Raleigh, North Carolina, where she recently moved to escape New England winters and be closer to one of her daughters, my Auntie Babs. Grandma is one of the liveliest, most vivacious people I know. She's hip, fun and personable, in a very loving, raw sense, and still wears real mink and high heels. Even her slippers have a stiletto look to them.

During dinner with Grandma my second night in Raleigh, I am reminded that she knows more about current issues and affairs than I do and has strong opinions on them as well. For an hour and a half, she talks nonstop about everything from Mayor Giuliani to Middle Eastern peace talks, as well as Madonna's new film and Ricky Martin.

"How about this Ricky Martin singer?" she says, while carving into her Outback steak. "Swinging his hips around and driving all the girls crazy. If I were just a little younger . . . "

Truthfully, as one of the most active and limber people in her age group, I bet she could keep up with Ricky. Grandma started taking aerobics classes in her late sixties and has been going three times a week, every week, for the past fifteen years. And even though she's eighty-three years old and quite plump, she still climbs out onto the roof of her townhouse twice a year to cover or uncover the big, box-shaped air conditioner in her second-story bedroom window, a stunt that I'm sure has caused several cardiac arrests in the neighborhood.

"I'm not going to sit around like all those old fogies, comparing medications and age spots, or letting other people wait on me," she says to me. "You have to get out there and live."

And live she does. Grandma is almost never home when I call her. Instead, she's either hanging out at her favorite diner—where she's befriended the entire staff, all eighteen- to thirty-year-olds—fighting some injustice at town hall or cruising around in her Buick Park Avenue. Born and raised in New York City, Grandma didn't get her license until she was forty. She frequently "overlooks" stop signs and totaled her last Buick while driving from her former home in Connecticut to my house in Massachusetts a few years ago. That's why I began picking her up for visits. At each major holiday, I would drive down to her house in Connecticut and bring her back to Massachusetts—three hours roundtrip—so she didn't have to deal with holiday traffic, snowstorms or stop signs.

Grandma loved our mini–road trips together. Since she lives alone, she is always starved for companionship or, rather, a good ear, someone who'll listen while she retells stories of her youth. I began using these trips as a way to record our family history. While Gram delivered her "when I was a kid" monologue, I used a mini–tape recorder to capture memories, stories and facts, occasionally slipping in questions to help direct the conversation.

I love Grandma's stories and admire her spunk, but I'm glad to get back on the road, where the only voices around are those in my head or on the CD player. My octogenarian grandmother exhausts me.

Jim, with whom I'm having breakfast two days later, says, "You gotta just take people for who they are." I figure he's probably right about this and consider it good advice, coming from a Methodist minister. I meet Reverend Jim, by chance, at a drugstore coffee shop in Sumter, South Carolina. After telling him about my family, I listen to his stories about life as a reverend, while I pack my cheeks with grits smothered in salt and butter, and sip sweet tea. Reverend Jim serves three churches, each separated from the others by seven miles. It's not a large territory, but the 186 congregants keep him busy. When he needs to take a break from what he calls "fighting sin, saving souls and spreading salvation," he goes out riding on a horse he's named Church Business.

"That's so I can tell everyone I'm 'out on church business,'" he says, adjusting the white, ten-gallon hat on his head that accentuates his striking brown eyes. He then talks about his degrees in psychology and sociology, and how these fields relate to his job.

"Everyone comes to me for confession and guidance," he says. "Mothers, daughters, fathers, cousins, everyone. So I get to see all angles of every story. And you wouldn't believe the stories—people sleeping with each other, lying, causing trouble, all these crazy tales. It would make a great book."

I swap addresses with the reverend and soon head west along Route 20, into territory where the majority of roadkill is sheep and there's a "wreck"—fresh or abandoned—every few miles. Although I'm on a main highway, weeds sprout from cracks in the road and I spot two as yet unsquashed turtles lumbering across the double lanes. For one long stretch, I don't even see another car. As I pass signs for Flat Shoals Road, I daydream about living in such a place and make a note to ask someone what a "shoal" is. Driving through Georgia, I come across billboards advertising corn dogs and concerts by Rick Springfield and Chaka Khan, a radio station dubbed "The Bubba Jam," cars with hairy tattooed arms hanging out their windows and lots of church billboards ("Have you read my bestseller? There will be a test.—God"). Bumper stickers have changed their attitudes, too: there are quite a few Yea God stickers and one that says, "Jesus: Don't leave Earth without him."

One thousand, six hundred and twenty-one miles from home, I finally give someone the finger. She's a bimbo in a white Saab and she just cut me off. So much for southern hospitality. I take down her license plate number, which gives me a momentary sense of empowerment. A few minutes later, another car cuts me off and up goes my finger again. Mr. Honda Accord was busy chatting on his cell phone and didn't have the energy to turn his head and see my thirty-five-hundred-pound, seventeen-foot mass of steel barreling down the fast lane.

My mom wishes I had a phone for this trip, in case anything happens and to keep in touch with her, but I'm adamantly opposed to portable telecommunications devices. As I watch Mr. Mobile Phone accelerate, my mind takes off, as it often does when I drive, and I create a brilliant poem (or so it seems at the time) to the rhyming rhythm of Dr. Seuss's *Green Eggs and Ham.* It's dedicated to my mom.

Cell Phones be Damned

I will not phone you from the car
I will not phone you from afar
I will not phone from here or there
I will not phone from anywhere

I will not call from I-95
I will not buzz you while I drive
From a mountaintop or by the sea
Or from deserted roads in Tennessee

And if I break down along the way
I'll wait until the break of day
Or I'll use those legs God gave to me
And find a AAA for free

So I will be just fine, you see
Without a cell phone by my knee

Maybe the air conditioner is getting to me. I swear I can taste Freon in my Subway sandwich. I tap a knob on the dashboard, shutting down the AC, and play with the windows, trying to get the right combination. Both front windows down results in Confused Hair Syndrome, which causes long strands of hair to stick to my Chap Stick and eyelashes, and thereby seriously impairs visibility. Both back windows down?

No good, no sign of air circulation. Driver's side front window down, passenger side backseat window cracked. Perfect.

When I reach New Orleans, I go driving in search of a bayou, because I'm not really sure what a bayou is, and find myself next to a beautiful estuary, which I use as a backdrop while photographing the Caddy. I have a big collection of car photos. I snapped my old station wagon in the Badlands of South Dakota, on top of Mt. Washington in New Hampshire and among the red rocks in southern Utah. I used to photograph the Mazda from my bedroom window at different times of day and under various lighting conditions—sort of like a Monet series. I captured it with sapphire-blue skies and dramatic storm clouds overhead, blanketed in snow and bathed in summer sunlight, and parked next to blossoming forsythia bushes. Now I'm working on my cross-country Caddy series.

The stretch of highway between New Orleans and Houston is the one place I fear breaking down. As a young woman from a big city, wearing a short, sleeveless dress and steering a Cadillac around eighteen-wheelers and pickup trucks, across an area devoid of trees and man-made structures as far as the eye can see, I sense that I'm a little out of my element. Nevertheless, I continue cutting across the dark, flat and desolate landscape, and decide that if I break down now, I'm crawling out of the car and into the bush, where I'll wait it out until morning. I'll probably be safer sitting among the prairie dogs and rattlesnakes than seeking help from a passing stranger in this isolated spot.

I am starving for sleep now and keep myself entertained by watching the miles-per-gallon indicator on my dashboard, which shoots up and down depending on how hard I depress the accelerator. I have been driving for more than seven hours already and I think I'm beginning to develop automobile ass. My rear end feels big, thick and rubbery. I can't imagine how truckers manage to sit for so long without moving their limbs. I am also suffering from several other afflictions, resulting from a faulty car accessory and a fundamental design flaw.

First of all, the Caddy comes fully equipped with beautiful, maroon leather seats and—here's the vital detail—a beaded seat cover on the driver's side, compliments of my grandma. This means that after driving, I typically walk away with dozens and dozens of perfectly red and round, knobby marks across my back, from my shoulder blades down to my knee joints. Red Knobby Syndrome, as I call it, usually occurs after about forty-five minutes in the driver's seat. As I said, I've been on the road for seven hours since leaving New Orleans, so you can just imagine.

The second major drawback is that the car was built for extraordinarily tall people (those folks who need three feet of head room and five feet of shoulder room), so the seat belt cuts right across my throat. For this reason, I have just driven 2,430 miles with a giant paper clip on the seat belt. It's fastened down near my hip and keeps the belt off my neck until it slips off, which it inevitably does every so often, meaning that I have to try to refasten it while I'm cruising at seventy-five miles per hour—not an easy task, but it's cheap entertainment and passes time.

Finally, around 3 A.M. and about 122 gallons of gas from Boston, I roll up to my mom and stepdad's home in Austin, where they moved from Massachusetts just nine months ago. I spend five days here, which feels strange after my days on the move, and then begin my return journey northeast along a different route that will take me across the flat plains of Texas, through the Bible Belt and up the spine of the Appalachian Mountains.

Back on the open road, I discover what the smooth, straight roads of Texas are ideal for—filing your nails. Now here's the thing about filing your nails while driving: it's all about temperature. It has to be hot enough that your legs stick to the leather or vinyl steering wheel, therefore enabling you to steer with them, but not so hot that your sweaty legs slip off the wheel. You just have to watch out for the highway cleanup crews. I file and shape my nails for about twenty miles, along a series of straightaways, until I reach the exit for a town called Emory—no joke. With the cruise control on and little traffic along Route 30, I could probably paint my toenails, but I don't want to push it. Instead, I decide to plan my schedule for the next year— baby showers, family vacations, work projects and travels—while Arkansas and its fiery fields roll past. The weather here is so dry and scorching, at times, that fields of grass and farmland catch fire. As I drive, I can see flames blazing across the flat, open landscape. I pass by a town called Bucksnort, just off I-40, and then a billboard advertising a "Cheep Sign."

With less than a week to go, I stop at my friend Katherine's parents' house in eastern Tennessee, just to pick up a guitar and lamp she wants me to bring back to Boston. Instead, I end up staying several days to visit with her parents and have my brakes checked by a guy named Larry, whom I'm told I can trust. My brakes have been soft and squeaky since Austin, which wasn't a problem as I crossed the flat plains of Texas and Arkansas, and the moderately rolling terrain of western Tennessee. But I'm planning to follow the Blue Ridge Mountains next and I'm beginning to wonder how much more these brakes can take.

Larry pulls off my tires and watches the brakes crumble to the ground. The total to put them back together with new pads and shoes, plus rotors for both back tires, is $310 with tax. I'm not sure what rotors do, but I hope that for $150, they're going to sing to me on the way home. I am still a good five hundred miles from home and, really, what choice do I have?

The third morning, I pick up my car and spend seven hours driving along the Blue Ridge Parkway—right along the top of the ridge, with sweeping views of the hazy and rippled Allegheny Mountains—and then make a detour to spend a night with my dad's brother, Uncle Paul, and his family in Pittsburgh. Due to lack of communication on that side of the family, Paul had no idea I was given Grandma's—his mother's—car, so he's understandably speechless for the first twenty minutes after I arrive. He doesn't want the car for himself, but he's spent years tuning and taking care of it for Grandma, so he feels a close attachment to it. He also knows a lot more about the Caddy than I do, and once he's over the shock, he spends a couple of hours giving me a full rundown on it—how much air its tires prefer, where the spare tire and jack are located (I still had no idea), the best type of radiator mixture to use and so on—and telling me Caddy stories.

"Gram and Gramps took this car all over the place, all around Connecticut, up to Canada to visit your cousins and great aunts and uncles, and down to visit us in Pittsburgh a bunch of times," Paul says. "They were pretty fast drivers, too. Gramps used to drive and it always amazed me how soon they'd get here. I remember Gram saying, in that soft voice of hers, 'Well, it's a little faster when you're doing eighty.'"

Though Grandpa loved driving the Caddy, these cars were too fancy for his tastes. He preferred his secondhand Ford Pinto or his Rambler Hornet.

"Grandma always wanted a Cadillac," says Paul, while we're eating dinner at Denny's that night. "Did you know she was the secretary at a Cadillac dealership, from the early sixties to, oh, about the midseventies?" That was news to me. "At that time, Caddys and Lincolns were the top dogs. If you wanted a luxury car, you definitely got a Cadillac. Gram always loved something with a bit of status to it."

My grandma and grandpa, whose parents immigrated to Canada from the Ukraine, grew up in Saskatchewan, where they got basic educations and learned English (Ukrainian was their first language), and spent a majority of their childhoods working long hours on their family farms.

"I remember hearing stories about how fresh fruit wasn't easy to come by and that getting an orange at Christmas was a big special treat," Paul says. Maybe their simple beginnings factored into Grandma's desire to own a "top dog."

That night, Paul, Aunt Leslie and I sort through several big boxes of Grandma's belongings, stuff she was forced to give up when she moved into the nursing home—a commemorative Queen Victoria plate, fluted wine glasses, an old juice presser that Paul, now forty-five, remembers using when he was five years old, and pots, pans and a glass rolling pin that are all probably older than I am.

Paul, a sentimental, keepsake type of person, has no need for these kitchen items, so he passes them on to me, glad to see them remain in the family. He's also pleased I have Grandma's car, he says again, genuinely, but also as if saying it out loud again will help him convince himself that this is the case.

"They had another Caddy before this one, you know, a second-hand Seville," Paul says the next morning, as he's packing my back seat with Grandma's pots, pans and wine glasses. "But they bought this one new. This one looks pretty tame from the outside, but it's a lot faster and has better pickup and handling than I ever expected. When you step on the gas, it's like, 'Watch out, hold on and make sure you're pointed in the right direction!'"

He's right about that. Although big and boxy, I'm always amazed at the Caddy's pickup, too, and frequently snap my head back over the headrest when I accelerate. I swear my neck muscles have doubled in size and strength on this trip.

I wave goodbye to Paul and Leslie, back down their treacherously steep, hidden driveway, stiffen my neck muscles and punch the gas pedal with my foot, praying that no cars come flying around the corner and strike the Caddy while Paul is still watching. Knowing how much value he places on this nearly two-ton piece of family history, I feel a greater responsibility toward it now.

After three weeks together, the Caddy now feels like an old friend. I know how it hums, what noises are out of place, how many miles over the speed limit I can drive on C-shaped exit ramps without making its tires squeal and how close to "0 gallons" I can get without sending the engine into coughing spasms. I can slide across the front seat and reach the cooler on the passenger side floor without even twitching the steering wheel, and I have totally mastered the art of consuming foot-long Subway sandwiches without splattering mayonnaise on the dashboard or letting one jalapeño hit the floor. Although the Caddy may not be something I'd choose for myself, I could never consider selling it now. Like family, it's what I've been given, so I'll just enjoy it for what it is because it won't be around forever.

Watch out and hold on, I think. Then I point the car north on Route 81 to begin my final leg home.

ride to live

anne stone

*M*ovement is touch, is horsepower, is between my legs, is where I sit. This is my heaven on Earth. I am on a road trip, on my Harley, without a helmet. I do not need to know if I am in Pennsylvania, Washington or Georgia, as long as miles of countryside surround me. Over the roar of the pipes, as I ease into fifth, the leather fringes on my levers dance in the wind, tap my wrists—love taps. The loose skin under my arms and along my neck billows in the wind, like water rippled by a breeze. At a bridge I pull in the clutch and give the bike a blast, and the roar of my pipes deepens as I pass under. My chest vibrates, my body vibrates and I breathe deeply. I stretch and hit eighty miles per hour, my favorite cruising speed.

Blue lights. Rats.

What's this guy's problem? It's nine-thirty on a Sunday morning, just me and about a hundred eighteen-wheelers rolling down the interstate at eighty in a fifty-five zone. I am a thousand miles from home, have fifty dollars in my pocket and never carry a phone. It's my first taste of the freedom of the road since I was a young girl hitchhiking across America. My freedom is new, though I have been a rebel all of my life.

A friend once told me that the average age for a woman to ride her own Harley-Davidson motorcycle is forty-seven. That made perfect sense to me. I'd been busy raising my son, on my own, the last twenty years. In my book, that means little free time and no money. Bits of free time came between laundry and dishes, and money came in spurts, such as lowered grocery bills when my son spent summers with his father. Forty-seven was just about the age I became free again, with my own time and money.

However, this freedom from responsibility was not quite enough incentive for me to ride on my own. At the time, as my son came of age and moved away, I began dating a rider. It was when he became very selective in taking me out for rides that I bought my own Harley and learned how to ride. He couldn't handle that and quit me. Riding is still a man's world, where women sit behind their men, protected from more than the elements. Back when I'd been a fender fox, I could smile and yawn and get a nice even tan and just follow the leader. My hair stayed in place with little fuss, and so did my popularity. Now my hair is shorter every year, and has a Don King style to it—lopsided and frizzy—and my popularity is gone, at least in the ways I knew it.

When my lover abandoned me, I was deeply sad. I took a million hot baths. I worked fifty- and sixty-hour weeks. I sat down to marathon movie weekends, immersing myself in favorite actors, actresses or directors. I developed a taste for Southern Comfort and naps. I felt sorry for myself—until I realized a woman doesn't learn to ride well when there is a man around. So I sought solace in maps, a habit from childhood, and I asked myself, What would it take to feel better? I can ride here, I thought, or there. I hovered over my maps, dreaming.

The cop gives me a ticket for loud pipes. He tells me it is the cheapest ticket I will ever get in Connecticut. He seems very serious. I thank him and ease on out of the situation with perfect and sincere politeness. My manners are impeccable when I am on the road. I don't ever forget that I'm a woman traveling alone, no matter how much fun I am having, no matter how tired I feel, no matter who approaches me. But as soon as I hit the road again and reach eighty miles per hour, I yell out loud to the wind. I scream a little bit. I am safe once more.

Two weeks of hugging my bike with my knees does more for my soul than two years of introspection. Real freedom is buying a Harley and flying down the road on a twenty-five-hundred-mile trip, alone. There is nothing stagnant about riding: every trip is a dance with the unknown. I leave behind my captivity—the routine, the mundane, the obligations, the duties, the phone call that never comes—and hit the road. I ride to live.

Along with the dreaming over my maps, it was love for a best friend living in New England that inspired me to go riding up the East Coast this summer. A solo trip from my home in North Carolina all the way to Portland, Maine, seemed a monumental and daunting endeavor. I took a deep breath and rode to her, one mile at a time. It worked. I did not fall down or crash; no one ran over me.

I am on the section of Route 6 between the Connecticut border and Providence, Rhode Island. The entire stretch is a heart-stopper with its hills and blind curves. Just outside the tiny town of South Foster, the speed limit turns to forty-five miles per hour and I am determined to reach and maintain that rate even though the road dips and curves and weaves around hills. Flying up one hill, I round a bend to find a dump truck blocking the entire road. There is a ditch and a downhill on one side and a ditch and an uphill on the other. Or I can put her down, slide under the truck and try not to decapitate myself. From far away I hear gears changing and my own tires squealing. Everything slows down and sound is muffled. I come to a gentle halt, my feet not touching the ground, and I hang there in a motionless balance as the truck moves forward. Then, everything starts to move forward and I find myself at the truck's rear bumper just as it gains speed and moves away. The sky becomes bluer, the clouds a sharper white and the road a darker black as tears fill my eyes. It is my closest brush with death on a bike.

When I bought my bike, four hundred pounds of twisted metal, she felt like a huge, loud and terrifying monster with a will of her own. Despite my heroic efforts to hold her up, her determination threatened to exceed my own as she sought to fall over. Despite all my explicit demands to go in one direction, she willfully countered me by going in another. During the first four months that she "owned" me, my knees shook whenever I approached her and remained spaghettilike long after I'd gotten off. It took six months for me to keep my eyes from staring in fascination at the treacherous road running beneath my feet and knees.

Not so anymore. I have become intimate with the value of speed, with having to make split-second decisions. Now, I fly by the seat of my pants. I have become one with my bike. In fact, I named her.

I named my bike Tinkerbell—causing a lot of raised eyebrows— because it seemed like I heard a bell tinkle whenever something dangerous was upon me. There was the shadow in the road that was really a pothole, and the dead animal hidden by traffic in front of me, blood and grease spread all over. There was the clueless, inattentive driver on the cell phone pulling out in front of me, and the sleepy commuter who couldn't seem to come to a stop but kept drifting . . . right up my ass. There was the hung-over churchgoer who straddled both lanes on a backcountry road, and the curve taken too fast, nearly impossible to pull out of—which left in its wake a desire to puke. Always, I was sure I could hear the tinkle of a bell.

But maybe, deep down inside me was the real Tinkerbell—the Tinkerbell that wanted to leave Peter Pan's bumbling, nurturing ass with his pack of sorry Lost Boys, and hit the universe at warp speed. Not that I go warp speed—ninety-two horsepower between my legs is wings enough for me.

The long Indian summer breaks as I limp onto the ferry, in fourth gear, headed back to Martha's Vineyard. There is talk of shutting down the ferries due to the high winds, but I get lucky one more time. I make the last ferry before the bad weather settles in for the remainder of the week. I park my bike, light up my Camel and contemplate what just happened.

One minute I was flying down the freeway, I-95 outside of Portland, Maine, and the next moment I was frantically steering down an off-ramp because I had no power and my shifting lever had quit working. I rolled to a stop at the gas pump and asked for help. The guy just stared at me. I asked again. He didn't speak English. So I did what I usually do in times of crisis—I smoked a Camel and surveyed the situation. It was not good. I was alone, miles from anywhere, with a broken bike and no clue how to fix it. When nothing fell from the heavens to help me, I turned and started across the parking lot to the phone. Two men were walking toward me and one of them was smiling. He said he'd like to be riding behind me. I smiled and asked him if he knew anything about bikes. He told me all about his restored 1963 Panhead

Harley-Davidson as he took the foil from my cigarette pack, helped himself to the few tools I had and repaired the spline on my shifter, just like that. With his help, I made it to within nine miles of the ferry before the lever broke again. This time I could figure out how to get it into fourth and that was good enough. It got me here to the ferry—to safety, to familiar terrain and to a belief in angels.

Live and learn and hope you live: it's one of my secret prayers.

My other secret prayer is: please, please allow me to park without dropping my bike. It's not easy doing things alone, but it is downright horrible to do something embarrassing—and dropping the bike is as bad as it gets. I fear arriving somewhere, alone and female, and dumping my bike. This is the material of nightmares, and if it were my nightmare, with my luck, I'd be naked, too. It took dropping my bike at home, alone, to know I could lift it back up, lickety-split, all by myself. Amazing, the power of pride.

For a man to drop his bike is a mortal wound; he never lives it down. There are clubs that pass a trophy around to the men who drop their bikes. Sometimes a man has the trophy for years, and he's required to prop it up where everyone can see it. He can only relinquish it when another member drops *his* bike. But women are *expected* to drop their bikes. I just heard that a local riding chapter instituted a new policy that all Sportsters (mostly women ride Sportsters) must be parked across the street from the annual bike show in case a woman drops her bike (this to avoid the domino effect).

I dropped my bike earlier on this trip. Dusk was approaching as I neared the Poconos. It was time to pull over and set up camp before dark. When a sign appeared for the Winding Hill campground, I pulled off. I turned left and rode a few miles—no sign. I returned to my ramp, turned right this time and rode through town—no sign. Two more times through town and I began to lose my enthusiasm. Bless the people who do not judge one by her looks, for I pulled into the Tasty Freeze parking lot with my Don King hair and approached a young couple having ice cream with their two children. They confirmed that there were no more signs to the campground and gave clear directions to a place that was not easy to find.

The route wound through hills, following the Wallkill River, and ended in the middle of a dense young forest. The Wallkill reminded me of the slow-moving rivers back home in North Carolina. It was thick, muddy, probably full of snakes, with tremendous overgrowth along the banks and clouds of mosquitoes hovering over the water. The air was so hot and wet it was hard to breathe. I followed signs to a boathouse to register for a site, but no one was there. The sign, however, was unmistakable: Reservations for Campsites Required. My heart sank. It was a long way back to town, and I wasn't going to pay sixty-eight dollars at the motel along the interstate. (I had checked the price when I went in to borrow their phone—they wouldn't let me.)

I sat at the boat ramp and lit a Camel. Mosquitoes were whining in my ears, my hair was plastered in dried sweat under my helmet, the sun was setting beyond the trees and I could hear the rumbling of thunder. I started up the hill where the sign said, Camping—In.

There is no sneaking in anywhere on a Harley; everybody knows you've come. I pulled into the first campsite on the right, counting on the fact that campers like to get way back and assuming no one had reserved this first one. It was steep, too. The path was straight down, and the site was too small for me to turn around once in it. I decided to back in, like a pro, and, hundred forty pounds of gear and all, I did so. Up until the rear tire hit a boulder at the same time as my left foot went into a hole: over the bike went. I helped her down as best I could to avoid breaking anything and then hit the kill switch. When I looked up, two guys stood above me and a third was running toward us. Unbelievable. In less than two minutes they had Tinkerbell parked at the picnic table and were off with a friendly goodnight.

My style of traveling puts me right in the thick of things: the weather, the landscape, the people. All kinds of people, like the guy who sits down beside me at a gas station as I head home through the mountains. I spend a lot of time at gas stations because I have to get gas every eighty miles and if they have a picnic table like this one does, I sit down for a smoke and a cup of generic cappuccino. (Actually, I mix the french vanilla and hot cocoa and cappuccino all into one cup. Sometimes, if it looks like the pot has been sitting there a long time, I pour regular coffee into that.)

This time, a guy sits down to have a cigarette and a talk with me. He's a bit scrappy looking, a bum actually, but I don't mind. I'm feeling road weary, digging black dirt out of my ears and from under my chipped nails and musing over the miles still ahead. He talks of his days working the chain gang and the Harley he used to own—his sister sold it while he was in prison for killing a few people. I like him well enough, about as much as I liked the cop who pulled me over at the start of this trip. Neither one would do me any real harm; each just had something he needed to say to me. I get a lot of that on solo trips, people needing to tell me something. All this guy wants to do is tell me how badly he wants to ride again, be in the wind again. I can appreciate that. I adore being in the wind.

My solo journeys have proved invaluable as preparation for another kind of riding. I'm not the type to leap blindly, so it took me quite a while to make the jump from riding solo to riding in a group. Group riding can feel like being watched, judged, commented upon. I was certain that if I had a partner or friend, this particular area of riding would be easy to get into. On my own, however, I was not about to attempt such a thing until I had a strong and deep level of confidence in my skills as a rider. And there were other fears: what if I get where I am going and no one likes me? I am poor, I can't afford to eat out often or pay for motel rooms unless it is raining. I fear missing the group at a meeting place and being left behind. These worries accompanied me on the biggest group ride I've ever done, the Trail of Tears ride, an organized ride of over fifty thousand bikes. But I have found that courage follows me as I make myself show up alone.

Prior to that trip, I thought of myself as an ugly duckling, not quite fitting in anywhere. I assumed all the women would have men to ride with. If they had their own bikes, they'd be custom and chromed out, not like my old, sturdy and hard-ridden Tinkerbell. But I knew it would feed my spirit to do the annual ride, which commemorates the route of the Cherokees, yanked from their homes in the eastern United States and forced to walk to Oklahoma. Someday, the organizers hope to have the ride go all the way. For now, it runs along Route 72 from Chattanooga, Tennessee, to Waterloo, Alabama.

Everything rippled in the Alabama heat. I'd had enough of camping. I was up at five every morning, packing in the dark cold after a long night. How appealing riding on the back now appeared! All but one of my fellow riders stayed in motels. They had expensive gear bags that snapped on and off their bikes. They were settled in each evening in one thirty-second trip, while it took me thirty minutes and three trips to undo one bungee cord after another and unload a cargo net, three bags, rain gear, tools and, finally, the saddlebags. They slept till the last minute, but I had to get up early, pack and then ride into town and find the meeting place on my own, in the dark, strange city.

Still, it was vastly more interesting my way. At the last campsite, I was next to a dozen guys. They drank, they sang, they yelled to one another—the Rowdies from Georgia, I called them. I felt comfortable next to them. My only worry was that one might fall into my tent, or worse, make the mistake of thinking my tent was theirs. The next day I made it to the meeting place in plenty of time, lined up with the others and rode all day in a pack that was thousands strong, two abreast and nearly fifty miles long. All along the route entire multigenerational families had set up coolers, canopies, barbecues and lawn chairs, to watch us go by. Grandmothers hollered and waved to me, young girls clapped their hands and jumped up and down. A woman on her own bike was unusual to see. They loved it.

On the other hand, the woman in front of me did not. At first I found her twisting and turning in her seat disconcerting, distracting. I imagine her partner did not care for that. Her scorn was apparent but I didn't realize it was directed at me until we pulled into a rest stop. With eyes half shut, her head lowered, she pointed a ghastly red fingernail to the ground behind their rear tire and literally barked at me, commanding me to back off. She then got off the bike and placed her body between their bike and mine. With folded arms she stationed herself so that she could keep an eye on me and make it clear she wanted nothing to do with me. I have come across envy and competition from younger women who ride behind, but this experience saddened me. She graded everything I did. In her opinion, women "play" at riding—they will never be real riders. She seemed to feel that I had no business being there. I moved on.

From there I leaped into the ride, knowing I had to prove myself. As a new member in a group used to riding together, I was under close scrutiny, as it should be. Over time they relaxed. I liked how everyone took care of each other, remained aware of each other's location at all times. We were eleven running to Cherokee. Like horses who are let full head, it seemed we raced the entire time. I was one of two women in the group and the only one riding her own bike. I felt deeply satisfied with my performance, with passing the tests, with feeling included in a group that stands tall in my eyes—strong, respectful, fun and at ease with themselves and the world.

In losing one kind of popularity, I gained another, and I liked this one much better. I rode well, I rode hard, I kept up with the big guns—the ones who have ridden all their lives, ride machines twice the size of Tinkerbell, have bodies twice the size of mine. With admiration and respect, they hugged me, invited me to ride with them again sometime. I felt like I'd found a home.

But tonight I am alone—on the last leg of my New England trip. Tough, sad thoughts crowd in and I am road weary. There's thunder, lightning, pouring rain and no bridge to pull under. I am soaking wet, filthy, cold and the sun is gone. I feel the fatigue press on my shoulders. I am still a long way from home. Will I ever get home? I berate myself for living on fairy dust and I pray. I figure I have seven more hours of hard riding—I'm so close and yet so damn far. I wonder why the hell I'm doing this. What has possessed me? Whatever was I hoping to accomplish?

Then I pull into my home state on a full moon, and what a moon she is. The color of a peach, she guides me and then drops below the horizon at seven in the morning. Dawn arrives. I murmur a big thanks to the moon. I have just traveled twenty-five hundred miles, on my bike, on my own, and I am alive. I have made it. I yell in the wind and dance a little jig on Tinkerbell—the two of us shaking our asses all the way down the road to home.

the punxsutawney pilgrimage

belinda farley

i celebrate Groundhog Day. It is a ludicrous ritual, I know. Ludicrous, that a Black woman raised in Chicago's inner city observes February 2 as a day of note. But I have my reasons, and I have my excuses—the kind that only make sense to me. Oh, and to one other person: Melissa, in Louisville, Kentucky. Annually on Groundhog Day, we exchange note cards and marvel at the lunacy of the interests we explored to pass the time during our brief encounter with small-town living.

Melissa and I were cubbies the year we hit the road. We worked as reporters for a newspaper in a small Pennsylvania town, so small that the entire town fit in one zip code. The newspaper required us to do everything besides make the coffee, which would come later, when we were "promoted" to head our own bureau offices. It was a paper notorious in the community for its bourgeois staff of fresh college graduates recruited from around the country.

Spurning the paper's hometown roots, the publisher (himself an out-of-towner) went out of his way not to hire the town's native sons and daughters. The intimate staff of his newspaper represented "fresh blood," save one reporter who was just too damn good a writer to sacrifice to the competition, which mirrored a high-school rag.

In some ways, the staff was spoiled. We knew of our status in the region, and reveled in being outsiders. We planned our tenure according to a stopwatch dictated by wet feet. One year—a year and a half tops—was standard residency. It wasn't just that we reporters were so ever mindful of the next best thing. We were all a bit overzealous then. Graduates of the top J-schools—Northwestern, Penn State, Drake—we wanted to crack corruption, investigate fraud, tell the story to beat all stories; we wanted our Pulitzers the very first year. But fresh blood or no, we were working in a small town for a small-town newspaper, and only so much blood was allowed to be shed. We only stayed as long as we could stand reporting on ox roasts and wooly worm festivals. We crashed and burned quickly. A year, a year and a half tops.

Melissa had already been at the paper six months when I arrived. She worked the night shift, happy for the perks of sleeping in on a daily basis and sitting cross-legged before her computer. She was short, blond and unashamedly country. Her boyfriend from back home visited often. He routinely drove a day's time to be with her, bearing dozens of Krispy Kreme doughnuts and a case of Big Red soda. This was before the doughnut franchise moved up north, and I had never tasted Big Red, ever.

Melissa laughed loudly, wore long hippie skirts that resembled my own and was a fan of foreign films. We became instant, inseparable friends, and our friendship would grow to become one of my strongest assets during my tenure at the paper. We felt out of place in a town that was inhabited by a few distinct families, whose last names ran for several pages each in the local white pages. That fact seemed to determine everything. Everyone knew everyone else, as well as who was known by no one. In the phone book, my name stood alone. And while the reporters I worked with at the newspaper were also outsiders from metropolitan areas, they were rarely game for any extracurricular activity beyond the occasional potluck holiday supper. Which left Melissa and me. We bonded in the way of junior-high girlfriends, but while Melissa consciously differentiated herself from the other staff members, the root of my alienation was chiefly a fact of biology.

In 1996, I was the first African-American reporter the newspaper had employed in quite a long while; possibly the first ever, everyone was too ashamed and shifty-eyed to say. No one expected me to be there. I was there because my father, born in Deatsville, Alabama, when lynching Black people was sport, went on to serve on a submarine crew stationed in Scotland, and because my mother, raised in the vicious housing projects of Chicago that have since been torn down, went on to own a house with my father in an integrated suburb where she later became a Girl Scout adviser. In other words, I was raised to be there, or anywhere a potentially rewarding opportunity presented itself. My parents were worldly people who subscribed to the philosophies and prophecies of Dr. Martin Luther King, Jr., including the rewards of self-application. So, in addition to being as ambitious as the other newspaper staffers, I was optimistic. I believed I could live anywhere for a year. Never mind that no matter where I stepped, I was stared at and met with a long and lasting silence. Once, in the parking lot of a supermarket, a woman stopped me for an autograph. She thought I was Oprah. After that, I was crowned *the* outsider, and joked about my experiences with my peers.

But everything wasn't always funny, and somehow Melissa understood this. As she lived only six doors down from our office, I would walk to her apartment at lunchtime to make sure that she was awake and prepared for her shift. We would use this time therapeutically, to decry the narrow-mindedness of our fellow residents and wallow in the sanctity of our common understanding.

We worked our first holiday shift together. Since we were the lowest on the totem pole, we spent Christmas that first year in a deserted newsroom, sampling the fare of the local soup kitchens from Styrofoam containers as we wrote about those who had no place else to go for a hot, holiday meal. We wrote about the displaced, about those who found themselves at the mercy of strangers. We exchanged notes. We bonded.

And then, approximately a month later, Todd belted out, "Hey, what do you guys know about Groundhog Day?" Because it was Todd doing the belting, our interest was piqued. But what of Groundhog Day? Who knew anything about it, save that it brought the annual announcement of how soon spring would arrive, predicated on the sight of a rodent's shadow? Still, Todd had hooked us.

Todd was a great guy to know. He edited the newspaper's webpage, had an awesome sense of humor and was far too informed for his own good. (He would be the ideal phone-a-friend for a contestant on *Who Wants to be a Millionaire?*) He informed us that Bill Murray's movie of second chances mimics events that occur in a knotty place not too far from where we were working. "Maybe a group of us should drive over, what with Groundhog Day being right around the corner." Melissa and I discussed the proposition the following afternoon over lunch.

Our daily meal was consistent. Melissa would boil a pot of spaghetti noodles, slap a slice of Velveeta atop the mound, then drizzle Ragu sauce over the pasta, straight out of the refrigerated jar.

"We would be able to say we'd actually been to Punxsutawney," Melissa said. "I mean, we're so close, we might as well."

"Yeah," I agreed.

Who knows what we were thinking. Why would we ever *want* to be able to say such a thing? (I've had occasion to reveal this startling bit of information maybe five times in my life thus far, and no one has ever been too impressed by it. "Oh yeah?" they respond, before quickly changing the subject.) But the thing was, Melissa and I were always bored—bored, restless and miserably city-sick. We were up for just about anything. Already we'd driven into Manhattan one Sunday evening, following a series of directions that promised to get us as far as the George Washington Bridge. We survived. Punxsutawney? Punxsutawney was nothing.

Still, we didn't decide until the last minute. We agreed the afternoon before the rodent's scheduled prognostication, "We're going." Todd and his wife already had a hotel reservation, and by then all of the rooms in the surrounding radius were booked. "We'll pull an all-nighter," we declared, and suddenly our random adventure was turning out to be a lot more fun. We bragged about our plans in the newsroom, where the copyeditors grinned and cheered us on. But they were all staying home.

We set out for I-80 west in the best of spirits. The weather was decent: cold and gray, but not frigidly so. The mountains of central Pennsylvania rose on either side of us, Dar Williams sang to us from the cassette deck, and we shared that mutual feeling of road-trippiness, that release acquired with the rolling of a few extra miles beneath us. We puffed up our chests, filled with our own sense of adventure and love for the women we were at the moment. But then, the drive grew less scenic, our snacks ran out way too fast, and it became cold and gray, though not frigidly so.

What we figured, and figured correctly, was that Punxsutawney would be small enough for us to navigate easily. We arrived at the town after being told only, "Take 80 till you see the exit." From there, we counted on our press passes to lead us where we needed to go. Small-town residents are notoriously free-tongued with reporters. They tell everything, and so we were guided first to meet the Inner Circle, who were scheduled to razzle-dazzle at the hotel in the center of the square.

Being newly introduced to this sheltered environment of revelry, neither Melissa nor I had any idea that within the U.S. of A. there was an entire population of people who made Groundhog Day a year-round celebration. To us (and, we presumed, our readership) the Inner Circle meant nothing. We were baffled, but that was why we were here—to get to the bottom of this story. And so, before proceeding to our first scheduled event, we compared notes to establish a bit of background.

Groundhog Day stems from early Christian beliefs associated with Candlemas, according to the official event website. (A fair Candlemas day predicted an extension of winter; a cold and rainy Candlemas meant spring was on its way.) Struck by the proliferation of groundhogs in the region, a number of Pennsylvania's early German settlers expanded their celebration of the European winter holiday to include the rodents, which resembled the European hedgehog, based on the belief that these creatures were wise enough to return to their winter's hiding at the sight of their own shadow. In an effort to bridge the present to a past when farm almanacs and natural phenomena played more influential roles in our society, Groundhog Day was born. The sun's appearance on February 2, which allows the animal to cast a shadow, forecasts six more weeks of winter.

While early predictions were conducted privately, the "grand prognostication," as it is known in Punxsutawney, has grown into what local residents like to call "one of the greatest ongoing publicity campaigns in history." And what is a campaign without a star? Never mind the groundhog, a campaign needs a human star. Or an entire group of stars, as we were soon to meet, organized as descendants of the Punxsutawney Groundhog Club, a group of local hunters who held groundhog hunts that began in 1887, before they took to the legend of the groundhog as a weather prophet and created a home for him on Gobbler's Knob on the outskirts of town. This latter group of stars has been dubbed "The Inner Circle."

The Inner Circle was a self-absorbed bunch. The group of mostly white-haired men wore top hats and those fancy swing coats reminiscent of a Dickens tale. They mingled in the crowded ballroom, posing for photographs and demurely declining to satisfy the common inquiry of whether or not America should expect an early spring this year. It was a bizarre sort of celebrity within the town. In actuality, the group consisted of politicians and businessmen, who took their positions within the exclusive clique quite seriously. They even had titles that they rambled to Melissa and me with pride: His Scribe, the Cold Weatherman, His Handler, the Cloud Builder, the Fog Spinner, the Storm Chaser, the Iceman, the Dew Dropper, His Protector and so on. I could barely keep my eyebrows lowered long enough to jot the names in my reporter's notebook.

At the hotel, drinks and hors d'oeuvres were served, and flashbulbs popped throughout the room. The members of the intimate conglomerate worked the crowd of local media reps, shaking our hands, slapping our backs and kissing their neighbors' babies. Kissing babies! In an effort to remain objective, I kept my reporter's notebook poised, but the validity of this event as a serious story was growing more questionable by the second.

I recently found a postcard that I sent to my sister during my visit. Its postscript reads: "They cheat. They decide in advance whether or not the groundhog sees its shadow." I ruined it for her, and for the readership of the newspaper when I later wrote my article. But the truth was, no one cared about the cheating. How silly is it, anyway, for millions of people to rely on the barometric skills of a rodent who could never help but to see his shadow, what with the glare of so many television cameras hovering over him? It was all in fun. But in observing the Inner Circle, I got the impression of just how serious this all was to Punxsutawney. Groundhog "Day" was groundhog *year* in the town. One day in early February made this locale the biggest fish in the small pond ninety miles northeast of Pittsburgh. It was surreal.

Famished, we located a diner a few miles away from the hotel. The restaurant was decorated in gingham, with checked tablecloths and Phil caricatures in every corner. Phil is the name of the star groundhog. I don't know who gave the groundhog his name, how many Phils there have been over the years or how long a run Phil gets in the spotlight. I do know this: Phil is housed in the center of the town's Barclay Square, his handmade tunneled home in full view behind a glass overlay. He lives there with his mate, Phyllis, and new Phils are bred on a frequent basis. Our waitress made us promise to go have a look.

Along the back wall of the diner, photographs of Bill Murray with just about every waitress in the vicinity were hung in a crooked arc. "Even Oprah came to visit us one year," the waitress said to me, and winked. (Phil made a guest appearance on the Oprah show in 1995.) I cringed as she cleared the mess we made with plates of fried chicken, mashed potatoes and fruit pies. We had eaten enough for the next two days, and used the opportunity to browse through the weekend's event schedule.

Despite the enormity of the event, there was surprisingly little to do. We could grab doughnuts at the local shop, where a giant wooden Phil cutout is lowered from the rooftop at midnight, à la Times Square. Or we could head to the all-night bowling event sponsored by the only alley in town, a smoky dive outfitted with disco balls and strobe lights. We opted for the latter option, in search of a few good quotes. Something by AC/DC blared through the walls as we approached the entrance. When we stepped inside, we were disheartened. A few scattered bunches of wild and whooping teenagers were holding court. We put our notebooks away, and began to seriously question our judgment. It was at that moment we met Phil himself.

He lumbered over to us with his bobbing head and personalized red T-shirt. Noticing our notebooks, he began to spout quotes at us, then asked over and over, "What newspaper will this be in?" He even let us try on his head—it's heavy—and offered us the scoop on his impending announcement.

Underneath the costume, Phil was just an ordinary guy with greasy hair. His blue jeans were too tight, and he shuffled back and forth as he smoked a cigarette. "You know, they make this down there where they make them Disney costumes," he thumped Phil's head. "Same place. Weighs about thirty pounds." I no longer recall the Phil guy's real name, but I do remember that he would not let me reveal it in my article. He wanted a pseudonym. He had been the Phil guy for years, and considering that he was rarely given the opportunity to reveal himself, it was a pretty thankless job. Not many others were vying for it, but he seemed to treasure it as an honor.

Phil's wife came over to us to find out what was going on, and why he was out of costume. He introduced her to us, and told her we were reporters from a paper outside of Punxsy. We all chatted briefly, and when she learned of our plans to roam all night, she frowned and shook her head.

"Oh hell," she said. "There ain't that much to do, not all night, anyways, in Punxsutawney. Y'all may as well come home with us."

I froze. Melissa turned to me and shrugged.

I was horrified when I heard her accept the offer. "We don't have a choice," she whined. "There's no place else for us to go. Besides, this is major." She suddenly lit up. "We'll be able to say we slept with the groundhog." I was sold. We vowed not to eat anything or to fall asleep, just in case the couple was a pair of mass murderers merely masquerading as rodents. But, of course, shortly after we arrived at their house, Melissa fell sound asleep while I counted down to the wee hours of early morning, when the "grand prognostication" was scheduled to occur. The reason, really, we were there: to get an up close and personal glimpse of the groundhog whose shadow was to determine my upcoming wardrobe.

At 3 A.M. we all loaded into a van and began the trek up to Gobbler's Knob. The Knob is located atop a mountain guarded by state troopers. It is the designated location of Phil's annual February 2 appearance, a splatter of clearing within a mess of surrounding woods. As the van approached its foot, Phil-the-guy stuck his head out the window and yelled, "I'm the groundhog!" There was a burst of cheers from the foot trekkers heading up the Knob, and Phil-the-guy waved and drove on.

Already, thousands of revelers were assembled, an estimated thirty thousand people were present that year. I was floored. Who were these people, and why had they come? Punxsutawney itself has an estimated population of sixty-seven hundred people. When I asked around, I found a number of the attendees to be college students from regional towns, but this many? I had clearly underestimated the appeal of drinking and partying in the woods all night, all weekend. It was cold and there was snow on the ground, but a hub of guys stood shirtless as they basked in the remaining coughs of a bonfire. "I hear MTV's here!" one frat boy yelled, setting off a whooping display for any possible camera crew that may have been lurking in the bushes. Our entourage was escorted through the mayhem to the stage.

All too quickly, Phil, the real groundhog, was snatched from his tree-trunk home, a creation that looked like it belonged in Winnie the Pooh's neighborhood. The three-foot-tall structure was mounted on a similarly sculpted tree trunk. Members of the Inner Circle gathered around it, knocked on Phil's "door," and wrestled him out of hiding. (I had been warned that Phil is known to put up a pretty good fight.) He was thrust into the air, and spring was declared, I think. By then, the sun had already risen, and no substantial attempt was made to locate any tail of a shadow. Melissa and I shrugged, put away our notebooks and joined the second wind of the celebration. From our prime location, Melissa spotted Todd and his wife in the crowd. We waved frantically, and Todd yelled, "Lucky dogs!" in admiration of our prime access. We smiled in modesty.

And then a hard snowball hit Melissa's arm.

"Nigger lover!" a white boy shouted at her and grinned.

We fell silent. We didn't know what to do. We pointed aimlessly in his direction. Nothing happened. At that moment, our trip was over. Groundhog Day was over, and we were in Punxsutawney once again, a hate group capital of the country. There was no adventure left in hanging around any longer. We hightailed it out of town, passing Todd and his wife on I-80 east.

"You guys sure were speeding," Todd said later.

"Yeah," we replied. And that was all.

We'd done what we said we were going to do. We'd taken our road trip, but it wasn't the trip of all trips. It was too fantastical; its abrupt ending way too real. Shortly thereafter, Melissa decided her time was up at the newspaper and moved back to Kentucky. I moved back to Chicago about a year later. We cried when we parted, and promised to keep in touch, and we have. On February 2, there's always a note in my box, just to say hello.

damsels on the highway

tara kolden

*t*he call came to my new apartment, which I'd moved into after finishing at the university. I was still living out of boxes and cooking in a half-unpacked kitchen. When the phone rang, I dug it out from under an avalanche of books and college notes I'd dumped unceremoniously in a corner. It was one of the first calls I'd received at my new number. It was Sylvie.

"Is it really you?" There was a catch in her voice, one I at first put down to sentimentality. She sounded weary. I assured her it was me. "I got the number from your mother," she explained.

Sylvie and I had been inseparable as children. When I moved with my parents to Seattle and entered a new school, Sylvie's was the most welcoming smile among the shy and curious looks I received from the denizens of Mrs. Blackwell's second-grade classroom. On the playground, she taught me to do cartwheels, and I showed her how to fashion French braids and play Crazy Eights.

Ours was a friendship of slumber parties, camping trips and shared crushes on Cary Adderholm, a boy a year ahead of us at the elementary school, and on a young man named Stephen, who worked at the pizza parlor near Sylvie's house and always gave us free Cokes. Life was good. It loomed large and beautiful, and Sylvie and I would take it all on together.

Her family moved after we finished the sixth grade, and though she was only a hundred miles away, to twelve-year-olds that was an insurmountable distance. At first we wrote letters constantly. We shared secrets, discussed the merit badges we'd earned in our respective Girl Scout troops, giggled over a few long-distance telephone calls. By the time we both started high school, though, our correspondence had tapered to a thin dribble of belated birthday cards and holiday form letters. Over the next few years I heard from Sylvie infrequently, and picked up scant details about her from mutual acquaintances, who told me she'd finished high school, started at the University of Alaska in Fairbanks, wanted to study biology. We'd become footnotes in each other's pasts. I never really expected to see her again.

She asked how I was, and I poured out a synopsis of the years she'd missed. I had the usual gripes about work, Seattle weather and trying to make ends meet. There was a lot to tell, none of it really important, but the sort of material a friend will treasure, no matter how inconsequential. When I finished there was a pause, and I expected the same regurgitation of gossip from her.

She sniffed once, as if she'd just been crying or was just about to start. "I need your help," she said. It wasn't just fatigue I heard in her voice, and it wasn't sentimentality. It was world-weariness. She said it again. "I need your help."

It came out in a rush, too fast for me to digest it all. A research grant exhausted. An expired lease on a despicable apartment. A boyfriend who hit her.

"I'm out of money," she said, the tears finally coming. "I want to get out of here. I have to. I have nothing. I can't ask my parents for help. They wouldn't understand."

I conjured up an image of Sylvie's parents, a surgeon and a stay-at-home mom who had been president of seemingly every church and volunteer group in our community. They had treated me with kindness tempered by a bit of condescension, as if I were a house pet that couldn't be counted on not to pee on their expensive Persian rugs. My own parents were blue-collar workers who didn't have time to show up for Scout meetings or school curriculum nights, and we weren't churchgoers. That, along with my Salvation Army clothes, made me an oddity in their home. When I asked her why she couldn't talk to them, she wouldn't say.

"Will you come and get me?" she asked. "I have a lot of books and things I don't want to leave behind. I can't afford to ship it all. Even just a plane ticket for myself—it's out of the question." She murmured apologies and blew her nose. "You're my oldest friend," she said. "Will you come?"

Of course I would. There was no question of that. I was working part-time as an editor for an online journal published by friends, and they could let me go for a week. And I thought my car could handle it. I drove an old Ford station wagon, inherited from my parents. It wasn't the chic sports car I would have preferred, but it was comfortable and reliable, and there would be plenty of room for whatever Sylvie had to transport. She seemed to think a great deal of cajoling was in order, but I wasn't having any of it.

"Just tell me where you are," I said.

She was living in a town called Homer in southern Alaska. Population: not many. Depressing: absolutely. That was how she described it. I got out an atlas and looked it up. I'd never been to Alaska, and my geography wasn't good. I found the town, and marveled at the maze of highways I would have to take to get there. It was going to be a long trip.

The first leg north, to the Canadian border, was familiar territory. The interstate took me through the suburb where Sylvie and I had grown up together, and past a host of other memories from late adolescence. I had packed a few supplies, thinking to make the drive up with as few stops as possible, but I allowed myself a brief respite in Blaine, ordering a coffee from a drive-through espresso stand and drinking it in view of the Peace Arch and its surrounding park.

I had been to Blaine once before, on a school picnic in the fifth grade. Sylvie and I had clambered around the base of the Peace Arch with our classmates, then shared a brown-bag lunch while straddling a low concrete wall that we believed marked the precise divide between the United States and Canada, now dangling one foot in each country, now hopping to one side or the other across the international border. It was a game then, crossing such an immense boundary with no more effort than a single skip. Were we too old for such games now? As I drove through the border checkpoint and into Canada, I was conscious of another crossing, one between childhood and an adult world, between friendship and the no man's land that can grow between friends who are long apart.

Evening fell as I drove toward the Alaskan border. The growing darkness shrouded what was by now an unfamiliar route, and left me with many empty hours. I thought of Sylvie, and of the impish preadolescents we'd been. I remembered making friendship pins and homemade brownies, staying up all hours playing games on her Commodore 64, getting into a play-fight with powdered sugar and earning ourselves a serious reprimand from Sylvie's mother, who found us collapsed on the kitchen floor, helplessly out of breath from laughter and coated head to foot in sugar. We put on skits and fought over who would play the princess in peril, who the hero. After such a long absence, it felt strange to be taking up the same shadow play again.

It was late afternoon on the following day when I got to Homer and found Sylvie's apartment. It was on the top floor of a dilapidated house that was sagging badly on its foundation. The staircase leading to her apartment was entered through a side door, and the dirty strip of carpet that lined the steps reeked of mildew. I tiptoed up to the landing and checked that the number on the door matched the one Sylvie had given me. She opened the door before I had time to knock.

She hugged me so tightly I thought I would break, and I could feel her ribs through the fabric of her turtleneck. She had always been petite, but I was stunned at how thin she had become. Still, it was my Sylvie. Her hair was shorter than she'd kept it as a child, and she'd grown into her long legs. The smile she gave me now was a tired replica of the one I remembered, but it was hers all the same. I'd have known her anywhere.

"You don't know how glad I am to see you," she said. "You're saving me." I stepped inside, far enough to see a dozen or so packing cases strewn about the cramped living room and covering an ugly pink sofa. There were a few nondescript posters tacked to the walls, and through an archway I glimpsed a tiny, disorderly kitchen with an antique refrigerator squeezed into an awkward corner beneath the room's sloped ceiling, and beside it a badly framed dormer window that looked out onto the small grassy patch that served as a backyard. Underfoot was the same green carpet that covered the stairs, similarly threadbare and in need of a vacuum.

Sylvie caught me looking at the packing cases and must have thought I was calculating how many would fit into the car. "They're not all mine," she said. "Our lease is up in a week. The owner wants to turn this back into a part of the main house, so Jackson's out, too."

I nodded. Jackson, the boyfriend. "Is he here?"

"No, he's at work. I really want to get out of here before he comes home. I don't want a scene. And he loves to make scenes." A crease appeared between her eyes. "I'm just sick of it. Of him. Of all of this."

I nodded again, trying to find the right words. A tortoiseshell cat appeared from behind a half-closed door that I assumed led to the bedroom. The animal wound itself around my ankles before sidling up to Sylvie. She picked it up and cradled it in her arms.

"Is it coming with us?" I pointed to the cat.

"No, she's Jackson's. Her name is Pansy. She's sweet."

I held her gaze. "So, is she coming with us?"

Sylvie looked momentarily confused. "No, she's—" Then she gave me her old sly grin, the one I remembered from sixth grade, when we sat in the pizza parlor and debated about asking Stephen for another round of Cokes. "I don't know. What do you say?"

I grinned back at her. "I say we liberate the cat."

In fact, most of the packing cases did belong to Sylvie, but she was too sheepish to say so outright. We made numerous trips up and down the narrow staircase, and I watched as the back of my station wagon slowly filled with the remnants of a disillusioned life. Sylvie wasn't very talkative at first, but her mood brightened as more and more of her belongings left the apartment. After I deposited a desk lamp and a potted ficus in the back seat, I returned to the apartment and found Sylvie rummaging around at the foot of a cramped closet off the kitchen. She emerged with a cardboard cat carrier, and after making sure that Pansy was fed and watered, we closed her protesting form into the carrier and transported it gingerly to the car. I asked Sylvie if she wanted to take a last look around the place, but she shook her head vehemently. She didn't bother to leave a note for Jackson, or even lock the door. I helped her remove the apartment keys from her key chain and she left them beside the kitchen sink. It was early evening, not really dark, and we were on our way.

I had consumed most of the supplies I'd brought with me for the trip north, and I suggested stopping somewhere to restock, but Sylvie was skittish.

"It's a small town," she explained. "People will recognize me and want to talk. Word will get around."

"Word's going to get around anyway. It's not like you're doing anything wrong. Tell me where we can get munchies."

She directed me to a mini-mart, where I picked up bread, cheese, apples, chips, cat food and a case of Coke. Sylvie waited for me in the car. I watched her out the window as the clerk counted my change. She looked small and nervous, engulfed by the brown plush upholstery of the station wagon. She also looked like someone who needed a hot meal, something more than the microwavable snacks offered by the mini-mart. When I got back to the car, I asked her if she wanted to get some real dinner before we hit the road. She said no, but didn't protest when I pulled into the parking lot of a Mexican restaurant. She still wouldn't leave the car, so I went inside and asked the wait staff if they could put together something to go. They did, and Sylvie beamed at me when I returned bearing chicken tamales and hot enchiladas. We pulled back onto the road, and Sylvie cut my dinner into pieces I could manage as I drove. She started to cry over her own food, and I put a hand on her shoulder.

"Don't mind me," she sniffed. "It's just been a long time since anyone's been nice to me."

I was tired after the long trip I'd made to Homer, and Sylvie conceded that she'd hardly slept the past few nights. The weather had been clear during the day, but it was a chilly night, and since we had Pansy, sleeping in a cold car in a parking lot didn't sound like an appealing idea. We found a cheap motel in Soldotna, and Sylvie pressed on me the last of her hoarded cash to pay for the room. It was detached from the main office, one of a row of one-story bungalows with their own parking spaces, so we didn't worry what the management might say about the cat. We fed Pansy, and Sylvie even rigged up a litter box out of supplies she'd taken from the apartment. We fell into bed too tired to say anything to each other but "Good night."

The next morning was the beginning of another clear day, cool, but with the promise of blue skies and sunshine. We made ourselves cheese sandwiches and ate them in the car as we headed east to the fork that would take us to Anchorage via the Seward Highway. Sylvie asked what I thought of the Seward Highway.

I laughed. "I have no feelings about it whatsoever. Should I?"

It was her turn to laugh. "You really weren't paying a bit of attention on the way, were you? It's a wonder you even kept the car on the road. Wait till you see." For the first time on our trip, she seemed to relax. I'd brought along various cassettes, and she dug through my collection and plugged one into the player. It was Tom Lehrer, a discovery I'd made during college and cherished ever since. "The Vatican Rag" began to play.

"You know Tom Lehrer?" I asked, surprised.

"Oh, sure," said Sylvie. "Especially this song. I used to play it when I lived at home with my folks. It made my mother livid." We sang it together and giggled over the lyrics.

"How is your mother?" I asked, thinking about my own parents and how negligent I'd been over the last few years, calling them only occasionally and conducting conversations that felt prefabricated and out of date.

Sylvie's face grew pinched. "I haven't talked to her in a while."

"Yeah?" I commiserated. "Me neither. I mean, talking to my mother. She hasn't even seen my new place yet."

"No," said Sylvie. "I meant I haven't talked to my mother in a really long time. Not since high school."

"What?" I counted back the years.

Sylvie sighed and looked out her window. We passed a sign that announced the turnoff for the Seward Highway. We drove in silence for a space of ten or fifteen miles. A few morning clouds had burned off, and the sun shone down on us unremittingly. It was almost warm enough for the air conditioner, except my car didn't have one. I rolled up the sleeves of my sweatshirt and waited for Sylvie to do the same with her turtleneck, a green twin to the blue one she'd worn the previous day. She didn't.

"What happened between you and your mother?" I asked.

I could see her purse her lips in the reflection on her window. "I don't want to talk about it."

"Was it about your going to college? Coming up here?"

She kept looking out her window. "I said I don't want to talk about it."

We were both quiet again, not even laughing along with Tom Lehrer. I could hear Pansy rustling in her box.

Surrounded by mountains and water, we sped along Seward Highway. To our left was the deep green of Cook Inlet, and to our right a breathtaking mountain vista. Railroad tracks skirted our route, and once a train passed by, traveling south.

"You're right," I said, trying to break the ice that was forming between Sylvie and me. "This is spectacular."

She stopped the cassette tape so we could enjoy the view quietly. "I was always sorry my parents never came up here. I think they would have liked it."

We stopped in Anchorage, filled the gas tank, and ate lunch at a McDonald's. Sylvie thought she remembered where there was a park, and we drove around town until we found it. We sat on the back bumper of the car and ate apples to supplement our hamburgers, and we let Pansy out of her box for a supervised exploration. She sniffed the car's tires inquisitively and was about to trot off for new adventures, but we corralled her beside a park bench and sat stroking her warm fur and soaking up the sunshine. Sylvie caught me rubbing the stiffness out of my knees, and she volunteered to take over at the wheel until our next break.

We had a long stretch ahead of us: the Glenn Highway, headed east. I settled into the passenger seat and put in a Beatles tape.

"So," I said. "Tell me things."

Her stories were as bland as those I'd shared over the phone. She talked of high school experiences similar to my own, skipping neatly over whatever had caused the rift between her and her parents, and described a run-of-the-mill stretch of time spent at college in Fairbanks.

"I'm sorry you won't see Fairbanks. I was almost happy there."

"We could take a detour if you want. You could show me around."

She shook her head slowly. "No. I want to get back south. I'm through with life up here."

I thought for a minute. "Is it Jackson? Is that the problem?"

She frowned. "He's a part of it."

"Well?"

"Well, he was a mistake, that's all. I've made a lot of them. I'll probably make a lot more."

She said it with a finality that indicated we were finished with the topic. Now I sighed. She glanced at me. "What's wrong?"

I hesitated. "You. I want to help you. Be your friend again, like I used to be. But you won't tell me what I can do."

She laughed incredulously. "This!" She hammered her hands on the top of the steering wheel. "You're doing this! You've been a knight in shining armor. If that's possible." She laughed. "Girls aren't supposed to be knights. They're supposed to be damsels in distress. I don't know what that makes you."

"Nix on the damsel, but definitely in distress."

Her brow furrowed. "You shouldn't worry so much about me."

"And you shouldn't tell me what I should or shouldn't worry about," I countered. "I used to know you as well as if you were my twin. It's hard to get used to things now. Us. Being grown up. Being apart for so long." I stretched my legs in the well of the passenger seat and leaned back against my headrest. "God, when we were in elementary school, people who were in their twenties were so *old.*"

She smiled wryly. "Sometimes I feel positively ancient."

She was quiet after that, and I watched the other cars on the road. Campers and RVs passed us going in the opposite direction, probably the beginnings of the tourist season. Most of the cars heading east had Alaska plates, and I wondered if they were like Sylvie, if they were trying to escape something.

"Please tell me why you and your mother don't talk," I said. In the silence before she answered, the cassette changed sides, and I flipped it out of the player.

Sylvie began picking at a place on the steering wheel where the plastic was peeling, then shot me a sidelong glance as if gauging my receptivity. "It's a long story," she said. "And at the same time, it isn't. Just another mistake I made. I told you, I've made a lot of them."

She spoke of her parents then, saying more about them than I could ever recall hearing in the past. I knew them, of course, had spent more of my preteen years in their home than I had in my own. I remembered them only vaguely, though, as quietly disapproving but never openly hostile referees of our various antics. Sylvie filled in the details that had escaped my juvenile disinterest. She talked about their impossible expectations, the grades that weren't high enough, the tennis team she quit, the growing résumé of after-school jobs that didn't measure up to her parents' standards. And I wasn't the only friend with whom her parents found fault.

"His name was Ryan," she said, "and he had red hair."

"This was when?"

"Summer after my junior year of high school," Sylvie replied. "Things were still on track. Sort of. I still had Key Club and student council, and I was working part-time as a receptionist in an architect's office. Things looked okay."

Sylvie tipped her head. "I wasn't such a hot commodity after that summer. All my time was taken up with Ryan. I started cutting classes, and my grades slipped. My parents were pretty furious."

The denouement to her story was predictable, but I felt myself wince as she pronounced it.

"In January of my senior year, I got pregnant. Ryan took off. Went to live with his father on the East Coast. I never heard from him again. And of course his bad behavior was all my fault. That's how my parents saw it. Suddenly I wasn't their golden child anymore."

We were quiet. A milepost streaked by, but I didn't catch the number. "So what happened?" I asked.

"I moved out," she said. "Found a part-time job. Got an abortion and would have called it a miscarriage. That's if my parents had ever asked, which they didn't. Decided to come up here to lose myself in the wilderness. And for a while it was good. It was good to be away from them, to live according to my own expectations, not someone else's. Then I fell into the bear-trap known as Jackson."

There was a hardness in her voice that hadn't surfaced before, a note of anger or discontent, I couldn't tell which. I had heard her speak of Jackson with bitterness, but this was a new discord, one I realized was directed at herself.

"But you're getting away from him," I offered. "This can be a new start for you."

She rolled her eyes again. Her voice went from matter-of-fact to plaintive. "Yeah, well, history has a way of repeating itself."

"What do you mean?"

She bit her lip so hard I thought it would bleed. "The golden child blows it again," she said. "I'm pregnant."

I gave her a moment in case she had more to add, but all she said was, "Open us a Coke?" I passed a can to her, and she took a long swig before looking fruitlessly around her seat for a cup holder. Finding none, she wedged the can between her legs and crossed her wrists atop the steering wheel. I opened one for myself and drank, more for something to do than for thirst.

I rolled the can thoughtfully between my palms. "Did you tell Jackson?"

She kept her eyes on the road. "He doesn't need to know."

"I understand."

"You can't possibly."

In the awkward silence that followed, I fished for a neutral topic. I reminded her of the sleepovers we'd had at her house, when we'd stayed awake all night questioning her Ouija board about which of the boys in our class liked us, and whether we'd grow up to be rich and famous.

Sylvie snorted. "I remember asking it for winning lottery numbers. We never won, though."

"I remember that," I said. "We were going to use our winnings to build a huge house on a tropical island and live there, just the two of us." I took a sip of my Coke. "With Cary Adderholm."

"Who?"

"You know. He was in Mrs. Naylor's class. Blond hair. Green eyes to die for. He hardly spoke to us, but I guess that didn't matter back then."

She shook her head. "I don't remember."

I was at a loss, feeling sheepish at my own recollections of our mutual crush. "It was in the fifth grade," I added weakly.

"Fifth grade," she mused. "That was a long time ago."

She told me her own memories of adolescence. Some I recognized, but most were strange, as if attending the same school had been the only common denominator in two alternate worlds, one hers, one mine. She talked of friends we hadn't shared, and trips she'd taken without me. I had expected to find in her memories a corroboration—more, a celebration—of my own. Instead, my recollections were merely footnotes to a life that grew more unfamiliar as Sylvie described it.

"I'll bet you're shocked, aren't you?"

I knew she meant about her pitfalls, about Ryan, Jackson and countless small but cutting misdemeanors that had formed the basis of an ongoing war between Sylvie and her parents. It was this rift that surfaced in all her reminiscences, while the happier times she and I had shared faded to the background.

"Aren't you?" she prompted.

I gave her a noncommittal shrug, unwilling to explain the way in which her stories had moved me. I felt a fool. I had hoped to break down the barrier we'd erected between our adult selves and instead found our childhood bond crumbling.

Sylvie looked over at me as if for encouragement, but I could offer her nothing. Somehow, my inability to sympathize or comfort seemed worse than the realization that we had become strangers. For so many miles I had carried a desire to help, to reach out, and now I was powerless. I looked out the window, registering an infinity of evergreen trees without really seeing them.

She laughed. It was a small, private sound. "You're not shocked," she said. "You know me too well."

We stopped for the night in Gakona. The motel we found was built like a log cabin, with a spacious lobby decorated with hewn pine furniture and an immense stone fireplace.

"We have a cat," I told the woman at the desk. She was unperturbed.

"We have a dog." She pointed to an empty basket beside the fireplace. It was a big basket, presumably for a big dog. "Best keep them apart."

"Not to worry." I handed over my Visa.

Sylvie watched me wistfully. "All my credit cards were joint accounts with Jackson," she said. "He controlled the money. I guess that was pretty stupid, huh?"

"Not stupid. Just a symptom of love."

We slept late and awoke to overcast skies. Sylvie and I didn't talk much as she emptied Pansy's litter box and I packed our things. When I suggested a hot breakfast, though, she smiled.

We packed up the car and checked out of the motel, then sat down for a breakfast of buttermilk pancakes and scrambled eggs at the tiny in-house restaurant. I was discouraged by the weather, but Sylvie shrugged it off. "It might get better."

From Gakona we had another long straight stretch of road northeast, to the town of Tok. I took the wheel again, and Sylvie let Pansy out of her carrier to roam free in the car. After a trying ten-minute period when the cat insisted on nesting beneath the brake pedal, Pansy settled into an empty space beside the ficus tree in the back seat. Sylvie took her shoes off and rested her feet above the glove compartment. We tuned into several radio stations, but the reception wasn't good, and soon we returned to my stash of cassettes. We'd replenished our food stocks at a gas station mini-mart in Gakona, and Sylvie sang along to my Eagles cassette using a salami as a makeshift microphone.

"I have friends in Tok," she said. "I haven't seen them in a while, but we can give them a call when we get there. Maybe they'll put us up for the night."

"You don't want to head straight through?" I asked.

"Maybe," she said. "But we could stop in and say hello. Use their bathroom, you know?"

The weather grew worse, and soon the patter of raindrops on the windshield became a torrent. I was grateful when signs told us we were nearing Tok.

"It's not much to look at," Sylvie warned.

When we got into the city, we pulled off the road and parked in a lot outside a grocery store while Sylvie fished in her purse for the phone number of her friends. She had a hard time finding it, and eventually I turned the engine off and listened to it tick as it cooled. Rain continued to drum on the metal above our heads. A sleepy Pansy wormed her way under my seat and then into my lap.

"Found it," said Sylvie, waving a scrap of paper triumphantly. She'd dumped out the contents of her purse, and her seat, not to mention the floor on her side of the car, was littered with papers, hair clips, loose change and used Kleenex. "Bad news, though," she said. "It's only the address. I could have sworn I had their number, but maybe I don't."

While I waited in the car, Sylvie found a pay phone with a phonebook and a map. She came back, map in hand, dripping from the downpour.

"Their number's not listed, but I think we can find them," she said. "This isn't all that big a town."

Perhaps it was these words, or the surety with which she spoke them, that jinxed our endeavor. We found the street that matched the address written on her slip of paper, but there was no house that corresponded to the number she'd taken down.

We drove in circles for nearly an hour on the outskirts of town, in a heavily wooded area that looked like it was trying hard to revert back to wilderness. We were on our fourth or fifth circuit of the neighborhood when Sylvie shrieked.

"A moose!"

Sure enough, a gigantic bull had wandered into the road ahead. It had stopped, and was looking placidly in our direction.

"This is great!" Sylvie exclaimed. "I'm so glad you're getting to see this!"

I tried to share her enthusiasm. "It isn't dangerous, is it?"

"No. I don't think it'll pay us any attention. It's just a good thing you didn't hit it with the car. People die that way."

I wished aloud that this one would move out of the road.

"Maybe we should turn around and go back the other way," Sylvie suggested. I gave the moose a long stare. Nothing happened. "Do you think?" she prompted.

I put the station wagon into reverse and backed it as tightly as I could in a half circle. There was a small shoulder at the side of the road, then a short slope into trees. I thought the shoulder would give us enough space to nose the car into an awkward Y-turn, but the rain had turned it to mud. The rear of the car sank into it before I could shift back into drive. When I finally did, the wheels spun.

We shut Pansy back into her carrier before getting out to assess the situation. The moose, meanwhile, shuffled back into the woods the way it had come. Sylvie and I were alone, and soon drenched to the skin. It was clear from the angle of the car and the weight of our cargo that the two of us would never be able to push it out of the mud. Sylvie held up her hands in a gesture of helplessness, and I kicked the back bumper in frustration.

"What now?" she asked.

"We walk."

We dug our jackets out of the car and put them on. Mine didn't have a hood, and we had no umbrella, but by this time I was too wet to care. We removed Pansy in her carrier and locked the station wagon. It was a quarter-mile to the first house, which stood empty. Further down the road, an old woman took pity on us and let us come inside to dry off and use her phone to call a tow truck. We were instructed to wait with our vehicle despite the fact that it was getting dark. At least the rain had stopped. The old woman pressed an umbrella on us nonetheless, and made us each drink a cup of scalding tea before we left.

Back at the car, we climbed inside and peeled off our wet jackets. Sylvie began to giggle. Then I joined in, and within minutes we were out of control. It was the hardest I'd laughed in a long time.

"Stupid moose," Sylvie choked. "We could have been over the border by this time."

I wiped tears of laughter from my eyes. "So much for my daring rescue, Princess."

Sylvie plucked a tissue from the collection of debris that still littered the front passenger side of the car and wiped her own eyes. "Good enough for me." She sobered. "I had a hard time asking it of you, you know."

"Why?" I exclaimed, unable to hide my surprise. "Did you think I wouldn't come?"

"It's not that exactly," she replied. "I just—I used to think I was the sort of person who didn't need anybody's help."

"Even mine?"

"Even yours."

"We don't know each other anymore," I said quietly. I had turned away from her, but I could feel her eyes on me.

She sighed, a sound of resignation. "I guess not."

"The thing is, I don't know if we ever did. You showed up and took the place of the girl I once knew. Now I've lost her, and I don't know who you are."

I held my breath. I expected her to argue with me, but instead she ran her fingers gently down my arm. The touch was unexpected, and with the surprise of it came comfort.

"Maybe you never did. Not really. Maybe I was never the person you thought I was." She sighed and tapped her fingers absently on the gearshift.

I looked over at her then, this stranger sitting in my stranded car. I took in the dark, shiny hair that I had once plaited, the hands that had held mine in playground games, the eyes that had winked at me knowingly over shared jokes. I wondered if I ever *would* know her, and whether mourning for my lost playmate was worth the effort and the anguish, when there was a very real woman next to me who had come to me for help and found in me everything she had expected.

"But we're still friends, aren't we?" Her voice was small.

"Of course," I replied.

It was the truth, a fact I was only gradually becoming aware of myself. We were friends. We would always be friends. And if we met again in twenty years and had to reacquaint ourselves, it would be the same. The idea of Sylvie that I kept with me in her absence might grow distorted or, as now, be left behind in a juvenile world that was no longer ours to enjoy. But I would find her anew. I realized then how you can love someone without really knowing them at all. I almost said as much, but my thoughts were interrupted by the sweep of headlights across the road.

"Looks like our tow truck's here," said Sylvie. She was smiling.

I smiled back. "An errant knight to rescue two damsels in distress."

"Definitely damsels," said Sylvie, "but nix on the distress."

The station wagon was towed out of the mud, and we were able to resume our journey without mishap. We never found Sylvie's friends in Tok, but we didn't feel like spending any more time in the town. We had better luck with acquaintances of hers in Bellingham, where I left her and Pansy in the care of a former research colleague with a spare bedroom and a possible job opening. Sylvie hugged me goodbye with the same force of that first hug in Homer, and she promised to call me as soon as she was back on her feet.

The phone call didn't come, but a few weeks later she sent a letter, and for a brief time we took up our old correspondence with a new vigor. We even got together for a hasty lunch in Everett, and Sylvie told me about a job for which she was applying, a research post at the local university. She liked Bellingham, she said. She might stay. I got a Christmas letter from her during the last holiday season, full of chat but not many details, and the postmark was from Bellingham. I don't know what became of Jackson, or Sylvie's pregnancy, or her relationship with her parents. She didn't say. But she always signs her notes, "With love," and sometimes she adds a postscript telling me to be wary of moose. I could ask for more, but I'm content with what she's given me.

driven

sharon b. young

*Y*ears ago, Chevy's advertising slogan was "See the USA in your Chevrolet." Well, I did see the USA, but it was from the back seat of a Ford and then a Dodge. Now it is from the driver's seat of a Mazda.

As a child, I spent much of my life in a car. My father was in the Army and we moved every thirteen months from one side of the USA to the other. And always we drove. Sometimes it was my father driving, with my mother relieving him in turns. Other times he flew ahead to the Army post and my mother drove solo, accompanied by my brother and me, but with no relief driver.

My earliest memories involve the smell of upholstery and the sound of soft music on the radio, as background to the American panorama going by outside my window. The Mojave Desert and the plains of Kansas, the Blue Ridge Mountains and the New York City skyline are snapshots in my mind—the car window framing

288

their colors and clipping their contours. Even now, if I close my eyes, I can feel the warmth of the sun through the windshield, smell my mother's soap wafting in the breeze and hear the reassuring hum of four wheels and an eight-cylinder engine.

For many years we moved and moved and moved again; houses and schools and friends came and went, but life in the car had a comforting sameness. After the movers had packed our household, and the trunk of the car slammed shut on the suitcases of favorite clothes and dearest toys, my brother and I climbed into our places. He always sat on the left side and I on the right. Just before she closed the door, my mother would hand each of us a brown paper bag filled with surprises that we opened one at a time as we traveled from Seattle to New Hampshire or Maryland or wherever we were headed. Hiding in the bag were animal crackers, Cracker Jacks, coloring books, new crayons, card games, books and small plastic toys—nothing that made noise.

While in the car, we followed an inviolable rule: the radio made noise, we didn't. My parents spoke to each other from time to time in hushed voices but the breaks from silence were sporadic. Sometimes we played time-honored games like "B my name is Barbara. I come from Baltimore and I sell balls"—an alphabet game I now play with my daughter. If a popular song like "Itsy Bitsy Teenie Weenie Yellow Polka Dot Bikini" came on the radio, we all sang along. Or we played a version of bingo in which the winner was the first to spot things from the car window. I was best at spotting airplanes, my father at spotting types of cars. He could identify a '56 Chevy when I could barely discern an oncoming car in the distance. At these times, our car would ring with raucous laughter and the groans of slower competitors. But when the games or songs were over, we would return to the silence of the view from the car windows.

☁

At fifteen, my longing for a driver's license became acute when my dad traded in the old Dodge for a fire-engine-red Ford Mustang. Both my brother and I drooled at the prospect of driving it. My brother's desire to drive a sporty car was accepted as a natural, male sort of thing. Mine was generally dismissed. My sixteenth birthday came and went with no offer to teach me to drive. By the time I was seventeen, my whining prevailed and, with the help of a high school driver's education class, I got my license. But a driver's license was not a passport to drive in my family. I still did not drive the Mustang. Even my mother barely drove it. My father took the car to work four days a week. One day a week, my mother dropped him off at work and kept the car for grocery shopping and errands. No one else drove.

I went off to college carless. My parents gave me a sewing machine as a graduation present. At the end of my junior year in college, my brother graduated from high school and decided to go to the same college I attended. There was no space in the dorms, so he enrolled as a commuter student. My parents gave him a used Mustang as a graduation present. I swallowed my feelings of injustice.

Midway through my brother's freshman year in school, a space opened in a dorm, but there was a catch: freshmen weren't allowed to have cars on campus. Only upperclassmen could have them. So I registered the Mustang and finally got to drive. And I drove. And drove. And drove. I was born to drive. I was not born to sew.

Early in my life, on those long trips crisscrossing the country, I learned that cars are a comforting place to think, plot and dream. Even now, when I am depressed, I hop in the car, turn up the radio and drive as fast as I dare without risking arrest. When I am happy, I hop in the car, turn up the radio and drive as fast as I dare without risking arrest. The sound of the wind and the road and the engine, not to mention music on a good sound system, carry me to a world that is my own. In the blur of stars or trees or telephone poles rushing by, I feel myself relax. My disparate feelings and experiences coalesce into something of substance and begin to make sense in some ineffable way. My deepest understandings and best ideas have come while driving. So have my craziest. Sifting the delusions from the epiphanies is a task that driving makes easier.

After I had grown up and moved to Massachusetts, my mother came to visit. It was her first and last vacation without my father. In her early life she had traveled widely on her own. In her twenties, my mother joined the Red Cross during World War II. Her eyes shone as she regaled me with stories of sheltering herself from enemy bombs and driving Army jeeps across pontoon bridges. But this was before she fell in love. After the war she traveled to Italy and to Korea, where she met my father in an Army hospital. Later, a wife of the fifties, she stayed home and raised children while her husband worked. Until this trip to visit me, the travels of her married life had been largely an adjunct to his.

We drove along the coast of Cape Cod in a companionable silence that echoed my youth. This time, I drove while my mother took in the sunshine and the salt air with closed eyes and a dreamy smile.

"I think that every ocean smells differently," she said at last, her eyes still shut. "The Mediterranean smells warm and spicy. The Pacific has a smell that is wild and complex. This smells . . . " she paused and inhaled deeply. "This smells chilly and full." Decades after her travels, the old smells still affected her, and she made me long to smell them for myself.

"Yes," I responded, at a loss for words. "I love to drive here."

"I can understand why." Her voice sounded almost sleepy as she continued. "Driving helps me remember things. It changes the way I look at life."

I was startled to hear her give voice to some of my own thoughts. "I didn't know you felt that way about driving," I said. "I thought I was the only one."

She opened her eyes and looked over at me. I saw disappointment in her face, as though my assumption diminished her.

"Oh, *I* understand how you feel about driving. It's *my* mother who never understood."

My grandmother was born in 1892. She grew up in a proper New England family, where she was taught to say "limb" instead of "arm" or "leg," terms that were considered crude. She didn't show any of her "limbs" until she married my grandfather in her thirties. In her lifetime she went from wearing long-sleeved, street-length dresses and buttoned shoes to nylon stockings and sleeveless dresses. She saw the invention of airplanes, radio, television and automobiles.

My grandmother graduated from Purdue University in 1913, with a degree in teaching. She was one of only a handful of female graduates. Her father had driven her from Massachusetts to Purdue's Indiana campus in 1909—a long trip in a slow car. She was driven back home again after she graduated. She moved to New Hampshire and taught for several years in a rural high school, where she met my grandfather. Once they married, my grandmother stopped teaching per the custom of the day: only single women could be teachers. And she never learned to drive.

In New Hampshire, she remained housebound unless her father or husband, or later one of her daughters, took her where she needed to go. Until I was fourteen, when my father retired from the Army, we often lived with my mother's parents while my father was stationed in some war-torn place overseas. My grandmother was an intelligent woman, who read widely and enjoyed discussing ideas. She loved aphorisms and taught me more pithy sayings and words of wisdom than any child has business knowing. Thanks to her, to this day I can quote long passages from Longfellow and Whitman.

She spent hours in her rocking chair, watching the birds feed outside the window, apparently lost in thought. There was little outlet for her eager but captive intelligence. As she got older, this inner world captured her more than the outer world. She ventured outside less often and, though she could be persuaded to go on Sunday rides through the countryside, she avoided stores and restaurants. At some undefined point, she became agoraphobic. Months and finally years passed without her leaving her property. When my grandfather died, a hired companion kept her company and ran errands in town. Eventually her body weakened, but she remained quick-witted and lively until she died at age ninety-four.

For years, my mother chafed at my grandmother's slide into helplessness and dependence. My mother saw herself as a woman who had left home and crossed an ocean, an independent woman who drove jeeps and half-tracks. She learned how to drive an ambulance in an era when many Americans still dreamed of owning a car. Few people had two cars in the 1950s, and when she married my father, her world began to narrow. Like most women of that era, she stayed at home, channeling her lively imagination and artistic flair into making creative suppers for children who didn't appreciate garnishes and a husband who preferred plain meat and potatoes. Gardening and decorating held little appeal for her. Like her mother and father, she taught her children to love books and learning, and her vast store of trivia extended from the scientific name for yucca *(Yucca filamentosa)* to the name of the faucet part that wears out and causes a leak (beveled washer). But like her mother, her talents were largely wasted.

By the time my mother entered her late fifties, shortly after our seaside conversation about the joy of driving, she seldom drove except for mile-long trips to a grocery store. Driving had not become a habit and so, as it had for her mother before her, the world began to shrink. Both women were somehow discontent with their lives but seemed unable to change them. How many times had I heard my mother's frustration with her own mother's self-imposed hermitage? Yet she too appeared to choose that same route until she died at age sixty-four of metastasized breast cancer.

"I'm sorry," she apologized. "Now you can't say that you have no history of cancer. I wanted to give you the best of me."

After her funeral, I drove like a woman possessed. I drove aimlessly for hours each day, comforted by the feel of the car wrapped around me and the breezes that dried my tears. Like so many women before me, I needed to figure out where my mother left off and I began. Much as my birth had cut a physical tie that bound us together, her death had cut some sort of psychological tie, and I needed to know I could survive without the security of a bond that had nourished me without my even realizing it.

As I drove, I felt myself letting go of more than just my tie to my mother. My view of my own life began to change. Gradually I came to realize that my husband, who hadn't suffered such a loss in his life, understood neither the depth of my grief nor the comfort that driving offered me.

"Stay home," he urged me. "You're thinking too much and driving yourself crazy."

No, I thought. I'm driving myself sane.

The more my husband urged motionlessness upon me, the more I realized that he had no idea what I needed. As though we were speaking different languages, neither of us seemed able to make the other comprehend. As I reveled in the rich complexity of the sights, sounds and smells that surrounded me when I drove, I realized that he had been slowly withdrawing from the world into the isolation of yoga and meditation. The more I drove, the clearer it became that this lack of communion had dogged the history of our relationship.

Three months after my mother died, I left him. Life is too short to sit quietly at home in a gulf too large to be bridged by words. My mother's death had taught me at least that much.

The first year after I left my husband, I drove nearly every back road and highway in southern New England. Hypnotized by the dotted white lines rushing toward me, my heartbeat slowed to the rhythmic *thump-thump* of my tires, and I felt my burdens slip away. I was grateful to my car.

Owning a car gives you options. I don't mean options like a sunroof and a lighted makeup mirror. I mean the option to see different scenery and to see life differently. The option to get a job or change one. The option to leave a relationship. Or choose to stay. Understanding that you have the option of changing things is powerful. But I suppose that it can be disturbing, too.

Did my mother stop driving because somewhere deep inside she was afraid that one day she would get in the car and not come home? It's something I didn't ask and now can never know.

One unseasonably warm spring day, while driving through the pine barrens of southeastern Massachusetts, I mused on the static, shrinking worlds chosen by my mother and grandmother. Why did theirs grow smaller while mine seemed to expand and transform? As I pulled into my driveway, I noticed the antique curtains that had belonged to my grandmother were flattened against the screen of my bedroom window, the breeze blowing in from the kitchen urging them to fly.

About fifteen years earlier, when my grandmother was living in a nursing home, she had written a note on a birthday card she sent me. In it, she told me that she loved me dearly and that she felt somehow we were kindred spirits. At the time, it had truly baffled me. She was an agoraphobic elderly lady and I was on my second marriage and eighth job. I had lived in six different states and more houses and apartments than I cared to count.

Now, as I looked at her curtains pressed against the screen, I felt flattered. My mother and grandmother were pioneers of a sort. I was the daughter and granddaughter of intelligent women who knew about all manner of things from Balzac to birding; from the wisdom of Brandeis to bowling. Women who had the gift of gab and hearty laughter. Women who had the strength to survive adversity and maintain a loving heart. But the one thing I had that they hadn't was a car of my own. And a road ahead that led any place I could imagine.

contributors

Marian Blue's award-winning essays, fiction, interviews and poetry have appeared in various publications, such as *AWP Chronicle, Snowy Egret , ACM (Another Chicago Magazine), Tiller and the Pen: A Collection of Sailors' Stories* (Eighth Moon Press, 1994) and *A Hundred White Daffodils* (Graywolf Press, 2000). She is currently an editor and writer for One World Journeys, an environmental/adventure website; she has also contributed to online productions for the LOOC (Lives Out of China) Foundation and the family-planning website Planet. Blue teaches for Skagit Valley College and Writer's Digest School and is the cofounder of Blue & Ude Writers' Services.

Kari J. Bodnarchuk is a Boston-based freelance writer who has mastered the art of filing her nails while driving—but only when the temperature is just right and she's cruising along wide-open highways. Author of *Rwanda: Country Torn Apart* (Lerner, 1999) and *Kurdistan: Region Under Siege* (Lerner, 2000), she is currently writing a book about her eighteen-month solo trip around the world. She teaches women's solo travel classes in the Boston area and has contributed to *Islands, Backpacker,* the *Christian Science Monitor* and the *Denver Post.* Her work also appears in *The Unsavvy Traveler: Women's Comic Tales of Catastrophe* (Seal, 2001) and *The Greatest Adventures of All Time* (Time, Inc., 2001).

Moe Bowstern worked nine years as a deck hand and skiff operator in the salmon fisheries of Kodiak, Alaska. She turned to writing because that seems to be the only place her friends will put up with her endless fishing stories. You can read about her adventures in her zine, *Xtra Tuf,* available from her at PO Box 6834, Portland, OR 97228.

Lorraine Caputo is a documentary poet, writer and translator. She has traveled extensively throughout the Americas, from Alaska to Patagonia. Her work has appeared in over forty journals in the United States and Canada, and her poetry has been published in five limited-edition chapbooks. In 2001 *Noches Latinas/Latina Nights,* an audio book of her poetry, was released by St. Louis-based DiMBy Productions. Ms. Caputo has performed at almost two hundred poetry readings in the United States, Canada, Mexico and Guatemala; more than eighty have featured her as a performer.

Shelly Whitman Colony lives with her husband and twin sons in northwest Oregon, where she grows wildflowers, herbs and drought-tolerant plants. She is the author of *Landforms/Lifeforms,* an exhibit and curator's guide at the Museum of the Rockies in Bozeman, Montana. Her work has appeared in *Woven on the Wind: Women Write About Friendship in the Sagebrush West* (Houghton Mifflin, 2001), *High Country News* and *Northern Lights.*

Alice Evans is a freelance writer and editor. Her outdoor essays have appeared in four Seal Press anthologies. She and her husband, Jon, live in Oregon with Ursula, their seventeen-year-old daughter.

Belinda Farley was born and raised in Chicago, Illinois. After receiving her journalism degree from Drake University, she dabbled in broadcasting before moving to a small Pennsylvania town to become a newspaper reporter. She has since relocated to New York, where she teaches English to middle-school students in East Harlem. She is at work on her first novel.

A fourth-generation Oregonian, **Martha Gies** began publishing nonfiction in the mid-seventies and later studied fiction with Raymond Carver at two

Centrum summer arts workshops. Her short fiction appears widely in literary quarterlies and in several anthologies. Gies received an Oregon Literary Arts fellowship for her creative nonfiction and a program grant from the Regional Arts & Culture Council for "Up All Night," a portrait of the city as told through the stories of twenty-three people who work the night shift. Gies has worked as a magician's assistant, computer programmer, deputy sheriff, masseuse, stage manager, waitress, bookstore clerk, arts administrator, interviewer and taxi driver. She currently teaches creative writing at Lewis and Clark College's Northwest Writing Institute and at Mountain Writers Center, both in Portland.

Deborah Gitlitz grew up in Bloomington, Indiana, where she learned to cross busy intersections without losing her place on the page. In her youth she roamed the world with her family in a succession of unpredictable vehicles. She and her lover Val are now parked in Portland, Oregon, where they live in a stationary house of several rooms and frequently leave the dishes in the kitchen to be washed later. The van is pastured in the driveway, dreaming of southwestern skies. Gitlitz can be reached at Debrarian@hotmail.com.

Jeffe Kennedy came to writing obliquely, via neurobiology, religious studies and environmental consulting. Her stories and essays have appeared in publications including *Wyoming Wildlife, Mountain Living* and *Redbook*. Excerpts from her work can be found at www.brightlynx.com. She lives in Wyoming with a fish pathologist, his teenager, two Maine coons and two Border collies. She drives an old Jaguar and owns a pair of three-dollar flea market shades that make her look *just* like Audrey Hepburn.

Tara Kolden recently completed a graduate degree in English literature at King's College, University of London. She is a freelance writer and scholar whose poetry, fiction and essays have appeared in a variety of publications. She is currently at work on a biography of Edwardian author Thomas Burke.

Tina Yun Lee is a writer and actress living in New York City. Her fiction and poetry have appeared in the *River City Journal* and *Kalliope* magazine. "My Mom Across America" premiered as a one-woman show with Here Theater and Lincoln Center Theater's American Living Room Series 2000 and ran at the Nuyorican Poets Cafe. Tina was profiled by BBC radio for her work with the show. For future performances, check out www.tinatrip.com.

Monifa A. Love received her Ph.D. in 1997 as a McKnight Fellow. She is the author of several works, including *Freedom in the Dismal* (Plover Press, 1998), *Provisions* (Lotus Press, 1989) and *" . . . my magic pours secret libations"* (University of Washington Press, 1997). She is currently at work on "Romancing Harlem," a cultural memoir, with artist Charles Mills, and "After the Rain: Life with an Extraordinary Man," a book about her late husband, visual artist and educator Ed Love. She is visiting professor of writing at Hampshire College.

Carolyn Mackler is the author of the award-winning young adult novel *Love and Other Four-Letter Words* (Delacorte Press, 2000). She has written feature articles, personal essays and short stories for numerous publications, including *Ms., Seventeen, Girls' Life, Fit, Self* and *Body Outlaws: Young Women Write About Body Image and Identity* (Seal, 2000). Her second young adult novel will be published by Delacorte Press in 2002. Carolyn has appeared on television and radio programs, on panels, and at schools nationwide, speaking about writing for teenagers. She lives in New York City.

Alexandria Madero is from New York City, Quebec and San Francisco. An avid knitter, smoker and Pez collector, she spends Monday nights with her Stitch & Bitch group, Tuesday nights smoking and Wednesday nights rearranging her Pez. The rest of the week, she pretends to write. This essay is her first published work; she is currently reading *A Course in Miracles,* hoping for a second. She lives with her monsters in an apartment in Los Angeles.

Janet Mason is an award-winning writer of prose and poetry. Her work has been widely published, most recently in the *Brooklyn Review,* the *Harrington Lesbian Fiction Quarterly* and the *Advocate.* Her writings have also been included in anthologies from Seal Press, Alyson Publications and Black Sparrow Press. She is the author of three chapbooks of poetry including *When I Was Straight* (Insight to Riot Press, 1995) and *a woman alone* (Cycladic Press, 2001). "Tequila Sunrise" is an excerpt from her novel in progress.

Kathryn Morton's writing career was launched the summer following the one described in her essay. She traded car travel for travel by freighter and bicycle; *Mademoiselle* published her accounts. Morton went on to write essays and articles for a variety of magazines and newspapers, including the *New York Times* and the *Washington Post.* Her work also appears in *Dutiful Daughters: Caring for Our Parents as They Grow Old* (Seal, 1999). Currently, she teaches Hebrew and is learning web design.

Andromeda Romano-Lax is a mother, traveler and writer who lives in Anchorage, Alaska.

Karen Sbrockey was awarded a Colorado Council on the Arts fellowship for a version of "Bridging the Waters" in 1999. Her stories have appeared in literary magazines and in the anthology *Walking the Twilight II: Women Writers of the Southwest* (Northland Publishing, 1996). Karen lives with her dog Cassie in Denver, Colorado. She travels the open road and mountain trails, camps, hikes and recently visited Italy (yes, alone!). She works full-time, writing employee communications. Occasionally she teaches writing; sometimes she even writes for herself.

Anne Stone has a bachelor's degree from the Evergreen State College and a master's degree from Duke University. She lives, rides and works in rural North Carolina and is getting ready to build her own bike, move to Charleston and sail the seven seas. She'll take her dog with her.

Sharon B. Young lives in Massachusetts with her daughter. She has a bachelor's degree from the University of Maryland and a master's from Trinity College. For almost ten years she worked as a researcher, studying whales in Canada and the United States. She now works for conservation and animal welfare organizations as a marine policy analyst, specializing in threatened and endangered marine mammals. She lectures about marine mammal policy at Tufts University and Boston University, among others. Her love of driving has led her to explore much of the United States and to fulfill her dream of taking race driving lessons.

*J*ennie **Goode** is the coeditor of *Gifts of the Wild: A Woman's Book of Adventure* and a founding member of the Northwest publication *Push: Queer Feminist Subversions.* Her writing has appeared in *Bitch, Feminist Bookstore News* and *Nebulosi.* An editor at Seal Press for four years, she currently works as a freelance editor and writer.

Her dented yet trusty Toyota has successfully transported her all over the United States, ultimately to her current home in Seattle, where she consumes slow food and fast music, tends her plot in a community garden and obsesses over serial commas. She lives with her partner and three cats.